MY LIFE WITH THINGS

MY LIFE WITH THINGS

The Consumer Diaries   ELIZABETH CHIN

DUKE UNIVERSITY PRESS   Durham and London   2016

© 2016 DUKE UNIVERSITY PRESS •
ALL RIGHTS RESERVED • PRINTED
IN THE UNITED STATES OF AMERICA
ON ACID-FREE PAPER ⊚ • DESIGNED
BY NATALIE F. SMITH • TYPESET IN
QUADRAAT BY GRAPHIC COMPOSITION,
INC. BOGART, GEORGIA • LIBRARY OF
CONGRESS CATALOGING-IN-PUBLICATION
DATA • NAMES: CHIN, ELIZABETH,
[DATE] AUTHOR. • TITLE: MY LIFE WITH
THINGS : THE CONSUMER DIARIES /
ELIZABETH CHIN. • DESCRIPTION:
DURHAM : DUKE UNIVERSITY PRESS,
2016. | INCLUDES BIBLIOGRAPHICAL
REFERENCES AND INDEX. •
IDENTIFIERS: LCCN 2015042545|
• ISBN 9780822361183
(HARDCOVER : ALK. PAPER) • ISBN
9780822361367 (PBK. : ALK. PAPER)
• ISBN 9780822374268 (E-BOOK)
• SUBJECTS: LCSH: CONSUMERS—
DIARIES. | ANTHROPOLOGISTS—
DIARIES. | CHIN, ELIZABETH,
1963—DIARIES. | ETHNOLOGY—
AUTHORSHIP. | CONSUMPTION
(ECONOMICS) | CONSUMER
BEHAVIOR. • CLASSIFICATION: LLC
HF5415.32 .C456 2016 | DDC 306.3—
DC23 • LC RECORD AVAILABLE
AT HTTP://LCCN.LOC.GOV/2015042545

Contents

Acknowledgments

Tom West, Brad Darrach, and Martha Ronk not only always treated me like a real writer; they also helped me to learn how to be one. The work done by Susan Ruffins to show me how a book could emerge was nothing short of heroic. Then there are readers and friends whose timely comfort or kicks in the butt kept me moving: Mary Weismantel, Gabrielle Foreman, Bill Talen, Arlene Davila, Sharon Bean, and Dàna-Ain Davis. Jeff Tobin and Marta Savigliano always keep me sane and honest, whether they are here in Los Angeles or in Argentina. A special thanks is owed to Anne Allison and the Department of Anthropology at Duke University, for providing a semester of respite and adventure; to Paul Smith and the Department of Cultural Studies at George Mason University for lively discussion and comments; to Kye Young Park and members of the consumption colloquium at UCLA for providing an "aha moment" in my figuring out what the point of this work really is. John Sherry and Russell Belk, along with Dan Cook, are among the most generous scholars and colleagues on the planet. Like a pesky tag-along kid, I try to imitate their generosity as much as possible. I also enjoyed great exchanges at the Child and Teen Consumer conference, especially with Ann Phoenix, Steve Woolgar; encouragement from James McKenna and Lee Gettler about the transitional object material kept me committed to that exploration. Portions of the book have been previously published as follows: diary excerpts "Shopping in Ikea" and "Capitalism Makes Me Sick," *New Review of Literature*

2, no. 1 (2005): 123–38; "The Consumer Diaries, or, Autoethnography in the Inverted World," *Journal of Consumer Culture* 7, no. 3 (2007): 335–53.

To all friends and family who make appearances here, thank you in advance for your forbearance.

Adrian Williams and Benin Gardner, without a doubt, you are my beloveds.

I owe enormous debts to two women, S.A. and P.B. The debts cannot be repaid but they can be paid forward. To honor them, the royalties of this book are donated to L'Arche, an extraordinary organization whose mission is to "make explicit the dignity of every human being by building inclusive communities of faith and friendship where people with and without intellectual disabilities share life together."

1

Introduction

The anthropologist Daniel Miller famously claimed that consumption is nothing less than the keystone in our understanding of contemporary society and culture.[1] Important questions remain as to the relationship between culture and consumption, people and things, capital and humanity, in part because the literature on consumption has yet to fulfill the program outlined by Miller over ten years ago. Many people who think and write about on contemporary consumption remain hampered by a strong vein of anticonsumption. In this project, I wanted to explore consumption more broadly than that, while simultaneously focusing down into the minutiae of consuming as a way of life. To do this, I began to take field notes on myself, documenting my own consumer life, not daily but nevertheless with a regularity that, over several years, yielded quite a virtual stack of reflections and observations. Opting to document my own dilemmas and obsessions involved releasing the imperative to make an argument or to establish a position. All the contradictions were left in place: for me consumption is maddening and joyful, scary and sexy, boring and fascinating, funny, horrifying, and, above all, unavoidable. This book has at its center the field notes documenting my own consumer life. These field notes take the form of diary entries, each of which is a self-contained essay written in a single sitting. My aim with this project is to explore a world of consumption in which I myself am—for better or worse—utterly culpable. Yes, I'm for social justice, and meanwhile I take inordinate pleasure in the few pieces of designer clothing I own. Yes, I'm against social inequality, and yes, my child was in private school through grade two. The larger point is that nobody is exempt, no matter how smart or critical, and realizing that ought to spur us into action rather than becoming an excuse for complacency or capitulation.

To hate a tradition properly, Theodor Adorno notes, "one must have it in oneself."[2] Oh, yes, I have the tradition of consumption in myself. This project is very much an exercise in hating tradition properly, one in which I have attempted to apply to myself the same theoretical and ethnographic tools we so often use to analyze and judge others. Using autoethnography, I turn my anthropological skills toward my own life and experiences, making myself the object of study, in the same way I once studied the consumption habits of a group of poor, black children from New Haven, Connecticut. If I hate consumption, and if I hate anthropology (as well as loving them all too much), I hate them variously as a consumer, an anthropologist, and a writer—and as a woman, a woman of color, and a mother. That the standards of serious scholarship are also heteronormative, patriarchal, and white should hardly be news to anyone at this point. In choosing to question the value of appearing objective, I am hating the tradition of positivism, a framework that in its worst instances can be reduced to what I call the "smartypants" principle. Positivism is so appealing because it is so clear and so definitive: as Vincent Crapanzano shows in *Serving the Word*, positivism is a literalist formulation; the kind of idea that runs through Antonin Scalia's insistence on the one-dimensional meaning of the Constitution is not all that far removed, rhetorically, from the assertions by evangelical Christians that the Bible must be taken at its word.[3] While I love the systematic investigation advocated by science, I do hate the simplistic kinds of analysis offered by an unreflective, absolutist positivism. By investigating myself, then, I am exploring how it is possible to reject positivism yet still remain meaningfully engaged with scientific and anthropological principles. For me, this has meant undertaking autoethnography, an ethnographic investigation of myself.[4]

Therefore, I confess: I am a commodity fetishist. I am made of the same failed and flawed impulses and desires as the children I studied in the early 1990s. eBay has been for years my not-so-secret vice. Certain hair products evoke in me a very particular kind of erotic excitement. A "made in China" label does not automatically deter me from a purchase even though I know slave labor may have been involved. I get a kick from Champagne, though lately Prosecco does it better. I will never spend even one dime at Wal-Mart, but Target is one of my ritual destinations. A Hello Kitty tattoo was not out of the question until Sanrio announced that she was a white girl. Sometimes I am afflicted with the overpowering feeling that the oranges growing on the tree in front of my house cannot be as clean or as good as the ones in the store.

My first book examined the consumer lives of poor and working-class African American children in New Haven, Connecticut.[5] In *Purchasing Power* I sought to challenge a number of myths about poor, black consumers, a challenge provided in large part through careful observation of what the kids I came to know really did and thought. Many people, when faced with my claim that the kids I knew were fiscally savvy and asked for few or no gifts, even at Christmastime, wondered about the scientific validity of my sample. Others quite plainly refused to believe that I had found neither closets full of Nike sneakers nor welfare queens driving Cadillacs. It troubled me that none of these doubters was poor, that none had lived or spent time in the hood, so they did not—to be perfectly blunt—know what they were talking about. These interactions rather painfully alerted me to the continuing power of narratives about wealth and poverty, about deservingness and punishment that circulate so freely around us. I was brought up short, again and again, to see how often such narratives are used as a substitute for knowledge in the face of facts. This sort of knowledge has real effects out there in the world. In my fieldwork, the geographic situation showed ever so starkly how closely great wealth and great poverty resided: in New Haven the city's most poverty-stricken neighborhoods bordered the wealthiest blocks, and people worlds apart lived cheek by jowl while somehow managing to avoid any sort of personal interaction. Walking nearly every day from one of New Haven's most well-to-do neighborhoods into one of its poorest areas, I was warned by Yale professors on one side and drug dealers on the other: "Don't walk over there! It's dangerous!" We are urged to believe that poverty and wealth exist at a remove from each other, but I am interested in exploring the ways they are connected. Connectedness is also about relations between people, and I am interested as well in the ways that consumption and commodities serve as bridges between people in ways that might not be scary.

Because I am an anthropologist and am always interested in comparing my own experience with others that might seem vastly different, I often reflect by thinking about the past, or about the poor, or about cultures other than those in the United States. The great wealth of the United States is profoundly connected to the crushing poverty of Haiti, for instance, and the consumption possibilities and limitations in a place like Haiti have deep connections to wealthy sites abroad. These economic connections are accompanied by those of the material sort: most consumer goods in Haiti are secondhand items that come from the United States. Take a moment and imagine what it might be like to go shopping when there are virtually no new clothes for sale in the entire country. What might not be emerging in your imagination is the reality in Haiti: that nearly everyone is impeccably dressed, in clothes that fit and styles that are hip. The worst-dressed people in Haiti, in fact, are international aid workers, whom Haitians view as hopelessly slovenly. Even more astonishing, at least to me, is that an incredible number of people wear white from head to toe—white that is utterly and entirely unmarked by dirt or dust. This ability to manifest style and to be fashionable speaks to me of very particular sorts of labor required by the context in which people get dressed in Haiti and places like it—a type of engagement with consumption very different from going to the mall.

These comparisons are especially important because so many recent accounts of consumption are centered on and in the United States, thus missing the broader connections that make the global economy what it is. The problem with being too U.S.-centered in thinking about consumption at large is that presenting the United States as the norm is a bit like saying Paris Hilton or Bill Gates has an average lifestyle. The United States, after all, is the richest country ever in all of human history. If, like me, you live in a household whose income is $90,000 a year or greater, then your income is in the top 20 percent of the richest country ever in all of human history. Households with incomes of $75,000 make up the top quarter of the U.S. population; at $55,000, a household is in the top 40 percent of the United States in terms of income. To use some clunky logic to illustrate, anyone with a household income of $55,000 or more might easily be framed as an "average" consumer, but to do that is taking the wealthiest portion of the wealthiest nation as a starting point, providing a monumentally skewed view of the so-called average life. It galls me to say it, but I am a member of an extremely tiny economic elite of enormous privilege and wealth. So are my students. So, perhaps, are you. Not feeling rich and elite does not mean it is not so.

For those with some measure of disposable income, the consumer sphere represents a nearly endless array of choices, which themselves are nested within choices of choices (options that somehow lead nowhere). No wonder so many rather frantically attach themselves to notions of moving away from consumer incursions: get off the grid, get back to nature, get a life. In recent years, we have seen an upsurge in documentary journalism in which writers (most from an economic segment similar to my own) attempt to reform or eschew their own consumption, buying locally or not at all for a specified time—typically a year—and then write about their experience.[6] This wave of experiential accounts arises, in part, from the growing sense of too-much-ness that pervades the United States, coupled with a heightened awareness of the global impact of consumer capitalism on the planet. There's an important element of walking the walk in these books, but these experiments also smack of gimmicks and tricks that are at once utterly hilarious and strangely endearing. I find it both interesting and instructive, though, that this position is one that is particularly strong among those who consume the most, comforting us even as we swipe the credit card one more time, chide China for its growing greed for fossil fuels, and chastise rural Africans for eating more meat in their diets,[7] because more people eating more meat spirals the price of wheat ever upward, since as everybody knows now, it takes four pounds of wheat to produce one pound of beef. No, I can't spare a dime, mister, I have a mortgage to pay, and that lease on my electric car isn't so cheap either.

I began this introduction with Adorno, himself a member of what is often called the Frankfurt School, a group of scholars who developed some of the earliest and most devastating critiques of mass culture and mass media. Their ideas remain useful and influential, and most anyone thinking about contemporary consumption has got to wrestle with the likes of Adorno, Herbert Marcuse, Walter Benjamin, and Hannah Arendt. Their critiques zeroed in on the powerful potential of consumer spheres for intensifying social control, intellectual anesthesia, and political shams—hardly a set of qualities worth celebrating. This point of view was impelled in part by the horrors of World War II, where film, radio, and music were used to promote fascism and racism and homophobia. Even Walter Benjamin's relatively enthusiastic defense of the culture industries noted the extremely powerful potential of these industries when put to nefarious purposes. His classic essay "The Work of Art in the Age of Mechanical Reproduction" is one of the best-known examples of this (measured) enthusiasm.[8] In a wide-ranging discussion that moves from cave paintings to fascist movie-making, he discusses how the ways that art is produced affects the way we see, understand, and experience it. Mass production, he argues, inevitably changes art from something unique and uniquely experienced (a piece of art), to something ubiquitous and reproducible (copies of an original). This ubiquity and reproducibility is not altogether bad—after all, it allows mass audiences to have access to ideas and resources formerly reserved only for elites. However, mass media's potential to reduce politics to entertainment, and war to aesthetics, was something that worried Benjamin deeply. One need only view the gorgeous black-and-white celebratory images in Leni Riefenstal's pro-Hitler film *Triumph of the Will* to get Benjamin's point. I'm not afraid to admit that somehow the film instilled a good feeling about the whole enterprise, much to my horror and disgust. Most horrifying was my own permeability, my own lack of immunity, my own inability not to "know better" except through disciplined, conscious effort.[9]

The distinctly alarmist fears of the postwar critiques continue to operate in much consumer analysis, complete with a sort of cold war rhetoric of good and evil and an "us" vs. "them" structure that assumes the centrality and normality of white, middle-class worlds. Few who grew up in the 1960s, as I did, could avoid reading Vance Packard's *The Hidden Persuaders*, which argued that ads are full of hidden, subliminal messages designed to rope people into buying. I still cannot look at a liquor ad without trying to figure out if there's an image of a penis hidden in the ice cubes.[10] This ultraparanoid point of view is a rather limiting way to think about the consumer sphere, and inevitably questions of resistance and agency emerged.[11] Writing on teddy boys and punks of urban Britain in the 1970s, Dick Hebdige showed how something like "style" can be enmeshed with politics of a powerful sort. With a tendency to be a bit over-hopeful about the potential for resistance to disrupt hegemonic processes, this work is nevertheless an important counterpoint to the "down with consumption" stance. The wave of resistance literature was inevitably tempered, and Lila Abu-Lughod's important article "The Romance of Resistance" marked an important shift into nuanced territory where colonialism, media, gender, religion, and other forces all came into play. In a detailed analysis of the contradictions of the desires of Bedouin girls to escape the oppressive patriarchal demands of family, Abu-Lughod shows how turning to mediatized versions of romance and an individually based love relationship leaves these girls often isolated in the city, and, ironically, in many ways they end up being more restricted than they were in the desert. Resistance, Abu-Lughod reminds us, is resistance to something; where it gets you may be somewhere new, but not necessarily somewhere where one is undeniably free.[12]

In the current moment, where a U.S. president can declare shopping as patriotism, the fears of Adorno and his colleagues seem utterly relevant.

These fears can be tempered, however, by paying attention to what people really are doing. After all, just because the packaging on the Barbie doll says "for ages 3 to 5" doesn't mean the doll will be played with only by three- to five-year-olds, or even that those who play with them will use the doll and her accessories as intended by the manufacturer. Of the millions and millions of children who have had Barbies over the last fifty-plus years, how many of them have used them *only* in the approved manner? And even if everyone did stick to the hegemonic script, how many kids who played with Barbies ended up actually being like Barbie?

Erica Rand's raucous and thoughtful book *Barbie's Queer Accessories* documents and explores such complexity beautifully, presenting a wide range of accounts from people whose remembered interactions with Barbie take myriad forms.[13] Her work shows that Barbie has been used by people to explore any number of personal or social issues, sometimes via play, sometimes via fantasy, sometimes by reworking the doll herself, whether when children or as adults. There is an enormous amount of kid- and adult-generated Barbie sex on YouTube, much of it hysterically funny, critically astute, and remarkably sophisticated in content and execution. Kids make fun of Barbie, and they do it quite a bit. (One of my favorite such YouTube Barbie sex tapes involves a Barbie who steps out on Ken and has sex with the Teenage Mutant Ninja Turtle. The jig is up when she gives birth to a little tiny Teenage Mutant Ninja Turtle figure that is swaddled in a piece of Kleenex.) There are scads of Barbie customization sites, where people transform existing Barbies into just about anything from a Diana Ross look-alike to a Swarovski-crystal-covered mermaid. Some people create and populate entire worlds with characters and story lines given to a cast of fashion dolls. One such world still sticks with me: created by a Filipino man, this world features Barbies in a Filipino world, eating tiny, hand-sculpted Filipino food, and wearing gorgeous handmade Filipino clothes. The cast of characters is almost in the triple digits, and each meticulously staged scene looks as if it must have taken weeks of preparation. The San Francisco–based event Altered Barbie encourages people to make Barbie what they want her to be—in whole or in part—and imagination and creativity hold sway here. Another favorite example is of the artist Margaux Lange, who makes sculpturally exquisite jewelry out of Barbie parts—bracelets made of dozens of amputated Barbie hands, neckpieces made of arms arrayed in spirals, bracelets of multicolored Barbie butts laid end-to-end. Perhaps more important is the everyday experimentation undertaken by kids, experimentation that shows kids are much less prone to robotic ingestion of mass culture imperatives than one might think: one girl I talked with while doing research on children and consumption told me she had at least ten Barbies. "What do you do with them?" I asked, imagining faux beauty contests and fashion shows. "I take their heads off," she replied, "and go bowling with them!"

So, as a counterpoint to the idea that consumerism and globalization means a tsunami of cultural sameness, we have the reality of a kid who goes bowling with Barbie heads: this nugget alone explains neatly why the consumption-is-sameness idea is wrong, and why fieldwork is so valuable: our own imaginations are not nearly rich enough to come up with all the possibilities that others have already explored. Immersed as we are in our own limited worlds, we too often imagine that our own understanding of the world describes the limits of the world itself. Cross-cultural and transhistorical research shows the surprising and powerful ways in which consumption is enmeshed with daily life. For instance, even the seemingly normative notion of the middle class is tremendously fragile and mutable, and looking at middle classes outside of the First World milieu shows how precarious middle-class life can be (and such is increasingly the case in the United States as well). One need only read Maureen O'Dougherty's powerful account of efforts to maintain middle-class identities in Brazil during periods where inflation often reached 100 percent a month to realize that even middle-class consumption takes widely varied forms and is often accomplished under startlingly stringent conditions.[14]

Focusing on the apparently mundane category of cosmetics and skin creams, Timothy Burke shows in his book *Lifebuoy Men Lux Women* how even a bar of soap or stick of butter can be a political tool.[15] Among the early twentieth-century Africans for whom an oiled and glossy skin was a sign of health and good hygiene, butter seemed just the product to rub into the skin daily to achieve proper grooming. The British, however, constructed this practice—and the Africans themselves—as dirty, going so far as to mount a public education campaign on the proper uses of butter. Beauty, attractiveness, and hygiene are not only culturally specific, but are also key elements in political regimes. Burke shows how in British colonial Africa notions of cleanliness and beauty were translated into zoning laws, medical practices, and vocational training—all of which profoundly affected people's lives and opportunities in enduring ways.[16]

Sidney Mintz's masterful book *Sweetness and Power* made a compelling argument for understanding how economy, consumption, and social change can all be intertwined.[17] The contemporary growth of human and organ-trafficking industries shows how much—and how little—consumption has changed since the slavery era Mintz focused on. For him, the hot, sweet tea drunk with increasing frequency by English laborers illustrated this principle beautifully. The tea leaves came from India, the sugar from the Caribbean, and in both cases large plantations using slave labor (or something close to it) provided the commodity. Sweet, hot tea, in turn, provided warming comfort to urban workers whose meager wages left them at the edge of survival. With its strong smell and shot of energy, tea was much cheaper than a cooked meal and substituted for more nourishing (and more expensive) foodstuffs. Thus tea and sugar were central in allowing urbanization and transformation of the labor force; the demand or market for these also stimulated the plantation economy, and the international market in labor such economies required. Mintz showed clearly the ways in which the "modern" world is tied to and even made possible by such "undeveloped" places as Haiti. Today with blood diamonds and international adoption, with Himalayan salt and sex workers trafficked worldwide, the developing world is no less a cocreater and coconsumer of those far away people and places.[18]

THINKING ABOUT THINGS

The diary entries are most fundamentally a series of meditations on specificities, whose purpose is to explore bits and pieces of my own human engagement with things, the ways consumption connects me at once outward to the world, and inward to my being. In so doing, I ask a lot of questions, of myself and, perhaps, of others. Striving to stay away from broad moral pronouncements about the goodness or badness of this or that technology, site of production, or consumer object, at the same time I do not hide my own thoughts and feelings about justice or privilege, guilt or pleasure, wonder or terror. That said, it is perfectly clear that I think capitalism sucks, while simultaneously pouring huge amounts of psychic energy into choosing paint colors for rooms in my home.

I have always been more than a little annoyed by so much of the scholarship on consumption that comes from left-leaning academics, the kind of work that implicitly or explicitly privileges "good" consumption over "bad" consumption. My objection is that too often the arguments ultimately reduce down to a criticism of popular consumption, critiques ungrounded by deep investigation into what moves those people who actually do those things.

These criticisms are often offered up by scholars whom I otherwise admire deeply; intruding like odd hiccups into otherwise smooth and cogent arguments, they strike me as moments worthy of attention because of their Freudian slipperiness. Sharon Zukin's book on shopping includes a few such moments, and I discuss that work in some detail here largely because this project was spurred to some degree by my own strong responses to the hiccups I encountered in Zukin's book.[19]

Taking a broad cultural and historical stance toward shopping and its role in the culture of the United States, Zukin's generally even-handed analysis disintegrated for me in her chapter on eBay and in her final conclusions. The book is wonderfully, unabashedly personal, drawing on her own experiences growing up in Philadelphia and living in New York. And yet she framed her broad observations in a universalist way, as if shopping in New York typifies shopping in the United States more generally. At the time Zukin was writing, eBay was pretty novel and still had that "this-is-going-to-radically-change-the-world" feeling about it. Zukin's assessment was that "eBay flies against traditional ethics: it encourages us to treat everything as alienable, to trade all the time, and to buy things only in order to sell them." The mention of "traditional ethics" made me immediately suspicious. After all, and keeping Adorno in mind, tradition is for hating. How much does eBay really reconstruct the social experience of shopping, much less the social relations of capitalism? Taken to its extreme, eBay certainly constitutes a new platform for and experience of shopping and selling, one that is experientially a relationship between consumer and screen, not consumer and embodied salesperson. At the same time, I found Zukin's nostalgia for the "romance of shopping" rather hard to swallow: is it really better somehow to be offered a spritz of perfume in the department store rather than picking the perfume you want on the Internet (in part because you want to *avoid* getting spritzed!), as she suggests?[20] Furthermore, I was extremely suspicious of Zukin's assertion that eBay goes against "traditional ethics" in which alienability, trading, buying, and selling of personal possessions is an anathema.

To explore these suspicions, I delved into an investigation of the pawn industry—a place and practice where people routinely partially alienate their possessions. Pawn historically and into the present has been an important economic vehicle for those too poor to access banking. Pawn is one area demonstrating that many people consistently view their possessions as potential sources of income, and have for centuries. From this perspective, "traditional ethics" are not disrupted when eBay encourages us to look at our possessions for their potential money value. The whole point of pawn is that possessions all have some amount of money value, and that is part of their social value too. This may not be the dominant middle-class, white orientation, but it is part of everyday life for significant slices of the U.S. population; in some countries, pawn is the closest thing to banking for the majority. The well-known song "Shake Sugaree" tells the story of a person who item by item sells everything: watch, chain, horse, buggy, the horse, the bed, the chair, until "everything I own is done and pawned."[21] The words to the song were contributed by Cotton's grandchildren, each of whom made up a verse. When little kids are spontaneously making up a song about pawning everything of value, the idea that your stuff can be turned into money must be familiar. If it is true that eBay encourages us "to treat everything as alienable" as Zukin said, one might ask, just whose "traditional ethics" are being disrupted, and how.

Understanding the specific dynamics of pawn in the United States also requires considering how Native Americans were enjoined into capitalist social and economic relations. At trading posts throughout the Southwest, trade in pawn was a primary means through which Native Americans were drawn into consumer spheres that reshaped their household economies and lifeways, while paradoxically ensuring the survival of numerous practices, particularly in jewelry-making and weaving. The trade of secondhand clothing, for its part, is another way in which possessions have circulated for centuries. It was not until the invention of the sewing machine, in the mid-1800s, that ready-made clothing could be mass produced and clothes moved from being repositories of value to increasingly disposable. Through these explorations of pawn and secondhand clothes, my attempt is to see how current forms of shopping and selling bear relationships to long-standing practices atypical of the middle classes, but nevertheless an essential component of many peoples' consumer lives, and particularly among poor and marginalized groups.

Zukin's epilogue, titled "What Shopping Should Be," states that farmer's markets inherently create community and are therefore good. The question might not be so much whether or not farmer's markets create community, but for whom, and how, and where. Like her, I aspire to value relationships more than shopping, more than consumer items. On the whole I agree that things that "create community" are usually better than those that do not. Yet it also is incredibly difficult for me to discern how to assign a particular thing to one or the other category. Once community "for whom" is brought into the equation, it rapidly falls to pieces. My experience of the farmer's market Zukin speaks of with such elegiac positivity is one where, as a graduate student, I rarely shopped because I could not afford to purchase most things on offer. In a city where grocery items are already premium-priced, the even more pricey farmer's market items were at most special splurges, not regular occupants of my shopping bag. When I meandered through the farmer's market, I felt more like the Little Matchstick Girl than a community member, looking in on a lovely world in which I could not participate. Neither of our divergent experiences stands as the truth about what the farmer's market is, or was; certainly that truth exceeds these two small facets of possibility, and it is precisely this expanded sense of complexity that it is important to foreground. For instance: what of the poor and working-class Latinos who were rapidly being displaced from their longtime homes around the Fourteenth Street hub at the time Zukin was writing? What kind of community did they feel with upstate New York farmers and Amish furniture makers?

New technologies lead to new socialities, which in turn usually lead to age-old critiques. The invention of the telephone was met with fears of wanton female sexuality, and the Internet has yielded similar fears, yet as Kramarae observed, "much of the seemingly revolutionary technology is actually conservative."[22] Twenty years after this observation, Margot Weiss, in a wonderfully rich and intrepid ethnography, documents how Silicon Valley professionals use a combination of technologies and communication media to participate in BDSM cultures, scheduling planning meetings at the local Denny's, even as they scope out the next slave auction.[23] Part of what she documents is how often the new exists cheek by jowl with the utterly mundane. As part of a long-arc project interrogating the relationship between affect, emotion, and capitalism, Eva Illouz examines, among other things, online dating platforms.[24] Amid a larger project outlining the emergence of what she calls "emotional capitalism" and the rise of sentimentality, her incisive exploration details the ways in which online dating sites encourage very particular approaches to the marketing of the self and the harnessing of emotion to capitalist imperatives. Those pressures no doubt exist, and people certainly respond to them, but are these sites really so profoundly different from the paper catalogs of Asian brides that have been around for decades?[25]

In Zukin's book on shopping and Illouz's analysis of online dating I am most troubled by assertions of taste embedded in the critiques. The most negative assessments are given for things or practices the authors themselves dislike or do not participate in (because they dislike them). For my part, my aim is to take on consumption in a way that exposes and implicates my own assessments of taste without putting them forward as principles to follow. This approach is an important part of my effort to "hate tradition properly." To make at least one early confession, and in the interest of full disclosure, I found my current husband on Match.com.[26] Or did he find me?

AN ENTRY ON HOW I MET MY HUSBAND

This is a story I have now told so often that it has resolved into a relatively stable narrative, though since it is a story that until now I have always shared orally, it has always been subject to storytelling's embellishments, extravagances, or elisions. It is usually a story I tell to girlfriends of mine, over a glass of wine; it's a girlfriend-to-girlfriend type story, the one about how I found my prince charming when I really wasn't thinking that was what I was trying to do. You know, the story that's along the lines of "I'd given up, and then there he was!"

My first husband and I had separated a couple of years earlier. I'd done a small amount of online dating, and faced the common crunch points: one guy used the word "perchance" and did himself in as far as I was concerned. Another, for a few months, was an occasional booty-call when one or the other of us felt so moved. Conveniently, we lived only a couple of miles apart. Another convenience was that our social circles had zero overlap and we never ran into each other in daily life (and never have in the years since). Neither of us seemed to invest any lasting emotion into our encounters. After him, I met an interesting man at a National Science Foundation event, and had been seeing him for a stretch of several months. It was a perfect rebound relationship: one that had no real long-term potential and had the added advantage of being long-distance. He lived and worked in Florida. We would chat on the phone pretty much every day, but we didn't see each other that often. He met my daughter only once; she still occasionally makes fun of the way he showed no interest in her that afternoon.

I'd gone to Florida for a long weekend visit. It was toward the end of the term, and I had a stack of papers to grade. He was at work all day, and I'd lie around his house in my pajamas, trying to force myself to get the grading done. I devised a plan where I would grade five papers, then get up to do a little household chore. Doing household chores in someone else's house has always been something I enjoy: whenever I go over to my dad's house, I clean the kitchen. Whenever I clean my own kitchen, I curse and complain.

So there I was in Florida with my routine: Grade five papers, wash the dishes. Grade five papers, sweep the porch. Grade five papers, empty the bathroom trash can. At which point I discovered some condoms that I did not recognize.

When he came back at the end of the day, I asked him about the condoms. And this is what he really truly said: "Yes, I am seeing other women. But you are the most beautiful. And you're the only one I'm having a relationship with." I love repeating those lines to my women friends, they sound like bad dialogue from a telenovela. My snappy answer was "Well, you're not having a relationship with me anymore!" I packed my bag and went off to stay at a hotel until my flight home a couple of days later. That night, I was on the phone with a good girlfriend of mine, one with a ton more online dating experience than me, and one with a no-nonsense approach to life. "You need to just get out there," she counseled me. "Just meet some people, go on dates, don't worry about whether it's a relationship." "Yeah, yeah, yeah," I was thinking to myself, with no intention of taking her advice. "*And I want a report by Monday,*" she ordered. Arlene is not the kind of person you argue with when she gives you an order like that.

So I'm there in my corporate-boring hotel room in Florida, with nothing to do, having managed to grade all those papers. And I'm taking my orders from Arlene seriously, but with a measure of bad humor too. I set up a Match .com account and tossed out a profile. In Match.com and other dating sites like it, you have to come up with a kind of headline about yourself. I was feeling contrary and cranky and uncooperative, so my headline went: HATES JACUZZIS. KNOWS HOW TO TAKE A BUCKET BATH. Then, when I had to write more about me, I just ranted about everything from how much I hated the gentrification of downtown Los Angeles to being mad that everybody's racist about Haiti. I uploaded a photo, of me, unsmiling but not looking too severe, I hoped—not that I had invested much energy in caring at all. I was *so* not invested in attracting people to my profile.

The upside of this approach was that anybody who did actually contact me struck me as really an interesting person. One guy wrote me a really hilarious poem; a few others sent thoughtful but not obnoxious or canned messages. The first guy I decided to have a phone conversation with was an accomplished photographer whose work I found interesting. About five minutes after we'd done our introductions, he said, "So, babydoll . . ." And with that, I had to cut the conversation short. *Babydoll?* Are you kidding?

Adrian was the next one I decided to talk with, and from the first, I just loved his voice (and I still do). There is a warmth to the way he talks, and from where I sit, it doesn't hurt that he has a lovely English accent. We had a nice conversation or two, exchanged a few emails, and decided to meet at a wine bar in Los Feliz, where he was living at the time. I sat down next to him and smelled cigarette smoke and thought, "Oh no, a smoker, no way. Gross." Then he said, not too long after that, "I'm a socialist." And then he pulled out a book of essays written by his hero, English parliamentarian Michael Foote, which he'd brought along to lend to me. And then I pulled out a book of essays written by George Orwell, which I'd brought along to lend to him. There we were, halfway through our first glass of wine, two nerds on the road to love.

I always claim that it was my I-don't-give-a-shit approach to my profile that yielded such excellent results. Adrian claims he didn't even look at my profile but gave me a ping because he thought I was cute in my photo and because he'd read my screen name, Babethe (a nickname given to me by a Haitian friend) as "Babe-the."

He has never once addressed me either as Babe or as Babydoll. He smokes one or two cigarettes a day but never smells of smoke.

Eva Illouz produces a sophisticated analysis of how such sites as Match .com use what she calls psychological technologies of the self to call forth or produce particular forms of emotional orientations.[27] The analysis is in many was a reading of Match.com as a text, much in the way that the Edward Hopper painting on the cover of her book can be considered a readable text. Her conceptual statements about the propensities of Match.com and the psychological technologies it employs are most useful when understood as readings of potential rather than actuality. Taking my own experience as a case in point, Illouz's analysis presumes an earnest engagement by Match .com users: that people will put energy into serious consideration of the profile questions and will likewise work to present themselves in ways designed to be appealing, to offer what they think those people out there might want to see. Luckily, my own engagement was not nearly so earnest.[28] The larger point I'm making here is one that hews rather closely to the kinds of cultural studies, subculture arguments that have been being made in the realm of consumption and consumerism for quite some time: remember resistance. Without over-romanticizing the spaces people find for pleasure, for off-label usage, and for contrariness, I find it fascinating to see that in the face of new(ish) technologies and platforms for social and consumer life, the response is often remarkably similar to so many responses before them to such novelty. First comes the claim, in one form or another, that Western civilization as we know it is doomed.[29] Then comes the continuation of Western civilization as we know it, pretty much unscathed: that is, sort of different, but mostly the same. Then emerge a whole mess of unimagined off-uses, unintended consequences, and accidents.

In a way, then, I am benefiting from the broad, critical pronouncements of those like Zukin and Illouz to advocate for paying attention to the unimagined and the unintended—something that I should also add is a typically anthropological strategy. In the case of Match.com, the question for me becomes, How much of the textual reading is reflected in people's lived experience? If the broad-level examination of society writ large is the province of sociologists like Illouz and Zukin, this micro-level intensity is the focus of anthropology.

I remember, for instance, when I showed undergraduate students of mine the free computer-animated version of *Alice in Wonderland* that was available on the iPad 1. They were appalled. "What about the smell of books?" said one student with great passion. In their minds, in that moment, they were seeing the end of reading as they knew it. As with so many other innovations the answer was both yes and no. For those with access to the Internet, iPads, e-readers and e-reading apps, reading has become even more democratized, being newly portable, instantly accessible, and much less expensive than it was previously. Worldwide, more people are reading than ever: the twenty-dollar phone I recently purchased in Uganda came equipped with an e-reader, a boon in a country where physical books are both expensive and scarce, and cell phones themselves are an important instrument in promoting literacy.[30] Plenty of people are still reading print on paper, especially if they live in places where being wired costs a lot or where wireless networks are an aspiration rather than a reality. What has changed more radically, but much less palpably than the act of reading itself, is the business model used by the publishing industry.[31] This goes well beyond the death of the (traditional) small, independent bookstore, which is being met with the rise of the (new) small independent bookstore in neighborhoods in Brooklyn, New York, and Highland Park, Los Angeles, by hipster gentrifiers of once minority-populated no-go zones. So yes, my students were right—reading is no longer the same. But I would argue they were not right about specifics, only about generalities.

The anthropological perspective emphasizes daily life and insists on understanding specificities in a context that privileges cross-cultural comparison.

This perspective is generally missing in newer work in the humanities that addresses materiality and things. Often viewed together as "new materialism," this vein of thinking and research is eminently of the present moment. All around us things that were clear are fuzzy; things that seemed distinct are intertwined; the differences between us and them increasingly difficult to name precisely. These blurrings come in all sorts of forms: transdisciplinary studies is an example from the academy. The growing scientific work on the relationship between the bacteria in our guts and our psychological states is another. What is a thing? What is human? What is the difference between humans and nature? Many scholars in new materialism take up these questions in deeply important ways.

As the world in which we live is palpably transformed by the accretion of our species' actions, the nature/culture dichotomy seems less useful than ever. The question "What is a thing?" has also broadened to consider systems of various scales from micro to macro, and, building on Bruno Latour's theories, exploring the ways "things" can be what he calls "actants" has been extraordinarily productive in reframing broad understandings of the dynamics of interaction and agency.[32] Drawing from the work of Gilles Deleuze and Félix Guattari, the concept of assemblage has been even more far-reaching in its influence.[33] Alongside these strains of theory, materialism itself has seen an upsurge of interest, across a range of (dissolving) disciplines. The titles say so much: *Hyperobjects*; *The Fragility of Things*; *Vibrant Matter*.[34] It seems no accident that as we recognize the current geologic era as the Anthropocene, the place of the human (with all its problematic baggage) in relation to all things is being anxiously interrogated. This interrogation generally draws exclusively from theories rooted in Western continental philosophy or social science.

However, my own position, with regard to thinking about things qua things, draws less from these theories than it does from my research with and my affinity for Haitian Vodou. I actively enter social spaces and experiences where things themselves can be enlivened by spirit, and my acceptance of this cosmology is one that renders me cautious about applying theory too forcefully to this project. Moreover, the animating force of the lwa, or Haitian spirits, is one I am disinclined to dissect using Western philosophical tools and traditions. Though the lwa are not a visible presence in this book, my orientation to thinking about objects is certainly shaped by my relationship with the lwa and the ways that I have seen and felt spirit at work. The black feminist archaeologist Whitney Battle-Baptiste is one of a growing number of scholars for whom acknowledgment of her African diasporic faith is part and parcel of her academic research agenda.[35] Battle-Baptiste, raised as an orişa traditionalist, opens each of her public presentations with a call to her ancestors. She further embraces and discusses the ways her faith shapes her relationships to and understandings of objects—something of central importance to archaeologists, whose engagement with material culture is foundational. In later parts of the book, where I take up the question of living things or move into a surreal imagining of enlivened objects, the influence of my own engagement with Vodou and the spirit has shaped my approach.

The personal nature of this enquiry bears relationship to the growing work on affect and emotion across the social sciences and cultural studies. Kathleen Stewart, Ann Cvetkovich, and Eve Sedgwick are some of the participants in the collective "public feelings" project who have gone a long way toward reclaiming affect and emotion on political grounds as legitimate areas for investigation beyond the confines of psychology.[36] Interrogating emotion as public and political rather than private and individual, they have also shown how feminist and queer theory can and should connect scholarship to gendered understandings of social theory and social justice. In their work on emotion and capitalism, sociologists Viviana Zelizer and Eva Illouz take pains to show that structures of emotion are scaffolded by the specific political economy of commodity capitalism. Like the public feelings project, this work removes emotion from the realm of individual psychology and places it into a broader social and historical context.

These streams of investigation are stronger on gender and sexuality than they are on race and ethnicity.[37] For my part, I offer the reverse: I am stronger in my examinations of race and inequality than of gender and sexuality. Ann Cvetkovich takes up race in a wonderfully thoughtful chapter and carefully plumbs the way black depression, in particular, takes on particular contours carved out by history and context that are too little assessed in psychological theory and medicine. Drawing especially on Jacqui Alexander's *Pedagogies of Crossing*[38] and Saidiya Hartman's *Lose Your Mother*,[39] Cvetkovich discusses the importance of spirit and the spiritual through thinking about race and depression, taking the not inconsequential risk of discussing her own emergent spiritual practices. This refusal to draw a line between the personal (spiritual practices) and the scholarly (psychological theory) is as refreshing as it is political. It is disquieting, though, that as Cvetkovich moves on to discuss other things in other chapters, questions of race are left behind; it is almost as if the question of race is segregated in the text, not through any particularly intentional strategy, but rather with the kind of nonintentionality that speaks of mechanisms of habitus and hegemony. Similarly, Viviana Zelizer opens her book *The Purchase of Intimacy* with an account of a complex Louisiana court case from the 1840s involving a plantation owner, his emancipated slave and sexual partner Patsy, debts, and the plantation owner's legal heirs.[40] Despite the centrality of the enslaved person in this case, the book never mentions the issue of race, a lacuna I cannot help but find astonishing. At the same time, Zelizer's analysis and framework for understanding the complexity of economics and family in the United States is tremendously important. Zelizer's overall concern is with the prevalence and intertwined nature of economy and intimacy, an intertwined reality that exists alongside strongly held notions that love and emotion are private and exist separately from the economic sphere.

One of the key issues in deciding economic questions in the case that opens the book is centered around determining Patsy's intimate status: was she to be considered wife, concubine, or slave at various points in the events before the court? These are important and fascinating questions, and alongside Patsy's case Zelizer juxtaposes the fraught calculations emerging from the 9/11 claims and decisions on who was owed what in terms of settlements, whether from survivor funds or insurance claims. Zelizer's analysis of the persisting discomforts and dilemmas around what she calls the "mingling" of the economic and the social is insightful and cogent. In this and other work, she has shown time and time again the textured and deeply felt ways our collectively held notions of personhood, sentiment, and emotion are produced in and through dynamic elements of capitalism itself. Yet the effacement of race as a key element in the formation and experience of those processes is something I find startling, especially given that *The Purchase of Intimacy* begins with a case concerned with precisely those questions: slave or free, person or property.

Mel Y. Chen is one of the few working in the vein of new materialism who consistently foregrounds both race and what she calls "politically suppressed cosmologies."[41] In a series of essays ranging across the linguistic animacy of the word "queer," the racialized animality of Asians, and the racialization of metals, Chen shows the intertwining ways in which living things are deadened and the unliving brought to life. Foregrounding how all of these situations involve fierce forays into biopolitics and lived experience, she argues that the world of the animate is staged along a hierarchy of moments of being, rather than existing as a set of discrete and concretized statuses. In this way the life-potential of lead or mercury is not less than that of a monkey or a human baby; all are scattered across the plane of animacy in which they endlessly swirl.

Chen's insistence that race and culture are central to questions of how we theorize and think about things and our relationships to them is one I share. It is striking that Chen's attention to race is nearly unique in the scholarship on new materialisms, even as a scan of that work reveals consistent calls to a generalized "we" whether that "we" is framed as stewards of the Anthropocene, actors in systems, or inhabitants of landscapes. But as Sylvia Wynter remarked to a symposium on ethnopoetics, "[W]ho are 'we'?"[42] The dominant colloquial "we" being invoked in both Wynter's critique and the new materiality work is without doubt white and Western. Invoking this "we" is an operative move, Wynter explains, and one that simultaneously identifies a "them" who are inevitably other, non-Western, and nonwhite. This apparently neutral "we," then, is in fact racially inflected as the result of sociohistorical processes long in the making. She describes this generalized "we" position as an example of "secular ethnocentrism." Calling attention to the scripted and inscribed white normativity of the "we" by naming it secular ethnocentrism is Wynter's move toward otherizing whiteness, making it visible as a contingent and problematic position. It is a decentering thrust at whiteness that names it as a thing, much in the same way that happens when Joanne Kealiinohomoku describes ballet as "ethnic dance."[43]

Although this book is not a book about race, throughout, race-consciousness is fundamental and crucial to my stance as it is in my daily life. In his critique of Michel Foucault and Giorgio Agamben, Weheliye shows how poststructuralism flung forth theory that at once apparently superseded and negated questions of race, even as scholarship and global conflicts demonstrated the continuing salience of race to questions of humanity. Weheliye adroitly identifies a peculiar persistence of racialization even in theory about cyborgs and posthumanism; even as racialization persists in these theories, they neither name nor purposefully take up the question of race. As Weheliye posits, the category of the human is not an "ontological fait accompli"—that is, the category of the human is not a coherent thing whose present manifestation is the end result of a developmental process.[44] Rather, the human, he suggests, has been revealed by black and ethnic studies as a "heuristic concept," an approximation, a best guess, an example. As such, it is problematic and contingent. This might seem entirely obvious, yet it is especially important to mark this problem in relation to the study of consumption, especially with regard to the literature collectively known as "new materialism," where questions of race have been virtually nonexistent and where race is implicitly whiteness.

For reasons that ought to be self-explanatory, the vast majority of black persons in the United States have a uniquely fraught relationship to capital, a relationship that, as Jamaica Kincaid succinctly reminds us, arises "because we *were* capital, like bales of cotton and sacks of sugar."[45] The specific ways the poor, black families I knew in New Haven experience the connections between emotion and capitalism look very different from those of the white middle class, who have a well-documented tendency of striving to shield their children from economic realities.[46] In the United States race inevitably contributes to the way emotion takes form and is given content, how it is enmeshed with capitalism, and how it is rendered public, and to which publics specific pieces of public feeling are made available. This is an eminently historical problem, in addition to being cultural and economic. One recent study found that African Americans consistently use images of slavery when discussing their day-to-day consumer experiences, describing themselves as "shackled" and "chained," words one would hardly expect to hear a white person using when talking about shopping.[47] It is for this reason that much of the broad generalization about the formation and content of emotion rings false when I attempt to relate it either to myself or to the people with whom I have long conducted research. As a sixth-generation-born-in-the-USA Asian American, I have ancestors who were born into and lived in forcibly segregated communities, who were not allowed to speak their home language in school, and who could not vote, own land, or marry whom they chose. While my Chinese ancestors were never bought and sold, they were held to be less than full persons and their status as citizens was precarious. Even my *Mayflower* ancestor, John Howland, was of the less-privileged sort, arriving in the New World as an indentured servant. Indenture, a form of bound labor, was something like a pawning of the self, and indentured people often suffered terrible treatment. The similarities between indenture and slavery in the colonies were powerfully explored by Toni Morrison in her novel *A Mercy*.[48] John Howland did well, marrying his indenturer and going on to have ten children who lived to adulthood, thus sidestepping the worst indenture-related experiences. My family history is part of my own being and consciousness, and I believe it is both possible and necessary to make such room for the breadth of their realities as necessarily part of the "we" to which generalizing statements apply. This can be accomplished without requiring that the substance of the work be fundamentally transformed into being *about* race, just as so many find incorporating feminism and queer theory easy to do without necessarily creating work that is *about* feminism or queerness.

It is impossible to speak of the human or humanity without affirmatively addressing the question of race because "humanity" was cocreated in permanent relation to "race." The two are bound together as surely as conjoined twins; any surgical attempt at separating them would kill them both. I will take up this problem specifically through examining the fetish and Marx's commodity fetishism, which are concepts overtly premised on understandings of African spiritual practices as primitive and backward. As the substrate on which ongoing materialist investigation into fetishism is built, the use of the fetish in social science can be framed as a racial encounter demanding closer interrogation.

THE COMMODITY AND COMMODITY FETISHISM

A book on consumption must talk about capitalism, and if you're going to talk about capitalism, you must talk about Marx. Nobody has ever cataloged the trouble with capitalism better than Karl Marx, and it is his concept of commodity fetishism that is responsible for establishing numerous streams of consumption studies. In a nutshell, the commodity according to Marx is an item produced under the economic system of capitalism. In this system, the average person must sell their labor power—that is, get a job where wages are paid. Workers do not own the products they make: they are alienated from the fruits of their labor. They are also alienated from their own labor, as it is this—their labor power—which they have sold in the first place. Under these conditions of alienation, commodities acquire rather magical properties, and the result is what Marx described as "commodity fetishism."

Where commodity fetishism exists, it is commodities that appear to have social lives and social being, not people. People are so completely and so powerfully alienated that they are reduced to things; in the meantime, the things they produce and the things they purchase have acquired all the livingness that people have lost: it is cars that are sexy and houses that are family; we have passion for shoes and yearning for cruises to destinations where love is.

On the radio or in the news we hear about commodity markets for corn or pig bellies, but more generally, a commodity is anything bought or sold. What is interesting about commodities is that anything can be one, whether it's animal, vegetable, or mineral; whether real or imaginary, factual or theoretical; whether physical or utterly intangible. A dog, a carrot, gold—all can be commodities, as can ideas, feelings, sounds, smells. What Marx tried to get us to understand is that what makes all this stuff special is not what it is, but rather what we believe it is. In becoming a commodity the alchemy is accomplished. "It is as clear as noon-day that man, by his industry, changes the forms of the materials furnished by Nature, in such a way as to make them useful to him." So far, so good, right? This is very simple, indeed, "clear as the noon-day sun": people take the raw materials around them and make things out of those raw materials. "The form of wood, for instance, is altered, by making a table out of it," Marx says, by way of example. By taking wood from a tree, making it into boards, or sanding it and staining it, we can transform wood into a table. Again, simple and straightforward. "But, so soon as it steps forth as a commodity, it is changed into something transcendent." With the added element of commoditization, we have gone from "clear as the noon-day sun" to "transcendent": the simple table is now by implication not so clear at all, and something much more complicated than its mere materials, its mere usefulness. First, notice that Marx has given the table agency, a kind of liveliness: the table actually "steps forth," though tables do not normally step anywhere at all. He continues: "It not only stands with its feet on the ground, but, in relation to all other commodities, it stands on its head." Now the table is performing acrobatics! In just the space of a sentence it has moved from stepping forth to standing on its head. This is getting strange indeed. Furthermore, it "evolves out of its wooden brain grotesque ideas, far more wonderful than 'table-turning' ever was." Heavens—that table now has a brain, and one from which evolve grotesque ideas. It is monstrous and magical, otherworldly and occult. There's an important double entendre here that gives added flavor to the mood Marx is creating with this description: "table turning" was a form of séance, so with this statement Marx has taken us, and commodities, into the realm of the supernatural. Part of what he is saying is that once the table has become a commodity, it has become as weird, eerie, and inexplicable as spirits from the nether realm. The table becomes something more than a place to rest a plate. It becomes many things; a symbol of wealth, a cozy reminder of home life, a thing of beauty, a "lifestyle" statement, an object given value beyond its simple ability to raise our meals up from the floor. In a world full of commodities, Marx intimated, things themselves—those very commodities—seem to come alive and to have properties that transform us or our world into something other than it is. We believe these things can make us happy or complete, sexy, healthy, whole. For Marx, the faith we place in stuff is utterly misplaced, and the ability of stuff to plug the holes of our despair or ennui is a figment of our own imaginations. What's worse, he argued, is that the more we believe in things, the less we believe in people. The more we love stuff, the more our ability to form human relationships is diminished.

As I have noted, Wynter, Weheliye, and others argue that the idea of the human itself was built on definitions of blackness that placed blackness outside the domain of the human. As a result it is not possible to speak in an uninflected way about a generalized humanity: humanity is white. Race, they insist, is part of the very birth of the idea and was, at birth, consigned to otherness. Similarly, race is at the very foundation of the notion of the fetish. The word "fetish" comes from the Portuguese and was used to describe the mistake animist Africans supposedly made in believing that tree stumps and the like were inhabited by spirits. In fact, it was the Portuguese who were confused when they witnessed African religious rituals. While animists might well believe that a particular rock or tree or whatever has a spirit residing in it, it is the spirit that is important, not the object that houses it; once the spirit leaves, the object is worthless.[49] The veneration that takes place is not of the wooden idols as objects, but of the spirits that animate them. That's the point of animism: veneration of the spirit. Veneration of the object is most certainly not the point of animism. So, from the very start, the history of the idea of the fetish is one of confusion and poor translations.

Marx's *Capital* was first published in 1867, well before the word "fetish" was applied to issues of sexuality. In the 1860s, the fetish was a specifically African thing, and fetishism itself was viewed by many of Marx's contemporaries as constituting the first stage of religious belief, a belief that was based in "sensuous desire" and manifestly unenlightened.[50] Thus Marx's use of the fetish invokes both race and primitivity. His concept of commodity fetishism calls upon something that distinguishes the African from the European, racially and along evolutionary lines, in terms of thought, culture, and existence. William Pietz observes, "His synopsis of the historical progress of religious consciousness from primordial fetish worship to an ironic deism that was the next best thing to atheism . . . bears an eighteenth-century pedigree."[51] In applying the term "fetish" to contemporary capitalism and the worldviews of Europeans, Marx was leveling an insult of mammoth proportions, stating directly that those who bought commodities were as primitive and backward as Africans. Embedded in Marx's notion of the fetish is the racial insult of comparing whites to blacks, declaring their thoughts undeveloped and primitive, their practices brutish and simple-minded. This smear of ideological blackness that clings to the fetish and to the concept of commodity fetishism itself should be kept in mind. Like white humanity, the fetish is a racialized concept, and because of this it is deeply problematic. The productiveness of the concept is undeniable, and the literature old and new on commodity fetishism or versions of it is large, rich, and provocative. Fully exploding the implications for our understanding of commodity fetishism through an analysis of its foundation in racist misunderstanding is not something there is space for here. Nevertheless, the importance of recognizing the centrality of race in creating the negative valence of the fetish, both as Marx intended it and as it has been activated since, seems necessary.

WHY MARX?

Ethnographers such as myself spend a lot of time observing daily life and writing field notes about it, but almost always about other people. In the diary entries, I was essentially doing anthropological fieldwork on myself. Anthropologists work via a strategy called "participant observation," which means that as we participate in the daily lives of those we are studying, we also observe and record as much as we can about what takes place around us. Even while attending a church service or going on a shopping trip with a family, an ethnographer has to have what I call "two brains": one that is participating, and one that is observing. So even as you are having a conversation, you have to think to yourself, "I'm having this conversation and I need to remember this and this and this about it." Once, years ago, I scandalized an audience of anthropologists by admitting to them that doing fieldwork makes me more than a little crazy. The specific word I used, actually, was "psychotic." How can it be that the main part of my work as an anthropologist is something I hate more than I enjoy?[52] It's this double-brain thing that I find both exhausting and crazy-making, primarily because during fieldwork one hardly ever gets the chance to just be a person engaged in doing whatever you are doing without having an agenda, without having to observe and remember to record it. To be blunt: the ethnographer in the field never gets to be a normal person, and I don't enjoy that, although I've learned to accept it and live with it when necessary. I wasn't surprised, then, when after having begun the diary project, doing participant observation on myself not only made me uncomfortable, but also, increasingly, began to make daily life something of an ordeal.

To get me to focus on someone *else*, I decided to look into the consumer life of Karl Marx. This was clearly something of a strategic choice. Anyone who seriously aims to understand capitalism or any of its elements must read Marx. His sweeping masterwork *Capital* outlines so many of the foundational elements of consumer society, none perhaps more important than his analysis of the commodity. Too many wish to summarily dismiss Marx because he was "wrong" about communism, which entirely misses the point, since he seems to have been quite right about capitalism. While we have yet to see a successfully communist nation or economy, capitalism remains with us still, albeit in ever new and changing forms of the same old thing. I turned to Marx in large part because his ideas about capitalism remain deeply important. I found myself really wanting to understand the man who wrote *Capital*, to get a clearer picture of the world in which he lived, and, ultimately, to imagine the kind of consumer life he might have had. How, I wondered, had he managed his own relationships with things like the family silver, furniture, medicine, even his own overcoat? My investigations into his life, and that of his wife and daughters, was focused on the kinds of important differences there might be between his historical moment, in the late 1800s, and my own, in the early twenty-first century. My real motivation, though, was trying to understand him and his family as real, three-dimensional people. At a very basic level, the point was to see in detail how Marx—like myself—was complex and contradictory, espousing one sort of vision of the world in his intellectual work, while immersed in an utterly different one in his day-to-day life. What kind of committed communist, after all, lives in an upscale London suburb, throwing coming-out balls for his marriageable daughters? What kind of serious ethnographer seeks to illuminate the harsh realities of living poor while refusing to sleep on anything less than 600-threads-per-inch cotton sheets? For Marx (and for me), the contrast is painfully clear. Yet these complexities and contradictions are part of the very humanness that drives the work we do, if I might be so bold as to claim some sort of solidarity with Marx. The contradictions are important and necessary, I think, rather than being pieces of evidence to throw, like stones, at the carefully constructed edifices collectively termed as "our work." Learning that people who have ideas may not always live in accordance with those ideas should hardly be a surprise, yet somehow it nearly always is. In seeking to find and understand these contradictions, my aim has been to contextualize the realness of competing demands, disparate desires, inchoate needs.

Even before their marriage, Jenny recounts how her morning chores involved cleaning up a trail of Marx's cigar ash and butts, loose pages from books, and wayward handkerchiefs. Then the barber arrived. Jenny's tone is sweetly loving in its attention to the material:

> I thought of putting it to great advantage and with rare amiability I asked him how much the Herr Doctor owed him. The answer was 7½, silver groschen. I quickly did the sum in my head and 2½ groschen were saved. [As I read it, she was happy that the barber's accounting of Karl's debt was actually 2½ groschen less than she thought it should be. I wonder why she can so quickly calculate the debt—she knows so much already about how often he gets barbered.] I had no small change and I therefore gave him 8 silver groschen in good faith that he would give me change. [What was Jenny was doing paying Karl's barbering bills, since they had not at that point married?] But what did the scoundrel do? He thanked me, pocketed the whole sum, my six pfennigs were gone and I could whistle for them. [Her tone is less annoyed than light or even silly.] I was still on the point of reproving him, but either he did not understand my glance of distress or Mother tried to soothe me—in short, the six pfennigs were gone as all good things go. [She bemoans—albeit charmingly—the loss of six pfennigs. The beginning of a lifelong pattern.]

What this detailed discussion is, really, is a prenuptial demonstration of her housekeeping skills and her keen eye for budgetary details. She knows what the debt to the barber ought to be; she knows how to use her "rare amiability" to elicit from him an accounting somewhat less expensive than it ought to be; she knows how to begrudge the six pfennigs even though there was a considerable savings overall [2 silver groschen as far as I can tell]. And here she is telling Marx something important about their future life together: I got it covered. She is also warming up to the more important topic, that of Marx's inability to shop properly. In a letter instructing him on how to shop for lace and flowers for her wedding outfit, she writes:

> If you cannot get them cheap or get someone else to choose them, then I ask you, sweetheart, to leave the matter in my hands. In general, sweetheart, I would really prefer at present that you did not buy anything and saved your money for the journey. You see, sweetheart, I shall then be with you and we shall be buying together, and if someone cheats us, then at least it will happen in company.

Her message is not only "leave it to me," but, ever so sweetly, she tells him (sweetheart) to keep his "dear nose" out of affairs into which he should not be meddling (especially if he cannot even manage to remember his handkerchief, which is the incident with which the letter begins). Her intent is unmistakable: she wants him to forget buying these things, since he really is not competent either to choose the best items nor to negotiate the proper price. She cannot come right out and tell him so. Rather, she urges him to save his money for himself, holding out the vision of shopping together as a more enjoyable way to either get cheated or, more likely, a more effective way to make a good purchase. Somewhat disingenuously, she even claims that should they get cheated if shopping together, at least it would be a togetherness experience. There is little danger, I think, that Jenny was likely to be cheated on anything she set her mind to purchase. The offer of shopping-as-togetherness was offered only as a sop to poor Karl's ego.

Marx lived during a time of extraordinary social and economic upheaval, and there's more than a bit of luck in this; thinking about Marx and his family also provides a point of comparison at two key moments when technologies and economies and people are facing change that proceeds at an astonishing pace. The industrial revolution changed more societies faster and more permanently than any other human sea change before it, and during Marx's life much of that change was characterized by industrialization and a massive shift from rural to urban life and living. Today the multiplying uses for social media from banking to terrorism are at the fore, as are the magnifying dangers from the globalized economy where the euro seems about as unsinkable as the Titanic. Thus although we live in very different times and face very different transformations, in some ways Marx's era and our own share more than might at first be imagined. Juxtaposing them is an exercise in exploring the kinds of gaps between then and now, and in feeling out the realms of sameness.

Immersing myself in his work, I got to know a different Marx, especially as I read his wife's letters to him, those of his daughters and friends, and his letters to them as well.[53] This Marx was of course a deeply committed communist, however, when writing to Engels about suppurating sores that plagued him through most of his adulthood, you can be fairly sure the labor conditions of the masses were not his first thought. Marx wrote movingly about commodities—that is, things bought and sold in the open market. Marx hated capitalism because of what it did to people, how it devalued them and invested that value instead into mere objects. I have tried to retrace some of the meanderings that Marx himself took as he moved from the poverty of London tenements to the velvety comfort of a Maitland Park mansion; of his wife, Jenny, as she purchased a coffin for her infant; of his daughter Laura, whose clothes were pawned to pay the family's rent. In many ways, this exploration is not new; feminist and queer appraisals of Marx as a man have examined his very human foibles in light of his intellectual production in important ways.[54] My aim is to attempt to place key moments in the consumer context, to see what other facets may be illuminated about Marx, his family, and their times. I'm interested too in what capitalism did to Marx, how it affected the life Marx led, the kind of person he was, and how his family's experiences are both like and unlike the experiences of life now, in the twenty-first century.

From constantly changing technology to global warming and the globalization of the economy, the irrevocability of changes sparked by capitalism inspires awe and terror. The unevenness with which capitalism's benefits are distributed is something I find maddening. Industrialization, globalization, and the rise of the Internet and wireless technologies have profoundly changed things around us and our relationships to them. They have provided many of us with unbelievably high standards of living and access to luxuries once reserved only for the very rich. They have fueled our imaginations and fantasies and present endless prepackaged stories for us to purchase or dream of purchasing. In limiting myself to a very mind's-eye focus on the intensity and details of my own personal consumer world, my aim has been to put together an account of life in consumer society that is at once something more than the empty promise of shopping, brand awareness, and advertisement-induced insecurities, and something less than the endless opportunity to experience, indulge, and escape. In other words, while it is true that just about everything we come into contact with in daily life is priced and sold just like any other, these things do not all have the same or similar meanings to us, and they do not affect our lives in the same way. For instance, how are things made precious to us by the addition of memory? Why is this particular broken souvenir something with which I cannot part, despite the painful scenes it brings back every time I see it? How have I changed when suddenly an object that used to mean something to me can now be put into the bag of things headed to the thrift store? When a pair of earrings or a coffee mug makes me happy, is that necessarily a bad thing?

These were the questions I wanted to explore. I tried to be as uncompromising as possible in my entries, to avoid portraying myself the way I might want to be seen by others, and endeavored to take on the hard stuff, the ugly stuff, and to be willing to show my ridiculous side too. Hence my embarrassing moments obsessing over kitchen cabinet knobs while failing yet again to schedule a mammogram, even though my own mother had a mastectomy in her early fifties. However, sometimes I would light upon a thing of mine and try to find out about its history, where it might have come from, the people who might have made it, and in doing so I embarked on a journey I would not have taken without this project to make me do it. Knowing there is no way to capture every single facet, mood, or nuance of shopping, of having, of wanting, I nevertheless did my best to cover as wide a range as possible of the kinds of moments that catch us.

A NOTE ON ORGANIZATION

I start papers in the middle and write my way out of them, which is my way of saying I am neither a linear thinker nor a linear writer. Throughout the years I was working on this project, the process was running along several lines at once, none of which was straight for any stretch of time. As with many other writers, there came a time where I felt stuck. I cannot call it writer's block, since the writing had not stopped exactly. The problem was that I really could not see how to shape what I had written into a book. My friend Susan Ruffins rescued me from that state. She took the manuscript in hand, laid out entries across her office, picked them up in one spot and put them down in another, and designated others for the "does not belong in the book" pile. Susan found and identified themes that were woven throughout the work. Her editorial labor allowed those themes to come into focus; I had not been able to see them for myself. We ethnographers spend months or even years documenting all manner of things that might or might not mean anything, but somehow in the process of watching, considering, participating, we begin to cut a path through the overgrowth of information. In my case I needed a guide through the thicket. Susan pointed out the themes of inheritance, survival, and love around which the book is organized.

Following this introductory section, part II of the book consists of the entries, punctuated by musings about Marx, and a couple of deeper digressions into the political economy of pawn, and children's comfort objects. The entries are not arranged chronologically; instead they are in an order that roughly explores the themes of inheritance, survival, and love. Because they were written over the course of a number of years, I had to do some light editing later to lessen confusion. This is especially the case with regard to appearances my daughter makes: in some moments she is two years old, and in others she is a teenager. In part III, I discuss more directly my stance as an autoethnographer and as a writer, taking up questions both personal and theoretical as they shaped the production and formation of the book and my own autoethnographic practice; some readers may want to engage with this material before diving into the entries in order to orient themselves with regard to how I approached the writing itself. Part IV is a surreal autoethnography of things that never happened, a fantastical imagining of where I might have ended up in an alternate or parallel universe.

Given what Marx had to say about our relationships with these commodity-things, it is hard to remember that Marx never abhorred objects in and of themselves: commodities do not create themselves; he was clear about that. A table is a table. It is people who make it into something with a life of its own. It is not the things in and of themselves that are bad and hateful. What is hateful and bad is the social system creating these objects, its contradictions and confusions against which Marx railed. He wanted us to see, most of all, how much the system costs us in human pain and suffering—to acknowledge that all the comforts and efficiencies afforded by the outpouring of luxury and wealth carries with it an unbearably horrifying disfigurement of humanity. To put it very plainly, he observed that we tend to forget that all the stuff we use, pine after, and shop for was made by someone and that more often or not, the people involved in bringing our stuff into being, whether that thing is a roll of toilet paper or a McMansion, reap very little benefit or reward from that process. Absorbed in the beauty of a length of linen cloth, his wife Jenny was unlikely to be thinking of the children tending the spinning machines, the fingers they lost, the schoolrooms they did not have time to visit. Consumers don't meditate on the life-force used up in making the cloth; rather, we imagine the lives we might lead in a dress, or fetching curtains, made from it. When we surround ourselves with stuff without acknowledging its human cost, we tend to get very, very confused. We begin to lose the ability to distinguish between things that have market value and things that have human value, to the degree that human value actually becomes market value—people are worth only what they earn, or what they can make.

It might seem strange, therefore, that even after developing these ideas, Marx stayed passionately attached to all kinds of stuff in his own life: family silver, Scottish napkins, seaside vacations, riding lessons for the girls, cigars, cigars, cigars. He treasured his three small pictures in their frames too, probably without thinking to damn himself or measure his culpability in the uglier parts of how they came to be. He kept these photographs with him all the time: one of his father, one of his wife, a third of his daughter, Jenny. At night did he let them nestle together in his breast pocket? If he did, did he think of the photographer's assistant breathing noxious fumes as the faces of Marx's beloved family revealed themselves on the chemical-bathed paper? Or did he take the photos out and place them beside his bed so that they might sit closer to his dreams? His memories of those he loved were not enough. Their photographs, in their frames, traveled with him, even into death, because he needed them and the comfort they provided, bearing witness to the love he bore them. His close colleague and friend Friedrich Engels placed those three pictures in their frames in Marx's coffin before he was buried. It was the love that mattered, not the objects.

I'm reminded of this every time my daughter snuggles up to me. She has this smell that I am sure I would recognize even if I were blinded and standing in a crowd of thousands, having to sniff each person's neck to find her. This precious, unique thing, my daughter, poignantly reminds me what I can and cannot buy. Shoes, yes. A chandelier, yes. Her, no. Even a perfume that smelled exactly the same—exactly the same! It would not do. But photographs of her matter, in a different kind of way than a pair of shoes, because they help me trace that connection when she is not right there to snuggle with me. When I am traveling, I can kiss her picture goodnight.

2

The Entries

Things are such a part of our lives these days that there isn't really a moment, not a single moment, that we escape from physical contact with one, two, or many of them. More to the point, we just cannot live without them and all that they do for us. Just as our thoughts have no meaning without language, our lives have no meaning without things through which to express who and what we are. I just have to wonder how bad this is—not a rhetorical "How bad could it be?" but a distinct and careful "Exactly how bad is it?" And of course I just don't know. It's certainly not something that can be quantified, as if loving my stuff (and coveting yours) could be, for instance, 87 percent bad and 13 percent good.

Two days after Thanksgiving (and the day after Black Friday) is the perfect day to begin this project of documenting my own consumer life. I read somewhere that on Thanksgiving, American families eat an average of 4,500 calories per person. It's easy to feel simultaneously overwhelmed and appalled by that. How many people in this world even eat 4,500 calories in a week? One of my anthropologist friends likes to point out that Americans love to think of themselves as average. But thinking globally, the average person in the world is not a middle-class American but, instead, a poor peasant in India. So, what reality am I living in as I mull over whether or not to get icicle lights for my southern California stucco home, a home on whose eaves real icicles will never find themselves hanging and melting into spring? Where does this desire come from and why?

One of the main things Marx noticed about capitalism is that it really encourages people to have relationships with things instead of with other people. This mistaking-things-for-people process is what he meant by the evil-sounding term "fetishization." Marx never explained how, exactly, fetishization came about, but I'm guessing that like labor, fetishization is a social process, one that is shared and learned.

LEARN TO LOVE STUFF

Yesterday it occurred to me that although I, along with everyone else, am surrounded in, swimming in, drowning in, wallowing in stuff that dances around us much like the otherworldly table Marx invokes, we have to learn and unlearn what commodities are. What made me think about this is when my then two-year-old daughter Benin reached for "Nightgown," her comfort item of choice, as I strapped her into her car seat. I realized in that moment that she had no idea about buying and selling or the promises of advertisements. This was a revelation to me. Even though the stuff of her everyday existence has the potential to dance like Marx's table, for her this is only stuff. For her, none of the objects populating her daily life really has those magical qualities Marx spoke of; for her there was not much difference between Nightgown, a snail on the porch, or an Elmo video. I was horrified to realize that in so many ways it was *me* who was teaching her to feel love for stuff.

I was looking through a Smithsonian Institute catalog, and my daughter was really getting into a page that had cat items—a pair of cloisonné cat Christmas tree ornaments, a cat lamp (she called it a squirrel), and some cat sculptures. She kept insisting we turn back to that page: "Where are the cats!?" But it was the images she liked, as if they were illustrations in a Beatrix Potter book (which she could pronounce, finally, after spending months saying "Meertrix Merpottis," which sounds harder to say, to me). She had no clue that the items in the catalog are real things she could buy and have at home. This became even more obvious to me when, finally allowed to turn the page, I uncovered a rather large photo of Dorothy-style ruby slippers for kids. Benin has a pair of "Dorothy shoes" that are white and covered with sparkles, bought at the thrift store for $1.99. She's been wearing them for months, since they were about three sizes too large when we bought them, and she searches the house for them, along with her "pink dress" and her blue socks. This outfit must be worn at all times whenever humanly possible. She's nearly worn all the sparkles off the shoes, and when she can't stuff her feet into them anymore, I'm afraid I'm going to have to cut the backs out so she can keep wearing them. I looked at the photo of the red shiny Dorothy shoes and thought, "I can't let her see that photo because she'll be asking for those." It took me several minutes to realize that even if she saw the photo, which she later did, she wouldn't be asking for the Dorothy shoes because she still has no idea what a merchandise catalog is all about. To her it's just another fantasy picture book, like *Peter Rabbit* (or her favorite, *The Tale of Two Bad Mice*). Of course, the catalog is indeed a fantasy picture book but of rather a different sort than *The Tale of Jemima Puddleduck*. The point is, right then, she didn't know the difference.

That realization led me to this idea: we teach our kids how to deal with sold-to-us stuff just as we teach them to speak and use the toilet. It's like the subtle (and sometimes not-so-subtle) ways we train them about how to use their bodies. That is, the process is largely invisible, even to ourselves. Some of it falls into the formal arena, just as teaching table manners (feet off the table) or grammar (don't say "ain't") is often a conscious strategy about training children to be who you want them to be, with manners and accents and ways of sitting that mark them as "one of us," whoever that might be. But the bulk of it is rather subtle. Already I've witnessed myself encouraging Benin to relate to people at the store by letting her hand over the money for a purchase and receive the change. What a big girl! I've noticed myself offering her a trip to the store as if it's something fun and exciting. That attitude is not just a matter of self-defense, that is, aimed solely at allowing me to get the shopping done when I want without a temper tantrum gumming up the works. By trying to get her to see mundane shopping chores—buying the milk and the butter—as exciting and a thrill I am also teaching her that shopping, in and of itself, for whatever item, can be seen as fun! She hasn't yet been taught about things like yearning and waiting—hoping that Santa will bring item X if only she's good, begging me or her dad to get her this toy or that. But I fear that time is just around the corner.

BANKY

Banky was, I think, my first love. I loved my Banky, loved it loved it loved it. It had a calming softness, worn into it by many washings and the brushing of my fingers, that I have never felt again. I slept with it, took it to school with me, and once even tried to go out to dinner with it wrapped around my body underneath my furry winter coat, one of those coats that had the white fur around the hood and woven ribbon at the edge. My parents, seeing my bulky middle, made me fish it out and leave it behind. Another time, when my stepdad was spanking me for something, he stopped and asked the usual rhetorical question, something like "had I learned my lesson." "I want my Banky," I wailed, and he spanked me again.

A pink-and-white square, white and pink on the reverse side, made of cotton. On it an image of a girl teddy bear in a skirt with a bow near her ear talking on the phone with a boy teddy bear, the phone line looping across my Banky in a sweet design, interspersed with hearts and flying birds. Who knows when I got it—when I was a baby, I guess—but all through my early childhood, Banky was a necessary thing. As it became old and worn and holey I could wear it in interesting ways. For a while, when I was in first or second grade, I turned it into a kind of doll, stuffed with underpants and wrapped into a kind of octopus-like shape held together with a rubber band. I drew a face on it with blue marker. I always liked making things.

At night, when I couldn't sleep (which was nearly always), I'd play a game where I would randomly crumple it up into a heap and then pretend that the layers of folds were a landscape to be explored. Grabbing little tiny dollhouse potted plants, dishes, stamps, whatever, I'd furnish the landscape and move about pretending my finger was a person lost among huge, strange objects. Then I would lie in bed and think to myself, OK, if the house is burning down, what things would I grab to take with me. Banky, of course, and that white lace dress that my Chinese grandma gave me before she died. Sometimes I would cry with the drama of it all, imagining the flames and the loss.

My attachment probably has any number of explanations—displacement, loneliness, immaturity. I took Banky everywhere and wanted it with me at all times. It was solid, dependable, and there only for me. I never really thought about it as having a soul or a being, didn't feel that it loved me back, but that wasn't the point. I loved my Banky, loved it true, and it never let me down. Once, when I had taken it to school with me in second grade, I found a note in my cubby that said, "Dear Betsy, you know I love you a lot but I would rather stay home during the day. Love, Blankie." That didn't fool me for an instant. First of all, I wasn't so stupid as to think my Banky was capable of writing. No hands, no muscles, no bones—it was a blanket, for god's sake. Second, the note was written in my teacher's meticulous cursive script. Third, my Banky, even if it could write, would never have asked me to leave it at home. And of course, Banky's name was Banky, not Blankie. Was my teacher so dumb as to think that Banky didn't even know its own name? Banky's place was with me. I got the message, but was deeply offended my teacher thought me so silly that I would believe that note. No, it was the teacher who didn't want me to bring Banky around. She would have done better by me to have signed the note as herself. That I could have respected. Later, when my report card noted that I was bossy, well, that was it. I never forgave her. (Anyhow, I wasn't bossy. I just knew the right way to do everything.)

I had my Banky right up until fifth grade, and if it hadn't gotten lost, I probably would still have it. I had taken it with me to a sleepover party at Michele Stefanedis's house. It was a party where all the girls put on makeup and I got voted prettiest, where we had a séance and lifted Julianne's body right into the air above us and where, the next morning, her parents got into a huge fight and we all went outside on the lawn while her dad threw the cookie jar collection around and broke most of them, and her mom stood in the kitchen and cried. In the tension of it all, where we ran around in the grass trying to distract Michele and ourselves from what was going on inside, I forgot to pack Banky up with my other things. The next day my family and I went out of town for a while. I have no idea where we went or why, but while we were gone, Michele's mom left Banky on the porch in a shopping bag. Problem was, that shopping bag was nowhere to be found when we got back from our trip. A secret part of me suspected a plan had been cooked up between the moms where Michele's mom would say they'd put Banky on the porch but they'd really just thrown it out, all with my mom's behind-my-back approval. I mean, who would steal someone's old stinky, holey security blanket off a porch?

Maybe at some level I was a little relieved that Banky disappeared. Now I didn't have to take responsibility for saying "I don't want you anymore." Banky was just gone and I had to move on and it wasn't so bad. But I'll always wonder where Banky ended up. Sometimes I find my fingers searching for a certain kind of softness in a piece of fabric and I realize I still miss Banky more than I care to admit. You never get over perfect love.

A DIGRESSION ON THE TOPIC OF THE
TRANSITIONAL OBJECT

Let me shift for a moment out of diary entry mode and into scholarly analysis mode. Reflecting on my relationship with my Banky got me thinking
about the "transitional objects." The concept of the transitional object comes
from the work of British psychologist D. W. Winnicott, who describes it as
"the first 'not-me' possession."[1] More broadly, object theory in psychology
is meant to invoke both material objects and the "object" of a child's (or
person's) desire, but I take it as no accident that Winnicott in his essay specifically uses the word "possession." Typically, he notes, this first "not-me"
possession is a soft toy, blanket, or other object, and it is through forming
a relation with this object that the child learns key elements in forming a
self-concept. Part of what is so provocative about Winnicott's notion is that
he views the transitional object as intimately tied up with key processes of
creativity, self-awareness, and the ability to think in complex symbolic ways,
as in the example of play. Object theory stresses that no one interacts with
the external world per se; rather, the material world is always experienced
through a set of associations, internalized images, desires. Object theory
also posits that the transitional object is central in allowing children to in-
dividuate and develop independent identity. Attachment theory draws on
similar ideas and issues. To be fair, the generalized use of the notion of the
"transitional object" does not limit it to a "possession." For most theorists,
the transitional object can vary; it might include body parts or even words.
Moreover, people may have transitional objects at various junctures. Nevertheless, I will focus on Winnicott's own definition of the term, which, wit-
tingly or unwittingly, makes possession a central aspect of the transitional
object.

In a nutshell, the notion of the transitional object posits that infants lack
the concept of "object permanence," so when the mother is absent they experience distress, anger, or other negative feelings. In Winnicott's model, the
mother's breast is, for the infant, the embodiment of the mother, providing
warmth, nourishment, and satisfaction. Transitional objects are something
the infant can draw comfort from in the absence of the breast/mother, and
it is through interacting with the transitional object that infants begin to
explore and understand notions of "not me," that is, developing as independent beings with their own motivations, ideas, feelings.

I am less interested in figuring out whether or not this theory is "true" than in examining it as a concept that naturalizes imperatives of capitalist consumer society. First, as I have already noted, the notion of the transitional object assumes that infants are entitled to private property. Second, "mother" here is singular, as is the breast. Third is the assumption that infants naturally form social relationships with inanimate objects. Perhaps the most central question that goes unasked and unanswered with this notion is "Why is the breast absent?"

In the 1950s, anthropologist Horace Miner identified a strange tribe whose ritualistic behaviors demanded documentation. Inhabiting the North American continent from the Atlantic to the Pacific, from the Canadian border at the north to the Mexican border at the south, this tribe was called the Nacirema. Miner focused his early work among the Nacirema on their mouth rituals; certainly had he examined child-rearing his findings would have been no less dramatic. The Nacirema turned out to be (of course) ourselves.[2] The presence of so much ritual around the question of putting children to sleep ought to be a strong indicator of the level of anxiety about the issue.

Miner might have written this, based on a survey of sleep manuals, magazines, and websites aimed at Nacirema parents: *Sleeping, for the Nacirema, is a dangerous business, especially for children. Nacirema believe that infants must be taught how to sleep and that following complex sleep rituals is a matter of life and death. Nacirema children are initiated into these sleep rituals from birth, sleeping in seclusion, in ritually prepared spaces that cannot be occupied by others. In the Nacirema view, having infants sleep in the same bed with others is a deadly practice. As one Nacirema chief stated, "We know the value of holding your child, cuddling your child, loving your child. But if you take the baby to bed with you and fall asleep, you are committing a potentially lethal act."[3] It is not until they are adults that Nacirema think of themselves as strong and experienced enough to sleep with others. As a consequence, the Nacirema are emphatic that young children must sleep alone.*

Sleeping alone is also thought to develop certain personal characteristics of value to the Nacirema, among these "independence" and "self-reliance." Nacirema believe that infants are naturally dependent and needy and must be taught how to tolerate being alone. The preparatory rituals for sleep help prepare children for these periods of solitude that are so central to developing Nacirema structures of feeling and identity. Especially important in these rituals are qualities of "warmth" and "softness." Accordingly, things the Nacirema identify as "warm" or "soft" are incorporated into presleep rituals. Typical elements include immersing the body in water that has been warmed, ingestion of warm drinks, or even warming of the ritual sleeping place. In addition, lighting that is "soft," music that is "soft," and even a "soft" voice may be used when singing ritual presleep chants known as "lullabies." Even among the nonreligious Nacirema the belief in the power of these rituals is deep-seated. Falling asleep "on one's own" is a central part of the presleep ritual. Once the ritual is completed, the caregiver leaves the infant on its own to fall asleep. Thus Nacirema strive to ensure that infants and children do not fall asleep before rituals have been completed. It is thought to be particularly dangerous for children to fall asleep while feeding, so Nacirema will wake a child who has fallen asleep at the breast, in order to perform the presleep ritual and ensure that the child falls asleep "on its own" and in the ritual sleep space. Occasional slips are accepted, but Nacirema parents who frequently fail to perform the ritual are often castigated by big men and chiefs, family and community. Children who are unable to fall asleep "on their own" must hide this fact, because it is very shameful for the entire family. Such children are considered open to a host of problems, including aberrant sexuality, and it is generally asserted that these children will remain forever immature, dependent, and babyish. Further, they are also thought to lack important moral characteristics, including "self-control."

Interestingly, while the Nacirema have a fear of infants being dependent on people in order to fall asleep, they encourage children to become attached to objects. Nacirema children are presented at birth with powerful ritual objects that embody the valued qualities of warmth and softness associated with successful sleep. Children are encouraged to form deeply emotional relationships with these objects and, like Nuer boys with their cows, may name them, sing about them, and draw significant social status from their display. The Nacirema believe the relationships children develop with such objects are important for many aspects of their lives, helping to develop imagination, language skills, and self-concept. The ritual sleep space, then, is to be occupied only by the child and its power objects so that these relationships may be energized, resulting in magical transformations leading to the growth of "independence" and "self-reliance" in the child itself. The importance of children's relationships with these power objects is so great that Nacirema place their children alone in ritual sleep spaces with them for at least ten to twelve hours per day. To be most effective, this time of communion between the child and its power objects should be uninterrupted, and Nacirema parents whose children "sleep through the night" take pride in this accomplishment, viewing those children as maturing well. Throughout their lives, Nacirema continue to commune with power objects, and such communion becomes increasingly public. Through these objects, Nacirema at once formulate and demonstrate their sense of "individuality" or "identity."

Clearly, this account is a bit tongue-in-cheek, but based on the extant literature, the portrait is not much of an exaggeration. What is distinctly absent—both in the literature and in the sketch above—is a sense of the diversity of practices that actually take place on the ground, in the United States and, perhaps more important, outside it. Despite the very strong prohibitions in the United States against children sleeping in bed with parents and caregivers, it turns out that it happens regularly in households of all types, and happens habitually in a wide range of communities, especially among immigrants and African Americans. In fact, this baby-sleeps-alone "ideal" is adhered to fairly inconsistently, and then is prevalent pretty much only among the upper and middle classes in the United States, and then primarily among whites. As with so much else, the ideals and practices of a relatively focused slice of the population becomes the model for all, and when people "deviate" they are portrayed as exhibiting pathology.

Anthropology has long taken psychology to task for being ethnocentric and ahistorical, and the question of early childhood development is particularly rich in examples of counterknowledge coming from ethnographic observation and examples. Malinowski famously challenged Freud's notion of the Oedipus complex by arguing that among matrilineal peoples, the fundamental conflict is with the mother's brother, not the father.[4] Recent cross-cultural work on infancy and childhood reveals similar problems with the underlying assumptions common to much psychological theory. For example, because such theory is built around a patriarchal, nuclear family, many types of social relationships and development are not taken into account. My position is similar to many of these ongoing critiques, but here I am concerned especially with the ways that this particular theory—the notion of the transitional object—is an example of making the workings of capitalism part of the natural order of things.

The situation, as I read it, is something like this: capitalism requires autonomous individuals; this leads to the mandate that from earliest infancy, children are to sleep alone; being alone causes infants anxiety; to soothe this anxiety, they are provided with security objects, many of which become transitional objects. The provision of these security objects is the initial instance of acclimating children toward forming social relationships with objects, and this is a foundational moment in creating a commodity fetishist. What is key here is that the object is intended as a *substitute* for the person/love object: rather than interacting with a person to gain comfort, the infant is encouraged to draw comfort from a thing.

Having a human baby in bed with a Heartbeat Bear is pretty similar to the set of conditions that Harry F. Harlow set up for rhesus monkey babies in a series of experiments undertaken in the 1950s and 1960s. While raising rhesus infants in captivity away from their mothers, Harlow noticed that they formed deep attachments to the terry-cloth pads in their cages. If the pads were removed, the baby monkeys would have temper tantrums. This got Harlow thinking about the connection between love and nourishment, and he devised a set of experiments in which rhesus infants were separated from their mothers between six and twelve hours after birth. For his initial experiment he constructed two types of "mothers" for the baby monkeys. "Wire mothers" were constructed of wire mesh; "unibreast" mothers were covered with terry cloth and heated with a lamp, thus providing both softness and warmth. Infant monkeys had access to both types of "mother." With one group of infants, nourishment came only from the wire mothers; with the other group, it was the terry-cloth mothers that provided nourishment. This experiment was called the "dual-mother surrogate condition." What Harlow found among infants with lactating wire moms was surprising: they went to the wire mother only for nourishment, spending most of their time with the cloth mother. Wire-mom babies experienced more diarrhea and other problems, leading Harlow to suggest that there is something about what he called "love" that really does make a difference. He did not conduct an experiment to see whether rhesus monkey infants nevertheless formed attachments to objects if they were raised in the presence of a live rhesus mother.[5] My guess would be that no such attachments would have arisen.

Of course human babies are not rhesus babies. Getting back to the transitional object, this substitutive element—where the object is a stand-in for the mother—is a feature that is virtually never built into gifts or material culture in noncapitalist cultures. Of course gifts may symbolically *represent* a person or relationship, but the gift is not understood as a substitute for people or relationships, as the transitional object is; alternatively, material goods often facilitate relations between people but, again, do not substitute for them. What is unique to capitalism is that people have social relationships with the objects themselves—a central part of what Marx meant by commodity fetishism. Marx also meant by this that objects appear to have magical qualities, and lives of their own.

Cross-cultural evidence shows that the amounts of time that Euro-American infants spend alone is at one extreme end of the scale. Studies have shown that infants in "developed" cultures are in close physical contact with caregivers about five hours a day, that is, about 20 percent of the time, including feeding and physical care. In contrast, among hunter-gatherers, infants are in close physical contact 85–90 percent of the time: they are carried in slings or tied onto backs; they sleep with caregivers and breast-feed at will. This is also true of a number of more sedentary groups, including the Yucatec Maya and the Gusii of East Africa; in an exhaustive survey of literature, Regine Schön and Maarit Silvén find similar figures for five other cultural groups.[6] Under these circumstances, absence of the breast/love object is infrequent at best, and this proximity lasts well into the first year, though it decreases a bit with time. In a comparative study of foragers and farmers in central Africa it was noted that "the Aka infants were substantially more likely than Ngandu infants to sleep, drowse, to be held or fed, or to be within proximity of their care providers, whereas Ngandu infants were more likely than Aka infants to be alone, fuss, cry, smile, vocalize to care providers, play alone, or play with objects."[7]

The authors of the above study used this difference to argue for the variability of child-care patterns in so-called traditional societies. However, I suggest that the difference has a great deal to do with sedentarism versus foraging and the forms of social organization that generally accompany those very different modes of production. It seems unsurprising that sedentarism would be accompanied by an increase in separations from caregivers, who now must engage in a wide range of work activities inside and outside the house; additionally, sedentarism generally leads to higher fertility rates and the presence of older siblings and other relatives who can stand in for the mother. Finally, the spaces in which settled people live, with their enclosed houses and cleared yards, are places where infants may be left on their own for periods of time without having to worry (too much) about their safety. (One example of this with an older child can be seen in the film *The Story of the Weeping Camel*, set in Mongolia. When the caregiver needs to do chores, she ties her toddler round the waist by a tether, leaves him in the yurt, and goes about her business.)[8]

The effect of subsistence patterns on infant-caregiver proximity and contact seems to be widespread, though difficult to establish given the very small number of hunter-gatherer and foraging cultures still extant today. In a study of 10 foraging cultures and 176 nonindustrial societies, B. Lozoff and G. Brittenham found that all of the foragers provided infants with close physical contact more than half of the time, while this was true for only 56 percent of the nonindustrial societies.[9]

For the transitional object to be culturally possible in the way that Winnicott describes it, people must have possessions in the first place, and also be relatively sedentary; as Engels noted long ago, sedentarism is a prerequisite for private property, and the two are deeply connected.[10] We know from the anthropological literature that these two elements (the individual and private property) are relatively recent, historically speaking, and in evolutionary terms the human species has possessed private property for less than 1 percent of its history.[11] That infants could even have possessions is an idea that becomes possible only in cultures valuing private property and, moreover, in cultures where children are viewed as individuals who have rights to private property.

Referring to hunter-gatherers provides a stark contrast that can help illustrate some of the problematic assumptions built into the notions of the transitional object. However, even in state-level societies, it is important to take into account questions of culture and poverty, and there are indications that the incidence of transitional object use has been rather strikingly varied.[12] Among the very poor, or in cases of great social inequality, where access to material resources is highly constrained, the conditions encouraging children to have possessions may well be absent. While my work with Haitian children has been primarily informal, I have never seen a Haitian child with a transitional object or security item. This is in large part because most of the children I interact with in Haiti are extremely poor, and, moreover, they are household slaves who are understood to have neither autonomy nor personal possessions; anything they do possess is entirely contingent and can be taken away at any moment. These children, often as young as three years old, have no rights, whether to possessions or to self-determination, in the households and communities in which they live. I would suspect that for such working children in India and Latin America, the situation is substantially the same.

Considering this variety in relation to the historical and cultural manifestations of the transitional object (which, I assert, is deeply connected to capitalism and teaching commodity fetishism), I come to what I consider one of the abiding problems in the way that Marxian fetishization needs to be investigated by scholars of children's consumption: how do we become commodity fetishists? Marx's point that all labor is social labor is an old chestnut, and much ink has been spilled to describe the complex ways in which social labor is put to use in the workings of the mode(s) of production. By contrast, there is little to no investigation of how the fetishization of the commodity is accomplished in individual or social experience except from the labor point of view. How does one *learn* to mesh self and sneakers, identity and eye shadow? It is as if the fetish erupts into social life already dancing (as in the case of Marx's famous table) on its own. This, following Marx himself, is by definition quite impossible. If, like labor, the fetishization process must be understood as social, we learn fetishization, and—perhaps more frightening—we teach it too, specifically through encouraging children to take up security blankets, binkies, and other self-soothing items whose basic need arises from the connected imperative that children sleep alone.

Thinking along these lines, it seems apropos to examine how our materially oriented capitalist society encourages children from very early on to form social relationships with objects—relationships that may well begin with Winnicott's transitional object, which then must be understood as a specific psychological phenomenon particular to capitalism and not a universal human process or problem. We make great sport in anthropology of knocking down straw men (economic man has been particularly violently battered). I make the point that the transitional object must be culturally specific not so much to discredit psychological theory but, rather, to understand that theory in historical context and, in particular, to emphasize the degree to which (if I haven't already made it clear) something like the transitional object, while a powerful notion, is profoundly enmeshed with contemporary consumer capitalism.

It would be overreaching to claim that capitalism and consumption are the only explanations for the notion of the transitional object. It is also important to distinguish a transitional object understood to be a possession from a self-soothing or calming tool that might be a thumb, a lock of hair, or an earlobe, whether one's own or someone else's. That is, while a transitional object may indeed serve a self-soothing purpose, its importance goes far beyond that in a way that self-soothing practices (twirling the hair) do not. The key thing is (of course) the nature of the relationship, not the thing itself. The threads I am attempting to trace here are the imperatives to develop children from earliest infancy as autonomous individuals in the very specific way in which both "autonomy" and the "individual" are understood in the Global North generally and in the United States more specifically. These are imperatives that have generated a large literature and professional discourse, both medical and psychological, on children's needs and proper development, and chief among these is the need for infants to sleep alone. Sleeping alone quite often provokes in infants anxiety and discomfort, and this is addressed by comfort objects such as pacifiers, teddy bears, and soft blankets, which the child is encouraged to relate to socially, in the absence of the mother (or love-object). Interestingly, according to the kinds of scales generally used by psychologists to investigate the question of children's attachment to caregivers, it seems to make little difference whether or not the child has a strong relationship to a transitional object. In a study of the relationship between children with security blankets and the type of attachment they had with mothers, the authors concluded that attachment to the mother and use of a transitional object operated independently.[13]

I am suggesting, then, that capitalism profoundly exacerbates the tendency for infants and children to develop social relationships with objects and that this takes place through a set of social practices involving adults who encourage infants to form deep emotional ties with these objects. To further highlight the historical specificity of the practice, I reiterate my hunch that in cultures where economies and social relations are more collective and egalitarian, we will likely find that transitional objects of the type we encounter so often in advanced capitalist societies are rare or absent.

The substitution of a thing for a person is commodity fetishism in a nutshell, and this is precisely what is understood to happen when a child acquires a transitional object. However, in cultures where the notion of personal property is not encouraged or valued, I doubt that transitional objects of the sort Winnicott has in mind are likely to be found. Certainly in all my reading up on hunter-gatherer children, and in all the ethnographic films I've seen, I've never come across an image with one of these children who has a comfort object. They hardly need them: it is quite common in egalitarian societies for women to breast-feed children other than their own (not to mention juveniles from other species). This more collective and flexible approach to breast-feeding also can be seen among more sedentary cultures, such as those in the lowland Amazon, where the economy revolves around gardening and hunting. In these cultures the mother or breast is not singular, and this situation is often reflected in kinship terminology. For example, in the Hawai'ian system all women in the mother's generation are called by the same term, which indicates a similarity in the construction of the child's relationship with each of those adults. While children know who their biological mothers are, they also can go to these other women as mother-figures, asking for food or for care, and expect to receive it. Consumption at every level, then, in such egalitarian societies tends to have profoundly collective aspects: everything is shared, from food to sleeping space, and those who seek solitary time are generally viewed as mentally unstable, dangerous, or both. Refusing to share is one of the central reasons an individual might be ostracized, tantamount to a death sentence in the harsh environments where egalitarian cultures persist. Thus in so-called traditional societies, where breast-feeding is often long-term and even collective, the child's understanding of breast and self, ownership and identity, are substantially different from those posited by Freud and Winnicott; recent work in Melanesia, for example, has revolved around the notion of the "partible body" or the "dividual" and centers on the idea that, as Marilyn Strathern says, "persons are not conceptualized, therefore, as free-standing" (588). Strathern and others argue that among the Melanesians they describe, the entire social body is experienced as a whole; specific people are "dividuals" within that whole, rather than "individuals" who come together as in common West/North/ Dominant constructions of the self. "Being" oneself, in such cultures, is a very different project than in the global North.[14]

The trauma of "losing" the breast either literally or figuratively seems possibly irrelevant in cases where private property is nonexistent, where hierarchy is profoundly mediated by egalitarian procedures, and where the self is experienced as partible rather than autonomous. Lest the argument about collectivity be mistaken as a nostalgic view of joyful togetherness, I want to point out that such cohesiveness is actively enforced and that the costs for stepping out of collectivity are substantial. Anthropologist Jean Briggs recalls in her book *Never in Anger* a moment when, while living among the Inuit in Canada, she is asked by a young child to share a small handful of her raisins.[15] Low on her raisin supply and frankly worn out with the porousness of collective life lived inside a very small space, she refuses the child's request. What for most of us might seem a perfectly reasonable and unremarkable instance of an adult asserting her rights over a child actually precipitates a crisis so severe that Briggs is nearly ousted in the dead of winter from the igloo home she shares with the child's family.

Contrast Briggs's experience with what I found in my own fieldwork in New Haven, Connecticut, among poor and working-class black children. Most slept in their own beds, and for the majority, these beds were in their own, separate rooms. Even the poorest children had a fair number of personal possessions, from clothes to toys and books. In New Haven, as in the United States more broadly, children are expected to sleep in their own beds, and for those children under the state's care (foster care in particular) this requirement is mandated by rules and regulations monitored and enforced by the state. Children are also expected to have their own possessions, and adults who do not provide private spaces and personal things for children are viewed as not providing adequately for children's needs. A lack of private space is one thing that can trigger the attention of social service agencies, and in general the failure to provide children privacy is viewed with extreme negativity and may even result in state intervention into the home. Thus even for the poor, for whom private space is often at a premium, maintaining private space for children is an imperative both for cultural reasons and in order to negotiate successfully with state observation and intervention. As with so much else, when their own practices diverge from those that are officially sanctioned, they must hide or deny them.

Many of the children I worked with showed me soft toys that had been given to them "when I was still in the hospital," that is, within a day or two of their birth. These first gifts were treasured (and may or may not have been used as transitional objects) in part because they marked the child's arrival into the family. As the child was born into the world, he or she was also nearly instantaneously presented with a commodity to mark the occasion. Baby gifts, of course, take a wide range of forms, as do transitional objects themselves. Nevertheless, typical gifts also make fantastic transitional objects: soft toys, blankets, and the like. Research has shown that mothers may well encourage their infants to move into relationship with specific objects by always placing them in the crib, urging children toward transitional objects by putting them in their hands.[16] Today it is possible to buy objects specifically manufactured to become transitional objects—a wide range of ready-made "lovies" and security objects are available for sale.

The ritual gift of that first stuffed toy is also the first step in training individuals to put their trust in things, not people. It's really quite a strange practice: we urge children to become attached to things from their very earliest moments by surrounding them with soft blankets and stuffed animals and encouraging them to love them. One of the wackiest examples of this is the Heartbeat Bear, which, when turned on, emits sounds replicating the mother's heartbeat as heard by baby in the womb. "Modern" parents, encouraged by a wide range of experts to train their children to sleep on their own, and to avoid cosleeping, put their child in a crib and then in order to soothe the child to sleep and perhaps to make it feel comforted and loved and not alone, plonk a plush bear in the crib, a bear emitting heartbeat sounds, with the idea that this will remind the infant of the security and comfort of being in the womb. The underlying concern about getting babies to sleep on their own is one of encouraging independence and individuation, and, from some perspectives, it is a question of whether the child will move on to normal adult sexuality.[17] I would argue, however, that this push for infant independence and the fear that a lack of independence might also lead to abnormal sexual proclivities is relatively recent and connected to both parental work schedules and the training of future workers. Interestingly, however, these rituals are very recent and can trace their roots to the 1920s or 1930s, when anxieties about sleep rose dramatically. These anxieties coincided with a marked rise in infants sleeping alone, and, importantly, with a marked rise in professional discourse about the importance of sleep schedules, providing specific sleeping conditions, and so on, a discourse dominated by doctors and psychologists. This shift with regard to child rearing mirrors that taking place in giving birth, where the process becomes increasingly controlled by certified professionals who dispense expert knowledge and advice. Notions of poverty, health, and hygiene were being refigured and redefined and, importantly, reinforced by a range of players including doctors, schools, and social workers. Manuals, magazines, education, and home visits all provided modes of entry into reshaping family life and practices.[18]

However historically shallow the idea that "baby sleeps best alone" may be, the notion is remarkably deep-seated in Euro-American cultures. On the whole, medical experts and public health offices seek to discourage cosleeping. Part of what is deeply fascinating here is the disorderly nature of the thinking, unless one takes capitalism into account as the driving logic of the arguments. The "baby sleeps alone" approach gives little or no credence, for example, to the fairly large literature attesting to the benefits of cosleeping, including longer and better sleep for everyone involved, significantly decreased incidence of crib death, and (not surprisingly) emotional benefits that are difficult to quantify. (Here I must admit that I coslept with my child, and did so unapologetically.) There is also a marked lack of evidence that sleep disturbance or abnormal sexual behaviors result from cosleeping. While evolution and genetics are often the keystone of today's scientific arguments, "baby sleeps alone" manages to overlook the pretty convincing evolutionary evidence that cosleeping likely typifies human behavior over the millennia, defining the norm rather than an aberration. Taken together, the evidence ought to lead to the conclusion that cosleeping is neither physically nor psychologically dangerous and may even be adaptive. Instead we get "baby sleeps best alone."

Evidence shows that the primary dangers of cosleeping have to do with inappropriate bedding and/or nonsober or smoking parents. It is not the cosleeping in and of itself that is dangerous, as James J. McKenna points out, using data from his mother-infant sleep laboratory.[19] Nevertheless, in 2005 the American Academy of Pediatrics Task Force on Sudden Infant Death Syndrome (SIDS) made the recommendation that infants should sleep alone, a move that connected bed-sharing to SIDS. However, most evidence seems to show that bed-sharing deaths result not from bed-sharing per se, as one study states: "Bedding-environment and sleep-position risks and higher ratios of demographic and lifestyle risk factors"[20] are by far the most prevalent issues. As McKenna has noted, the single most common factor in bed-sharing deaths is that children were bottle-fed. Moreover, since 1992 when the American Pediatrics Association began advising that infants sleep on their backs, along with sleeping alone, research shows that a large part of the lowering of SIDS deaths is actually a result of changed classification categories, one of which is the quickly growing category of infant deaths attributed to cosleeping.[21] At the same moment, then, that cosleeping has been identified as a dangerous practice associated with SIDS risk, it has also been disaggregated from SIDS statistics, emerging as a cause of death all on its own—while still being considered a risk factor in SIDS. The way I see it, bed-sharing is being double counted (a methodological problem) and doubly blamed (a conceptual problem). In Los Angeles County, for example, forty-four infants were found to have died "after sleeping next to an adult," and this was identified as a 76 percent increase from 2005. These numbers led to a blanket call for parents to refrain from cosleeping with infants. It is not clear, however, when Los Angeles County began tracking such deaths, what measures have been in place for identifying such deaths, whether such deaths were due to problems with unsafe sleeping environments or parental sobriety, or whether or not these deaths are being identified in conjunction with SIDS. Was this increase really a side effect of a reclassification rather than a jump in similar types of deaths? What role did bedding, parental sobriety, or bottle-feeding play in these deaths?

Lee Gettler and James McKenna have carefully analyzed the rhetoric around cosleeping in the United States and criticize key players for either overtly or covertly creating policies and public health campaigns that discourage any kind of cosleeping at all. In particular, they note that rather than responding to the evidence with education campaigns about safe cosleeping, the response is to call for infants to sleep alone.[22] These campaigns can be dramatic indeed: a 2010 public service ad from the city of Milwaukee shows an image of a queen-sized bed whose headboard is a gravestone on which is engraved the message "FOR TOO MANY BABIES LAST YEAR THIS WAS THEIR FINAL RESTING PLACE." One would expect that an objective, non–ideologically driven science would seek to clarify the causative factors and respond accordingly, yet the imperative is nearly always expressed in terms of avoiding cosleeping as if it is the cosleeping itself that is dangerous and deadly. The persistence of the perspective makes me suspicious. The emphasis fits in surprisingly well with the priorities of capitalism, with the pressure to become an autonomous individual, a pressure that, apparently, can never be brought to bear too early. The vehemence of the push against cosleeping seems to come less from a rise in infant deaths and more from the rise in the cosleeping practice itself—something that perhaps could be viewed as a hopeful surge of sociality in the face of the individualistic autonomy demanded by capital.

Interestingly, newer evidence shows that babies do best when sharing a sleep space, that is, when sleeping in the same room as a caregiver. In a solomonic declaration that managed to acknowledge the evidence without entirely giving up on the idea that cosleeping is dangerous, the American Academy of Pediatrics policy statement on SIDS advocates that infants sleep in the same room, but in a separate crib or bassinet. The policy statement also advocates the use of a pacifier, which seems to lower incidence of SIDS, and, interestingly, for many children the pacifier becomes the transitional object.[23]

The child's first "not me" possession, then, is at root something arising from infants sleeping alone, and this is the result of the combination of private property and capital's need for independent individuals. As cosleeping becomes more common (or at least more commonly admitted to), the efforts to clamp down on the practice strike me as deeply revealing of the anxieties provoked by the sociality and intimacy embedded in this practice. The professional discourse against cosleeping is so oddly out of sync with its own data that it seems virtually impossible not to analyze the rhetoric against the practice as a symptom, a cultural and historical artifact. Cosleeping is constructed as life-threatening, and along with that, sleeping alone becomes medically necessary, as does, to some degree, the transitional object itself.

In the end, then, Winnicott's notion of the transitional object is incredibly useful because it helps us understand the social processes through which the imperatives of capitalism shape our most fundamental being, the way we experience ourselves, naturalizing our alienation to the point where we experience it as proper parenting, as citizenship, as patriotism, as love. The child's relation with the transitional object is about the transition into consumer capitalism, not away from the mother or the breast, except insofar as those are symbols of humanity itself. And who needs humanity? Capital can always provide a Heartbeat Bear to make us feel secure and loved, and not alone.

As I was working on this argument, which I wholeheartedly think makes absolute sense, and so at least in that way I believe it, I went to a conference in Sweden on child and teen consumption, where I delivered a talk based on these ideas. My travel time to Sweden was quite long, with a nearly three-hour stopover in New York. While killing time between flights, and while worrying a bit about the length of the travel time ahead of me, I decided to buy a traveler's neck pillow, this one in plush fabric and in the shape of a panda. The fabric was deliciously soft and utterly reminiscent of my Banky. I spent much of my time on the plane, and elsewhere, touching and feeling the softness of that panda, and it was almost as if I had my Banky back again.

CEBEBRATE!

My daughter grew up in the era of pharmaceutical television advertising. In contrast to the cute depictions of mental depression and songs about arthritis that have surrounded her, my childhood soundtrack was the Oscar Meyer baloney song and the "Ay, yi, yi, yi" of the Frito Bandito. Admittedly this is probably not worth romanticizing, but obesity issues aside, the problems that come with a lifelong trigger memory for deli meats and corn chips seems just a tad less problematic than one for poorly tested painkillers and mildly habit-forming sleep aids with very scary side effects. These are the commercials sealed into my daughter's mind. When she was about two, and the Celebrex commercials would come on, she was mesmerized. "Celebrate, Celebrex!" went the soundtrack, to the 1970s tune of "Celebrate" by Three Dog Night—a tune the target audience of arthritic oldsters might recall with happy memories. As smiling, gray-haired men and women went through their tai chi moves, Benin would be standing in front of the TV, swaying back and forth, waving her arms, smiling and singing "Cebebrate, cebebrate!" It was so sweet to see her enjoying the music and at the same time moderately horrifying to see her loving a drug commercial as much as she did, regardless of whether she understood that the point was to sell Celebrex, a drug that turned out to have some pretty bad side effects, due to a somewhat rushed FDA approval process backed, no doubt, by pharmaceutical-company-induced urgency aimed at making lots of dough.

A couple of years later, she came up to me and said, "Mommy, I think I need Lunesta! I have trouble sleeping and if you give me Lunesta I will go to sleep at night!" Really, I try to be with the times and not to read too much into cultural change. I don't want to be a wet blanket or a party pooper, but it is disturbing to be living in a time when a four-year-old child comes up to you and asks for prescription drugs. Of course the lovely animation in the commercial probably had something to do with it. The Lunesta commercials showed people snoozing comfortably in bed, lulled to sleep by a beautiful pale green moth that flew above them, and then up into the sky. I wanted to explain to her that probably the main reason they're using the animation is because they're too cheap to hire actors, who, if they say anything on screen rather than lying there asleep, would have to be paid more than the animators they likely hired in China to do the work.

It is certainly true that my daughter has never been big on getting to bed. She is a party girl and does not want to miss the party under any circumstances. I have only once in her entire life heard her declare that she was tired, and she resists sleep (on the front end, anyway) valiantly. On the back end, she cannot stand getting up in the morning. What a struggle. So in a way Lunesta might even make sense—not that I ever considered it—but the commercial did address the ongoing battle in our house over getting her to sleep at a reasonable hour. My response so far has been peppermint and chamomile tea and a touch of melatonin before bed, which seems to work fine.

However, I need to get her off the Lunesta kick because I really don't want her to think that every problem can be solved with a pill. Plus Lunesta too seems to have some fairly disturbing side effects, including doing all sorts of things while not entirely awake, from raiding the refrigerator to having sex and driving around town. While I'm not prepared to have a detailed discussion with my four-year-old about side effects and double-blind clinical studies and the political economy of the pharmaceutical industry, I am prepared to issue a mommy-sized "no" and that ought to do it. I am not ready, after all, for her to be having sex and driving around town.

In a way medical advertising seems more problematic, more dangerous, and maybe even harder to address than the more basic stuff like toy ads or clothing brand billboards. The commercials I think are the most ridiculous are the ones that ask, "Do you suffer daily fatigue?" which I take to mean: Are you tired at the end of the day? My answer to that is, in a nutshell, "Hell, yeah!" Apparently, though, "daily fatigue" is a recognized syndrome, where someone feels dragged out all the time. (Wait, that's me!) On a lark and because I didn't want to grade papers, I started chasing the concept down across a bunch of websites that explained what might cause "daily fatigue." Hypothyroidism? Check. Busy lifestyle? Check. Depression? Check. Hmmm, I start thinking, maybe there is a pill that might magically make me happy and energetic! What are the options? It's no surprise that a wee web search turns up all sorts of options, from the herbal to the utterly synthetic. There are the "try this, it's totally natural" products, and there are the "ask your doctor if it's right for you" products. And it's exceptionally easy for a little exploratory jaunt to turn into a several-hour odyssey that involves putting things into shopping carts in multiple online stores, reading articles, cruising blogs, double-checking research, and on and on and on. I start out by trying to smartly critique the invention of a disorder and end up thinking I ought to try to address my own daily fatigue. While I'm at it, I think my hips and knees are getting arthritic and some Celebrex might not be a bad idea, after all. Cebebrate!

MY PURPLE SHOES

There's a way we work to make things ours. Some of it's in the choosing: I'm me because I bought this and not that, and because as those choices begin to congeal into a pattern, they take on a me-ness that is utterly unique. Like a lot of people, I get a kick, a certain kind of personal pleasure, from choosing things that other people notice and appreciate. Or that make them laugh. Yes, it makes me feel like more of an individual to have things that other people don't have—though sometimes, when my choices (particularly in clothes) are way out there, I do suspect that people are just staring because I really look like a clown. One day, on my way home from dance class a few years ago, I had stopped at the store to get some milk and stuff, but halfway to the door realized I *actually did look like a clown*, and got back in my car and went home. I was wearing a jacket I'd made when I still lived in New York (when I still had time to sew my own clothes) that was from children's upholstery material, a design that looked like a child's drawing of animals at the zoo. Very big crayon-y outlines in bright colors, elephants, zebras, and so on. Underneath that, I had on my blue-and-black-striped dance pants. I really did look like a clown. Seriously. I couldn't quite face going into the supermarket dressed like that.

But my purple shoes. The first thing I have to say about them is: $8.99 at Ross! I could probably look at any piece of clothing I have and say where I got it and how much it cost (if I bought it). However, telling people those kinds of money secrets is a little bit like telling them which sexual positions you prefer. I don't actually feel that talking about prices is dirty, but sometimes people respond to me as if I've told them what I really like is hot sex doggie-style in the guest bathroom.

So, these purple shoes. Some people tell me they look like "space shoes." Really, people have actually said they remind them of that show Lost in Space. Personally, I don't think they look like space shoes at all. They're not really purple purple, but more a lilac color, and here's the good part: they're shiny metallic and kind of shimmery like a butterfly. They're loosely in the sport shoe vein, though not quite; the soles are a little high, so they don't look like a sneaker at all. You slip them on, and there's elastic that holds them on. Am I imagining things, or has shoe design really undergone some sort of radical transition in the last couple of years?—they're like these amazing sculptures! I had gone to Ross to buy long-sleeved shirts for work and since it's winter I always wear about three layers (witness today's undershirt, T-shirt, and sweater). I spent a long time finding a few shirts that were inexpensive that I liked and could wear to teach in, since I like to dress up a bit when I teach, not in suits or anything, but a change from what I normally wear at home. Formal-ish, without being stuffy and boring. I wasn't there to buy shoes, but I have a shoe thing and cruised the shoe section while I held seven shirts, having decided I would only allow myself to purchase five of them. I tried on a pair of zip-up boots that were $16.99 with that fake pony-fur stuff, very fun, but the heels were way too high. Then suddenly I saw those lilac shimmery shiny shoes and I couldn't believe they were in my size. I grabbed them, snatched them from that lower shelf, and thought: this is why I came here.

Years ago in Seattle, when I was in my senior semester of high school, I saw a pair of shoes I desperately wanted. It was an awful year. I'd headed out to Seattle to live with my dad, but he ended up in LA, so I stayed with friends of his, living on their enclosed porch. The public school I attended was a bit of a shock for me, coming from what I call "hippie high," a tiny, experimental high school in Connecticut I'd been at for the preceding three years. I'd gone into a store to look for some shoes to wear to the prom, which I was attending with my gay friend Apollo as a joke. My other high school didn't even have a prom! I had made my prom dress and I even made Apollo a little boutonniere in the shape of pansies. That day, the shoes that caught my eye were little ballet flats, and like my lilac shimmery shoes, they were metallic and in bright colors like bold magenta, pink, green, and blue and so beautiful, like butterfly wings. They were too expensive and I just couldn't buy them. There are some things I have seen and wanted that I just can't forget, like those little ballet flat shoes from Seattle. It's actually something I think about with many purchases I make now: is this something that I'll think about in twenty years and still wish I'd gone ahead and bought? Or will I forget about it and it won't matter at all? How do you tell the difference between those kinds of wanting and wishing in the moment?

Wearing my purple shoes around campus, I don't get many remarks, but when I wore them to Washington, DC, for the annual anthropology meetings, it was hilarious. I had them on with black tights and a skirt, and the whole day I could see people tracking the shoes with their eyes. They weren't looking at my legs. I can't recall ever having a piece of clothing that got that kind of attention, and I've had some doozies, as most of my friends can tell you. My winter coat gets a lot of attention because it really is quite beautiful—it's made of Chinese silk brocade in a bright emerald green (I made that too, and I'm very proud of it, even its soft blue silk lining), but the purple shoes really do make heads turn in a way I've just never seen before.

Recently in San Francisco, I was in a Chinese restaurant with my Auntie Vi and my cousin Jon (my dad's aunt and cousin, really). They both keep asking about my brother, whether he has tenure, and how successful he is. "I just wrote a book," I say quietly. "I have tenure. Plus I'm chair of my department!" I add brightly. There's a big black guy with dreadlocks sitting at the next table with some friends. As we're getting up to leave I hear him say, "Did you see them?" I know what he's talking about, so I say, "$8.99 at Ross!" and lift my pants leg and turn my foot on its toe to show the shoes better. They laugh, because they were scouting the shoes. Everybody else looks, too.

When we were teenagers going out at night, Jon often made me change my clothes before he would drive me to our favorite club, the I-Beam, for a night of dancing. Off with the spider-web-print vintage dress, on with the preppiest clothes he could find in my suitcase. He's a doctor. I call him the meanest ob-gyn in all of San Francisco. I'm a doctor, too, but the wrong kind.

It's a guilty pleasure, but there's real pleasure in making a choice that gets you noticed like that. Maybe people see the shoes and think: now there's a woman who knows how to put things together. Maybe feeling good about the shoes will help me feel better about not being very good at being Chinese.

When I first moved to Los Angeles, I knew I needed to subscribe to a newspaper, and what I really wanted was the *New York Times*, but I knew it would make me just too homesick for the East Coast.[24] I didn't want to read about all the shows at the Met that I wouldn't be able to see, or the new restaurants I wouldn't be able to try, or the things happening in New York that I wouldn't be able to experience. I was happy to be in Los Angeles, to have a job, to be near my dad, but there's something about New York that makes doing all the cultural stuff just a lot easier. More important, I needed to be really committed to Los Angeles, and that wasn't going to happen if I had a subscription to the *New York Times*. So I subscribed to the *LA Times* and concentrated on reading local-interest stories so I could fall in love with the city, and to my surprise, I learned that Hollywood and the film business were pretty fascinating too.

This was when Manohla Dargis still worked for the *LA Times*, and she was by far the smartest film reviewer around. Later the *New York Times* snapped her up, so I didn't get to read her reviews as often. I actually had met Manohla a few times in New York, because the boyfriend she had then, a very cool and smart guy named Lou, was a grad student at the same place I was studying, and we took statistics together. Sometimes I used to think, "Hey, I should send Manohla an email and maybe we could hang out," but I never did. Anyhow, I got used to the *LA Times* style of news and reporting and enjoyed the paper a lot.

For the first few years I was working at Occidental I had a two-hour morning routine that involved getting up at six, taking the dogs for a long walk in Elysian Park, then coming back, making coffee, and reading the paper. What I loved about reading the paper was the smell of the paper itself, its sounds as pages turned or sections were tossed onto the floor. It was like getting a present every day and reading the paper was a combination of unwrapping the present and using it up at the same time. It did feel a bit wasteful, and the papers would pile up awfully quickly, especially when I was still living in my little hillside cottage, which could only be reached on foot via a switchback trail. Carrying the papers up to the recycle can was a bit of a chore. But worth it.

Then of course the Internet revolution really hit and papers began to be disemboweled in the process of becoming disembodied. I stuck with the physical paper as long as I could, into 2010—longer than a lot of people,

I suppose—largely because my morning routine, even the truncated one, still depended largely on being able to smell and handle the newspaper. It was as important to me as that first hot sip of coffee. Eventually, though, I could no longer see the point. The coverage was so spotty, the paper itself so shrunken, mostly I would just give it a glance and really, not wanting to get more annoyed, wouldn't even go much further. No more would the paper surprise me by revealing interesting secrets about the city, or shine some light on something I hadn't considered before.

I still haven't been able to make the transition to the online version of the newspaper, though, and since I don't have cable, the only places I get my news these days are NPR and BBC radio, which is what I put on while I'm working. To be specific: I listen to NPR in the mornings, and while I'm working I put on BBC radio. Never the reverse. The satisfaction I get from looking at the news online just pales in comparison to reading the physical paper, and maybe I'm an inflexible old fart (which probably explains a lot about me at this point, such as why I almost never go to parties or out to clubs—too many people, too much noise!), but I cannot seem to adjust my habit to a mouse-and-click experience. In most other areas, I've taken to the web like a duck to water, but not when it comes to the news.

I love telling my students about what email was like back in 1986 when I started grad school. You had to go to a special room to log on and access your email. You got about three emails a week, all of them boring. If you wanted to print your email, you sent the command and the message got printed in another room on red-and-white striped paper with those tear-off strips along the sides. The printout process usually took a couple of hours, so you had to come pick it up well after you had sent the command. One of my friends was, I'm sure, among the first people on the planet to have a passionate email romance that blossomed into a long-term partnership and happy marriage that persists to this day.

Many people get their knickers in a knot about the ways technology is changing human communication, but I admit I'm not especially bothered, or at least I'm not generically bothered, because what people are actually doing is often incredibly interesting even if it's in many ways very different from what happened before. Although the tendency is to think that something like texting is impersonal and isolating, I'm just not sure that is the case. I think about what a godsend the cell phone has been for Haitians, and other people in the less-developed world, who had little hope of ever getting a landline given the corruption and inefficiency of their local telephone companies, and I just love the way kids use YouTube to do all sorts of wonderfully creative and nutty things, from spoofing movies to creating programs of their own and making "how to" videos for everything under the sun from homemade mermaid tails to using glue to create a double eyelid for Asian girls. Actually, those double-eyelid glueing videos are really pretty scary-looking. Even more scary are the Ulzzlang videos, where girls transform themselves into anime characters using special contacts and makeup. With newspapers, there is no doubt that the Internet has rewritten the rules of the game. The news business has yet to figure out how it will respond, reshape, reinvent itself. As a harried, time-pressed academic, I don't want to read a jillion blogs here and there on specialized topics, and I don't want to post comments on news stories. Plus I don't want to have an interactive relationship with the news. I don't think Internet news means the end of meaningful news or anything remotely so dire. Perhaps I'm naive, but I have a certain level of trust in journalists and journalism, hoping that they'll figure something out and the news will still do what it's supposed to and journalism will retain its integrity and exposés will still be published and journalists will still risk their necks to find out things the rest of us are better off knowing. Still, I nostalgically yearn for news delivered the old-fashioned way so I can put my coffee cup down on top of it and, once I'm done with it, crumple it up and use it to pack boxes or start a fire. I miss that part of my life, that plain act of reading the paper in the morning. I find myself wandering around looking for a paper to read even though I know there isn't one. Mornings will never be the same, that's all there is to it, and I think that for the rest of my days I'll spend at least a few minutes roaming around, looking to pick up the day's news off the front step, and the day will always be just that little bit off-kilter because I haven't been able to adjust, change my disposition, be flexible, and twenty-first-century enough to read the news online and convince myself it's as good as or better than what I had before.

ROSE NAILS

My office is being moved. My entire department is being ejected from our current building where we now are into a teeny, tiny little house. Both of my colleagues are away, and they both will be gone all fall, so it's up to me to order all of the furniture for the entire department. Mailboxes, bulletin boards, lamps, desks, chairs, meeting tables, filing cabinets, bookcases. I have spent most of nearly two weeks compiling lists, marking pages with sticky notes, weighing the virtues of size, taste, and workability, trying to stay within the budget. The house is so tiny that "executive"-size desks are out of the question: one of the offices is eight feet by nine feet. Everything in the office catalogs is so ugly it brings tears of frustration to my eyes. Even the best-constructed desks are veneer over plywood. Dreadful. This kind of shopping maybe could be fun, since it's about spending someone else's money, but it's mainly more miserable than I can say.

The elements to keep in mind are so numerous, it's got me tied in knots. Style over functionality? Can we live with stuff so ugly? Can we afford to buy the cool-looking stuff? The nine-layer molded plywood chairs are cunning and cute, but will we be able to sit in them for longer than ten minutes without squirming? If I buy the padded retro-diner-y chairs, will everybody hate me? Every day I find a new lead on something promising, like the high-tech modular furniture from tekniondia.com. But should we instead go all wooden and old-fashioned and make it very homey? Should we do some stainless steel Moderne touches to show we have style and irony? Or should I just order the easiest and ugliest stuff, melamine coated, and save myself the time and heartache?

This is why, really, I find myself driving up and down my neighborhood looking for a place to get my legs waxed.

After spending hours and hours and hours immersed in evaluating prices and aesthetics of one highly ugly office chair versus another, what I really need is to spend some time and money on myself. I've never been to the beauty parlor. My mother always cut my hair for me (since I wear it long and straight, this really just means cutting a straight line at the bottom every once in a while; sometimes I even do it myself) and I've never had it professionally colored, though every once in a while I do an at-home job with a box of supermarket stuff.

In part, turning toward myself by getting my legs waxed was to ease the anxiety of having to make all these office furniture decisions without my colleagues around. Making decisions of aesthetics and taste for other people is fraught. When people make such decisions for me, they're usually wrong. Luckily, my colleagues aren't as picky as I am. I think if I wasn't making the decisions, I wouldn't be as picky either. I'd just be glad someone else was doing it.

When I was younger, my mother used to go to New York to get her hair cut. She went to this hair salon on the Upper East Side that had a big motorized sculpture of a comb made of overstuffed fabric and the fingers of the comb waved around. It was orange and kinda funky. Once I wanted a manicure there, but they wouldn't let me get one. It was a big extravagance for my mother, going into the city to get her hair done. It's hard to imagine she was that devoted to that kind of luxury, because my mother nowadays is entirely low-maintenance, barely wears makeup, and keeps her hair very simple. No hair color. Her hairdresser now is a guy who spent the last ten years caring for people in the terminal stages of AIDS in his home.

I ended up in a place called Rose Nails, the o of "Rose" shaped like a heart. It was in a small, grungy strip mall right near my house on Figueroa Avenue, one of Los Angeles' main streets that runs and runs and runs from the mountains to the sea. The parking lot is baked and crusty, so awkwardly designed that when I was trying to leave I had to back out of the driveway three times to let other people enter in.

When I opened the door to the place, steamy waves of acetone-laced air sliced up into my nose.

All of the clients were Latina or black. All of the workers were Vietnamese.

There's something about the manicure and pedicure postures that are the embodiment of labor exploitation. It's so direct and physical, a woman with a mask on, hunched forward, holding another woman's limp hand in her own, picking at cuticles, filing nails, painting on varnish. Or squatting down the way Vietnamese people from Vietnam do, in front of someone whose feet are soaking in a warm-water bath, bringing a dripping foot to rest on her knees, wrapping it in a towel.

But all of this was taking place in a kind of chaotic mess. This was no quiet oasis of creature comforts. It was incredibly noisy, kids running around, women talking to each other, fumes making everyone a little light-headed. I can't remember exactly what was out of place, but it all seemed messy. The Vietnamese women were all tiny and looked like they had just gotten out of bed, maybe because putting the face masks on and taking them off messed up their hair.

Sometimes it's so easy not to see what's right in front of our faces. The gender stuff was bad enough: Mister V. was certainly in charge of all the money, though he, too, was wielding an emery board when the customers were lined up.

When it was my turn to get attended to, Mister V.'s wife, a tiny woman with a long ponytail she wore draping forward over her shoulder, had me follow her into a back room. I felt like nothing so much as a massage parlor customer. The pink room, with its reclining chair, windowless walls and fluorescent lights, seemed like one of those seedy places for illicit sex. I wanted to walk out. Shortly after, another customer came in, a woman who was getting her eyebrows waxed. I both wanted my privacy and was relieved by the company.

The procedure itself was all business. Her face was blank. I didn't really know where to look. I wondered if her blankness was personal. I wondered if she would talk to me if I talked to her, but for some reason I couldn't think of anything to say. I thought that maybe if I came back and she remembered me she might smile and say "Hi" and things might get more friendly. She'd wipe the warm wax on, rub a strip of cloth over it and, zip!, pull it off along with the hairs. Afterward, she massaged my legs with oil, and then with a pair of tweezers looked all around for missing hairs to be tweezed out.

Nobody's getting rich here, I thought. The owner, a skinny man in his thirties, kept track of how much money each woman brought in, lines of numbers running down a page in his wobbly handwriting. Leg wax: $20. But even in that atmosphere of run-down chaos, of Vietnamese women waiting hand and foot on Latinas and African Americans, I wondered if those customers would be the same people who might confidently claim over dinner that Asians are rich. I wondered if the customers might really think that the women scraping at their nails and calluses were better off than them. Maybe, in part, what the customers there are buying is the opportunity not just to be waited on, but to be waited on by those other people who seem higher up. It was like a chance to reverse hierarchy. All parties seemed to ignore each other doggedly. There was the human world of the customers, and the human world of the workers, and neither would step over an invisible border of incomprehensibility, one that could be blamed on language or culture, but was really just intransigence.

Here on a Saturday, women off work after a long week were treating themselves to a nail job, maybe getting ready for a big night out. One woman sat at the nail counter with her little girl in her lap, bright round eyes watching the magic of the nail job, and, I guess, learning a little bit about the magic of being served, being waited on, how to make that part of yourself exist that requires the work of other people to be brought forth.

I slipped the woman a five-dollar tip. Her face stayed blank as she filed the nails of the customer in front of her.

A few days ago, I was at Home Depot and spent about $150 on various things for the house: caulk for the roof (lucky, because a leak sprang up yesterday during the rain), a file to sharpen garden tools, energy-saver attachments for the refrigerator and freezer (the freezer has yet to be plugged in, so the attachments are connected to the dryer right now), and a bunch of other stuff, including a few plants for the garden. I also had stopped by the home design center, or whatever it's called, and had decided to go for broke (there's a capitalist/consumerist idiom for you, which reminds me to make a list of *all* of them someday) and order a shade for the bedroom window. The window is on the large side, about forty-five inches wide and fifty-two inches tall, a real wooden sash window with old glass in it that's been part of the house since it was built in 1941. But in the winter, the cool air just comes gushing in and since I'm often sleeping on that side of the bed, it's miserable. Last year I kept wearing a hat to bed.

Of course we could just turn the heat up, but that's my Yankee roots— OK, not that I have real Yankee roots, but I grew up in Connecticut living in a number of households where the one thing they all had in common was that they were too cheap to pay for heat. That trait seems to be something I've inherited, despite being uncomfortably cold all winter. I usually wear an undershirt, a turtleneck, and a sweater when in the house, and I carry a cup of hot tea at all times from about Thanksgiving till Easter. Sometimes I stick the cup under my shirt.

At least I could cut down on the window draftiness in the bedroom, I thought. Besides, the window faces the street, and although I really like the vintage (and free!) tablecloth that I've got hanging in the window now (its red and green pattern miraculously matches the paint job that the former owners left us with—and that, surprisingly, we like a lot), it isn't really wide enough to cover the whole window. There's about an inch on either side that's uncovered, and I'm convinced that my neighbors have probably seen me changing clothes more times than either they or I would like.

So I decide to order the shade. Between the size and the cord and the spacer block and the color and the double-air cell construction (to conserve heat!), the price came to a hundred and seventy-some dollars and I'm writing it out because the words take up the kind of space that a price like that takes up. I have these moments a lot, as I suppose many people do: a quasi-out-of-body experience where I'm making a purchase I feel incredibly ambivalent about, but am sucked into incremental decisions (what color, what size, what kind of cord) and then suddenly, somehow, have an invoice in my hand. I left the store after paying $150 for my other items, and a few days later came home to find a phone call from Home Depot asking if I still wanted the shade, since I hadn't paid for it. I'd been experiencing buyer's remorse but had decided not to worry about it since it was a done deal. Meanwhile, last night it was bitchin' cold and I put the fleece blanket in the window just like I did last year. That solution didn't cost me a thing, and I even got even smarter than in the past and clipped the blanket to the holders that are holding the tablecloth in the window. At this rate, I can efficiently store all my linens as window treatments.

So now it's almost as if I have a hundred and seventy-odd extra dollars. I have a friend who always says that when you get money in a windfall, you really end up spending it three times because you think of so many things you want.

Which is really the basic question. What do you want? What do you really want? It's a question we avoid as we busy ourselves buying all the crap we do and fretting, as I did the other day, about whether the pull cord should be on the right side or the left side. We're afraid deep down to really think about what we want in our souls and our spirits. It's much easier to wonder: fizzy water or flat? Nose job? New car? And so I find myself drawn again to the simplicity folks because their message is so transgressive and, ultimately, so dangerous: stop wanting all that crap. Why work? Why buy? Don't you have better things to do?

So today, if I really think about it, I don't want to spend that phantom windfall of one hundred and seventy-odd dollars even once. I'm trying hard, really hard, to just get out of debt, since a crummy auto mechanic and my own procrastination led me to spend over two thousand dollars on my nearly new car recently. Please don't ask—explaining would be really humiliating. Let's just say: clutch and transmission.

What I really want, really really want, is to work less. It's hard to concentrate on that when I also decide I really, really want an antique rug. But it's equally hard to keep the credit card stashed in my purse when my electric toothbrush dies unaccountably, or when yet another person thinks I've left the planet because there's no answering machine at our house and how would you know if you have the right number if no answering machine picks up? That's how you know, I tell people: we're the only ones on the planet who don't have an answering machine. Except for the millions without phones.

I'm afraid to work less mostly because I'm not sure who I am if I'm not working, working, working. I'm also not sure how we would pay all our bills if

I took a semester's unpaid leave, or dropped down to 60 percent pay for a year, or for several years. Not that I've sat down and done the math. I'm afraid to. I'm afraid to find out that it would be possible: that I'm more free than I think I am. I'm so locked into feeling like there's never enough even though I scrimp and save and economize, but maybe it's all an illusion. What if my life is full and abundant but I only see it as falling short? What will I have to face up to then?

It's like when I'm going around in some tony neighborhood where the houses are huge and everything is beautifully tended and money seems to be coming out of everyone's ears. Going by those houses, or apartments (if you're in New York, especially), I'm convinced that those people have it all, all that abundance I long for and crave. Who passes my house and thinks I've got it all? More people than I'd care to admit, and I say that not out of any kind of smugness. When I step back and look at myself, I realize, what's there to complain about? Then I wonder: where does the overwhelming daily feeling of inadequacy, loss, yearning, and of desires unfulfilled come from?

Marx wrote about table-turning and the grotesque ideas emanating from the enlivened table-as-commodity. I can only imagine that he was able to write about this so well not just because he had reasoned it out logically, but because also he had experienced it emotionally. Certainly the table in the rooms where Marx lived with his family in London were rather (clandestinely) famous, being described in meticulous detail by a Prussian spy who was appalled at the state of housekeeping in the Marx household.[25] It is more than a little amusing to see this spy account, which focuses so much on such details as chipped teacups and stray dishtowels, and one can see in his description a kind of horror that the Marx family does not take better care of its possessions. Maybe he was just spying on them on an especially messy day. Maybe they really didn't care, or had not yet learned to care, since, like so much else, activities like dusting are not exactly evolutionarily determined.

NAPKINS

I have a "thing" for vintage table linens, and rescue them as often as I am able from thrift stores. A few years ago I received an especially fabulous trove of nineteenth-century linens from a friend who had inherited them and didn't want to keep them. There were hand-embroidered matching sets of place mats and napkins, tablecloths in lace and embroidery, some with initials. These belonged to my friend's grandmother, a well-to-do woman from the Orr family, for whom the town of Orrville, Pennsylvania, is named.

Included were also a set of six very fine, light-textured linen napkins, hand-embroidered and bordered in handmade bobbin lace. These are upper-crust napkins. The lace is of a type called Bedfordshire, which was popular in the mid-1800s and named after the English town where this sort of lace was made. Bedfordshire lace is often described as having a heyday beginning around 1851, when it made a hit at the Great Exhibition in London, and ending in the 1890s, when machine-made laces decisively killed the industry for similar handmade goods. My friend's grandmother was a young woman in the late nineteenth century. Perhaps these napkins are very like those that the Marx family had at their table; at least they are from roughly the same time period.

From their size, about fifteen inches square, it is clear that these are luncheon or tea-time napkins. Dinner napkins of the era were usually at least thirty inches square (a size that to my eye seems huge), in part because women's voluminous skirts needed a lot of coverage. What is perhaps most striking about my napkins is the amount of labor that must have gone into making each one of them. The embroidery alone must have taken hours upon hours. With a combination of satin stitches and cutwork, the stitches are unbelievably tiny and even, a tracing of curlicues, flowers, and graceful shapes. There's something compelling about a household full of objects—like these napkins—each of which embody days and days of painstaking work. The Marx household was like that, filled with items that were handmade. This was a time when everything was dressed, decorated, and just so: there were window dressings and different table linens for each type of meal, and even much of the food on the table was clothed. Those little white frills on the ends of the turkey legs (the turkey ankle, to be specific) are a Victorian invention, a wonderfully prudish covering up of a racy part of the bird's body, something too indelicate to leave revealed at the dinner table. These objects did not just display wealth, however; they also embodied it. Like Navajo silver buttons fashioned from coins, these objects could be turned into money if need be via a visit to the local pawnshop. This is a cycle quite different from the eBay-ification and Craigslist-ing throughout so many cities and neighborhoods today. eBay and Craigslist have made it much easier for people to sell their possessions rather than giving them away or just tossing them out or having a yard sale as they might have done before. In this sense people may view many of their things as potential pots of money, whether large or small. The difference is that in selling something, you send it out of your life forever. My sense is that with many eBay and Craigslist sales, people want to recoup some portion of their original purchase price. With pawn, the item remains under your ownership until it is redeemed or goes dead. The goal is not to get some money "back," but to get the item itself back.

The lace border on the napkins is about three-quarters of an inch wide, with a lovely arching design with little picots all over. Not being a lace maker, I cannot guess how long it would take to make enough lace for one of those napkins—a day, two, three? Bedfordshire lace makers, the majority of them girls, began learning their trade by age five or six, leaving regular school to attend special lace schools, since the belief was that young small hands learned how to make lace better than others. Five- and six-year-old children worked between four and eight hours a day, while older children might work as many as fourteen hours in a day, depending on demand. This sort of lace was also called "pillow lace" because it was made atop a straw-filled pillowlike form; young lace makers bent over these pillows as they twisted the bobbin threads into the required patterns, inhabiting a posture that was at the very least uncomfortable. Some inserted wooden busks into the front of their bodices to help support them in this odd leaning-over position with the result that the still-developing bones in their chests and sternums often became permanently deformed.[26]

With the deformed bodies of young girls to answer for, Bedfordshire lace is tainted. The problem with Bedfordshire lace, as with all things made through use of child labor, is not in identifying "the bad guy," whether this might be the parents who sent their children out to work, the lace school mistresses who beat the children if they did not produce enough, entrepreneurs who sold materials to lace makers at inflated prices, or fashionable ladies purchasing lace for their clothes and linens who didn't seem to care how those items came to be. The problem is the larger context in which families find themselves so poor they must rely on children's earnings, in which it is believed that children are better workers for some industries, and in which certain people are considered to be disposable, and their disposability exists in direct relation to the comfort and leisure of another slice of the population. There is something perverse in the white purity of the napkins, their crisp freshness when newly ironed (itself a painstaking and time-consuming task that I perform lovingly before and after every Thanksgiving, the one time a year I put the napkins to use), and the juxtaposition of this fresh purity with the ghosted labor of long-ago children. More perverse, I think, is the intimacy of it all, as the linen brushes across my lips, picking up stray crumbs and blobs of grease, to be crumpled up and left on the table after a holiday feast.

MY WHITE MAN'S TOOTH

No talk of Christmas, shopping, or presents. It's all too much, even though we try to keep it low-key and healthy. Maybe later. Besides, I'm all backed up.

In the week before Christmas, I find myself practically living in my dentist's office, frantically trying to get my front tooth fixed before our insurance changes over and I'm left high and dry. There's still that way in which our bodies, at least the bodies that "god gave us," are the last horizon. What parts of our bodies are no longer up for intrusive improvements that cost us money and make other people rich? Plastic surgery of the labia, and what is known as "vaginal rejuvenation" (read: tightening you up down there), are quickly becoming the most common forms of plastic surgery. Then there's anal bleaching and "Vajazzlling." What's next? Designer-patterned intestines?

I hadn't realized, despite regular nightmares in which my teeth are falling out, how attached I am to my teeth. Not only am I attached to my teeth, but I like them just exactly the way they are. My one front tooth is a little crooked (or was, I should say) and chipped from running down the sidewalk and tripping over another kid and landing right on my face when I was eleven. Then it was chipped even more about fifteen years later when I walked—strode, very fast—into a plate-glass window I mistook for an open door. For a while, the tooth was bonded, but the bonding fell off while I was waiting in some government office in Ecuador in 1988 for some sort of paperwork. I remember sitting on a wooden bench in a dim room, holding this triangle that had just fallen off my tooth, and whenever your teeth change, even if it's just a tiny little chip or something, it feels like a cave was gouged out in your mouth.

About a year and a half ago, I casually mentioned to my dentist that when I blew my nose, sometimes I had a little tenderness up above that old tooth. She took an X-ray and found an abscess. Root canal! Having never had much dental work, suddenly I was initiated into the world of why people hate to go to the dentist. Then she wanted me to bleach my teeth and to get not just the one tooth done, but both front teeth, paying out of pocket for the one, a hefty seven hundred dollars or so plus the semi-subsidized cost of the other. No way was I going to pay over a thousand dollars for my two front teeth. Plus the whitening. I don't want a movie-star mouth anyway, but I did begin to feel more and more self-conscious about my snaggly front tooth as it began to darken down a bit. It wasn't just a sales pitch, although I guess the pressure was partly a sales pitch, but all put in terms of my own good. "After all," the dentist tells me, "this is the smile you present to everyone in the world, and don't you want to look your best?" "Debatable," I think to myself. I'm sitting there with all this undyed gray hair, and my main hairdo is a kind of ponytail thing where I only pull my hair halfway through the rubber band so it's kind of looped around and hanging out. I mostly never wear makeup. My boobs are sagging since I breast-fed my kid. My nails are bitten and I've been walking around for over twenty years with this big old snaggletooth. Obviously, I don't care about my looks that much, or not in the way that some people do, anyway.

Part of me is thinking: maybe I really do need to do both teeth?

I march in and tell them no, it's only the one.

Plan A. The veneer. A veneer, as far as I can figure, is a kind of lesser tooth cap where they grind your tooth down. You can smell that burnt bone smell as the drill is drilling away and frankly a basic animal response to that smell when it's coming from your own mouth is to want to run away really fast, but you have to just sit there and tell yourself it's OK. My tooth is ground down flat in front, smaller all around, but there's still about three-fourths of a tooth there. It's apparently very discolored, so they do some on the spot bleaching right there and tell me that most places would charge $250 but I'm getting it for free. I leave the dentist, grateful and less brown in front. No smiling. Lip down. Self-conscious.

Two days later I meet Brixie, the woman who makes the teeth, and in her wonderfully messy lab are lots of interesting gizmos and machines and color pictures of mouths open wide in grimacy-smiles. With her frazzly hair and big glasses and eastern European accent, Brixie could play the part of "mad scientist of incisors," if she was ever asked. She turns me this way and that and decides I'm a $D2$ in tooth color, absolutely not (as the dentist said) a $C1$. She explains that when she makes my new tooth she will add imperfections so it will look right in my (imperfect) mouth. Little white spots, some staining. I think, I should stop drinking coffee, but having gotten it down to one maybe two cups a day, I can't think I'll really get it any lower. I'm very confused, though, because I have to go back to the dentist, carrying a little cardboard box with a cast of my front teeth in it and some other little things rattling around.

"Nope," the dentist tells me, "Plan A won't work." Turn to Plan B. The cap. No veneer possible, tooth too brown. Shots, drills, and gum trauma. "Tom Cruise has one cap that's higher than the other," my dentist muses looking inside my mouth, "but we might have to cut the gum on the other side to get them to match." Since that last visit, I've been telling my gum to go down, go down, but I've also decided even if it doesn't go down, I'm not going to slice up my gum on the other side just to get them to match. When do we cross the line from doing things we really need to and when is it self-mutilation? Still, plenty of blood was going into that gurgling drain thing dentists have you rinse into.

The point is really this: for the three weeks between the start of Plan B and when I get my real tooth, or my new tooth, I have a white man's tooth in my head. I don't care that the color doesn't match; they tried hard. They don't make these temporary teeth special for each patient—they're prefab, "right from the box." But there's an array of shapes and sizes. Now I know I'm not supposed to believe in or subscribe to this racial biology stuff, but I do remember learning about tooth shapes in physical anthropology class, and I remember learning about the shovel-shaped incisor, which is what I have in my head. Asian people have them. Native Americans have them. White people don't have them. Now I don't know for sure that the temporary tooth in my head is from a white person, but I do know that it's the wrong shape in back. And I can tell from the way it has little curves and bumps that it's a cast of a real tooth.

Dentists call the inside of your teeth the lingual side, the side where your tongue is. On the lingual side my front teeth up on the top are straight down, or actually slightly concavely curved, smooth cliffs with a little ridgy bump in the back where they jut out to meet the gum. I wish I could draw the shape, but the shovel analogy is pretty good—its like a flat-ended shovel, curved that way, but also straight. My new tooth, the one colonizing my mouth, is more like a ski jump, or the long side of a triangle, tilting across the front of my mouth at what feels like 45 degrees. Meanwhile, my other front tooth, the normal one, is almost straight up and down. My out of the box tooth juts into the roof of my mouth maybe an eighth of an inch farther than my own teeth, but it feels like a foot. There's a promontory of bone in the roof of my mouth and the whole back edge of the tooth is just further into my mouth. Grrr, I just hate it. It's rabbity and long.

From the front it looks just fine. The only question I had for them was, will the tooth that Brixie makes match in the back? I don't care if the color is off, but it needs to be a nice, vertical, curved-like-a-cup tooth, not this long, thick, rabbity tooth. It makes me lisp. It holds my tongue down. Maybe I'm oversensitive, but in my imagination, white people aren't getting Asian teeth stuck in their mouths and having to reorient their speech around foreign teeth.

The thought of having a white man's tooth in my mouth for longer than three weeks is just more than I can take. I hate race, I hate it! And I hate even more that it invades me at this tender and public point, but in a way that nobody but me even notices. It's a nice-looking tooth, all right, but it's all wrong.

Marx did not have medical insurance, and doctor bills plagued the family during all their time in England. His daughter Jenny in particular was often sick with lung complaints and persistent coughs; the stress and strain of their lives and conditions also affected Mrs. Marx negatively, and she was often ill in bed. One terrifying year smallpox hit the household. And then there were those carbuncles. When reading Marx's letters, one of the things I couldn't help noticing was the frequency with which he suffered from carbuncles. First of all, I didn't know what a carbuncle was, so I had to look it up. A carbuncle is a form of staph infection that is usually below the skin and often starts from an infected hair follicle—or in the case of a carbuncle, a few hair follicles—and can range in size from that of a pea to that of a golf ball. Carbuncles are red, inflamed, and full of pus and dead skin cells. They might open and weep of their own accord, or they might need to be opened up by a scalpel-wielding doctor. Men are especially prone to carbuncles. In a letter to Engels, Marx remarked jokily that a carbuncle "has had the impudence to emerge just above my penis."[27] Yuck. Still, the thought of having to lie on a bed for weeks while suffering from painful, oozing sores that could lead to worse infections, and even death, is grisly.

The London rooms where the Marx family lived until 1856 certainly had no washing machine and no hot running water either. Even in the posh homes on Grafton Terrace and in Maitland Park, where they lived after London, what counted as clean probably would not qualify as clean these days. How often did they wash the sheets? The towels? How often did they wash their clothes? Their bodies? Not too often, or not what we would consider too often, anyway, with our bleach wipes and antibacterial soaps and bottles of hand sanitizer. No wonder Marx kept getting carbuncles—between his sheets, jammies, towels, and whatnot, he was continually swathed in a sea of Staphylococcus aureus. In terms of cleanliness and healthiness, technology and medicine together have made huge strides, changing not just cleanliness itself but standards of cleanliness as well. (There's a theory gaining ground that the upswell of allergies and autoimmune disorders might be because we have kept our environments too clean and our immune systems, with too little to do, go haywire.) Whatever the housekeeping standards of the Marx household, they would fall short today, but only in part because of so-called objective standards that might call for hand-washing, disinfecting, and so forth. On the personal front, carbuncles aside, I suspect that, meeting Marx now, he would be judged to suffer a whole range of maladies nonexistent in his time: morning breath, halitosis, BO, bad teeth, bad skin, toe jam, hairy back, and greasy hair.

I raise these issues about Marx and his personal hygiene to highlight that it is not quite so easy to figure out the distinction between need and "need"; the slippage between a changing need facilitated by advances in healthcare and one sold to us as a profit-making item seems to be increasing in ways at once fascinating and disturbing. After all, just look at the booming business in braces.

SHOULD I BE STRAIGHTER?

A report prepared for the Southern Association of Orthodontists attributes the relative lack of evidence-based orthodontics to the fact that few third-party payers include orthodontics in their suite of benefits. The report notes that "there has not been an organized challenge to the widely held belief that outcomes depend more on the art of the practitioner than any norms that science might identify."[28] In other words, for much current orthodontia, despite the sense that medical need makes braces necessary, there is little evidence as to whether many techniques actually work or whether the effects are long-lasting. One such practice includes the (highly remunerative) strategy of encouraging parents to have their children wear two sets of braces, one when the child is about eight years old and another when the child is twelve.

The powerful imprimatur of medical necessity seems to remove many decisions from the crass world of consumerism to which other procedures, such as nose jobs, more clearly belong. Yet to what degree is this difference in fact an illusion? At what point are braces fashion or vanity? As an anthropologist I hardly want to give short shrift to cultural influences in terms of standards of beauty—there is no such thing as a human society that does not engage in some form of body modification, whether this is cutting hair, filing teeth down, or removing pieces of flesh—but not all beautification processes mean the same thing; they cannot be reduced to their surface effects. It matters, and it matters quite a bit why, we do them. To bring it back to Marx, much as a table is always a table and it is us who make it appear to be full of its own life, so is that true of what we call a "need." It is certainly a cliché to talk about "basic needs," which are often boiled down to food, clothing, shelter. However, as with body modification, there is no such thing as food that is not always and already cultural, human-made, and the same holds for shelter. Thus these things already exist in and speak to complex systems of meaning, forms of social organization, and are entangled with specific histories and politics. What I am saying here is that to attempt to determine whether a given procedure is "needed" misses the point entirely and, more important, is an exercise in futility. A more productive approach is to ask why it is understood as needed, who needs it, and why. What are the alternatives? What are the implications for failing to address the need? We find braces necessary because orthodontists tell us so, or because we fear our children might have ugly teeth and then be perceived as ugly and we don't want them to suffer.

"Why do you have braces?" I ask my students. "I needed them," they reply with defensively indignant tones. "Why?" I ask. As a way of encouraging them to think about what need means regarding their own orthodontia, I ask: "Would you be dead or unable to eat if you hadn't had them?" A common comeback is "I had way too many teeth for my mouth." Translation: my teeth looked really wonky and bad.

An admission: I never had braces and my teeth are perfectly, wonderfully straight. I also have all of my wisdom teeth. It is therefore quite easy for me to view braces as wholly unnecessary: after all, I never needed them.

The truth is feeling ugly sucks. What matters more, I think, is why someone might feel ugly, or others find them so. The American obsession with Mack-the-Knife teeth is pretty long-standing, but the marketing of smiles so white they can only be achieved by the application of veneers, implants and lasers, special toothpastes and toothbrushes is a magnification of this initial nice-smile impulse that comes straight out of the principle that a fool and his money are soon parted. That sounds very judgmental, I know. And because my teeth are perfectly straight and I never had braces, I know it's easier for me to spout off that braces are an utter scam. I am not talking here about people for whom messed-up teeth create unending physical pain. I am talking more about the fuzzy line between medical necessity and a beauty-oriented procedure where the standard of what is beautiful has been created by the very people who want to earn their living by beautifying you.

We live in a society where orthodontia is justified because it's deemed medically necessary. Yet clean, bright, straight smiles quickly are becoming an index of privilege and a requirement for certain lifestyles. Following a certain logic, one could say it is becoming medically necessary to be wealthy or at least middle class, and it's already pretty clear that one must be middle class to have access to decent medical care. At another level, orthodontia is constructed as something that is "needed" by everyone, the way vaccines and eyeglasses are viewed as necessities and not luxuries. Notice what you see at the movies: poor people have bad teeth, and so do the bad guys, Austin Powers excepted—but he's English, and English people have bad teeth. Bad teeth are quickly becoming a social liability, with real effects—not just on ephemeral issues like self-esteem, but on the prospects of getting a job or landing a spouse. The Institute for Alternative Futures writes:

> In today's appearance driven American society, a healthy smile with straight teeth is becoming necessary for success. Adults will be willing to invest in their own orthodontic maintenance, and less affluent families will want their children to have access to affordable orthodontic treatments. Getting access to orthodontic treatment will shift from a privilege people elect to a "right" they expect.[29]

A look at some basic statistics tells an age-old story: that people of middle and upper incomes get braces much more often than those of lower incomes, and that white people get braces at rates far higher than African Americans and Latinos. Fully 14.3 percent of people who have incomes that fall below twice the poverty level are edentulous—that is, *they have no teeth at all*. Having teeth becomes much dicier as people age, reported the surgeon general in 2000. Among those who are age sixty-five and older, nearly half the population is utterly toothless in West Virginia (47.9 percent), Kentucky (44.0 percent), and Louisiana (43.0 percent); in Arkansas and Maine the figure remains startlingly high at 39.2 percent and 37.8 percent, respectively.[30] At least they don't need braces, right? It is painfully obvious that there is not some big push to provide teeth for those who do not have them, but rather a huge market for perfecting the teeth of those with the disposable income to pay for it. Including my daughter. And yes, I'm going to pay for them.

CYBERFUCKED

When I was about four years old I used to have this nightmare. I was in a sunken courtyard of cement, long and rectangular. The rectangular space had two steps up that went all the way around it. At each end of the rectangle stood a door and in each doorway was a preschool teacher, or what we called nursery school when I was little. The teachers wear sensible shoes, hose, skirts, and twinsets. They have brown hair, cut short. I walk up to one of them, eagerly, excitedly, about to start nursery school, and she bends over to me and says, "No, you're not in this class, you're in the other class," and points me back to the teacher standing in the doorway at the other end of the rectangle. I turn around, looking down at my dimpled knees, eyeing my socks and red shoes. (I have always loved red shoes.) I mount the steps at the far end, looking eagerly into my teacher's face, and she says to me, "No, you're not in this class, you're in the other class." Stunned, I look over my shoulder and see the first teacher standing there looking at me, hands on hips, slowly shaking her head as if to say, "Nope. Don't come over here." I'm trapped. Nowhere to go. Nobody wants me.

I felt like I was in that dream today as I wrestled with my stupid Target Visa card. I had been trying to pay my bill on the phone, and had to input my routing number and account number. But they couldn't make the electronic debit. Of course they didn't bother telling me. Now I have been paying my bills online for a long time and have never had a problem, so it's not like I don't know what I'm doing. I called the credit card people and they said they didn't know what the problem was. I called the bank and they said they didn't know what the problem was. Well, at the bank they said maybe I should add the "2" onto my account number, which would indicate my checking account, but I've never done that before on any online payments and never had a problem, so why did it matter now?

Via phone, I boinged back and forth between the bank and the credit card people, trying not to cry, which I often do when I'm really frustrated and emotional, and trying to avoid getting all yell-y and making things worse. I got more and more boiled, just this close (this close!) to losing it.

So I closed the credit card account. They didn't try very hard to keep my business. All those bounced check fees due to some computer glitch, when the money was sitting right there in my account, made me feel just as powerless and trapped as I did in my dream when I was a little girl.

That powerless feeling is absolutely the worst—they can just charge you up and that's that. There's not much one can do in response except jump up and down like Rumplestiltskin, saying, "You cheated!!!!" They reel you in by appealing to your vanity, as if you've been specially chosen for the privilege of membership by having the card. But once you're suckered in, you become just a number. The personal connection is utterly gone—not that it was there in the first place, not really—and the curtain pulled back to reveal that there is no there there and the point is for them to make money, not to have a relationship with you. I tried to make myself feel better by getting it all out in an email to customer relations. As if.

KNOBS

My kitchen has forty-two brass door and drawer pulls. They are round. They are old, or at least as old as the last major kitchen remodel, which, as far as I can tell, was in the 1970s. The kitchen has an abundance of storage: pantry shelves, cupboards above and below the cooktop, to the right and left of the cooktop, to the right and left, up and down of the sink. There are four wide drawers at the right of the sink, and the cupboards below the counters have cunning little shelves that pull out, lined with 1970s cheery contact paper in a pattern of daisies with yellow petals and orange centers. That paper will not be removed from the kitchen on my watch.

At present, two of the knobs are missing. One is broken off at the shaft, an accident that happened before we owned this house. The other I lost, somehow, when in a new homeowner burst of energy, I decided to clean the knobs.

The main reason I decided to clean the knobs was because they were, one and all, covered with a thirty-five-year accumulation of grease. Melding with the metal itself, the layers of scum had taken on a greenish hue in addition to their greasy blackness. The knobs had to be removed from the doors, and the grunge had to be scraped off with a knife. Sometimes it was dry and flaked away. On other knobs the grunge consistency was more gooey and goopy. In either case, it was disgusting. I'm not a squeamish person in general, though I'm not fond of picking up the dead animals the cat drags in, and I really hate ticks with an atavistic revulsion I am at a loss to explain. Spiders don't bother me a bit.

It took weeks to remove the knobs, a few at a time, soak them in concoctions I created of Simple Green or Windex, or whatever I had around, reminding myself not to mix ammonia and bleach because that can create toxic fumes. Somehow or other, one of the knobs went missing. Not sure how. Maybe my husband threw it away—he's not the most observant person on the planet. This is a guy who managed to wash not one but two pairs of earrings down the sink because he didn't notice them soaking in alcohol in the little rice bowl.

I never managed to finish cleaning all the knobs on that first go round. Lost my get-up-and-go. The monotony of it had certain meditative charms, but eventually, I just forgot to snag the next few knobs. Around New Year's, in another fit of house beautiful after a three-year hiatus, I became interested again in the forty-two knobs and drawer pulls and cleaned almost all the remaining ones.

With most of the knobs now grease-free, the task remaining has been to shine them up. Why I have decided this is a necessary work effort, I really can't explain. Like the grease removal, it has a certain meditative element. And the results are unmistakable. Taking a knob from dull and lackluster (wait, is this a shampoo commercial?) to shiny and perky is a really satisfying thing to do while I wait for my coffee water to boil in the morning. Alone in the quiet, with Benin and my husband still hunkered down in the bed snoring in stereo, I can get a little shining-up done. In the process, however, I have come across the last few knobs that still need grease removal. For now, I'm avoiding them. So far, in about two weeks punctuated by many interruptions, I have shined about twelve knobs. Each knob takes five or ten minutes. The knobs are not flat; they have raised ridges in concentric circles, and getting in the crevices requires some finger gymnastics. My hands are getting stronger.

The trouble with the growing army of shiny knobs is not just that they seem to observe me like a lot of expectant eyes. They also make the brown cabinets look decidedly shabby in comparison. So now I'm thinking a lot about painting them—not the knobs, the cabinets. I can't afford new cabinetry, no way. See how one thing leads to another? The knob shining is one little part of a transformation that's been happening between me and the house. I am finally, after three years, beginning to take possession. I've been afraid to invest in the house—in part financially but mostly emotionally—maybe because I've been a renter all my life, but also because the house has not yet become something other than a commodity to me. I read the real estate section much too often and it always urges you to view your house as an investment. That perspective keeps me seeing my house as just a house, so I miss its larger potential as a home.

Cleaning the knobs is changing me as I change the house—my fingers are newly strengthened—not quite as strong and quick as they were when I was playing the piano as a kid, but stronger and quicker than they have been lately. I've been afraid to love my house, to form a passionate attachment to it. This is probably one of the fundamental problems of my life. Not specifically my inability to be passionately attached to my home, but my fear of being passionately attached to anything and more important, anyone.

To the extent that forming a passionate attachment to my house, healing its cracks, polishing its surfaces, filling its spaces with special and meaningful objects, is a ruse for me to continue avoiding passionate attachments to the people in my house, there is no doubt that shining knobs is not a good thing to be doing. But I wonder—maybe it's easier to start with those inanimate things. Maybe it's a first step. Love the house, love the people in it. Certainly, a house can't let you down the way a person might, unless it fails to stand strong in an earthquake. People have more ways to slip from your grasp.

GLASSES

Since fourth grade I've had glasses, and I'm a maniac about seeing clearly. I want to see every little detail and to have better than 20/20 vision. It's the perfectionist in me. When I was little I was always complaining that I needed stronger glasses, and I'd go get my eyes checked and the doctor would say, "We don't make prescription changes that small," and I'd be thinking, "But I'm blind!"

My first pair of glasses had gold-toned wire rims in a kind of aviator shape, but small. I remember realizing I needed them because sitting in the back of my little fourth-grade classroom I couldn't read the board. I think the lesson that day was about gorillas, but maybe I'm wrong. Fourth grade was my best and favorite year in school; my teacher, Mrs. Johnson, was a strict taskmaster from England who stood at the classroom door at the end of each day and would shake our hands, one by one, as we left to go home. "Good evening, Miss Chin," she'd say, and we'd answer her, "Good evening, Mrs. Johnson."

Just a few years ago it occurred to me that a person might have a wardrobe of glasses. Lord knows why it took a clotheshorse like me this long to figure out that glasses are clothes too. It might be because they're so expensive, but when my friend Jackie told me that her very cool I. M. Pei–style glasses cost her fifty cents at the thrift store, I knew I had a new mission.

With glasses, it's a love-hate relationship. They're so expensive, and I've only ever had one pair at a time (though now I'm considering many, many more pairs . . .). It's compounded by the fact that since graduate school, I've had some functional problems with my eyes that involve extreme eye strain, the kind that left me feeling like someone had punched me in the face, hard. For a few years there I stopped all reading except required reading, a drastic move for a girl who would read three mystery novels in a night if left to her own devices. My eye troubles led me to vision therapy, and Melvin Schrier, in reverse order. Melvin Schrier was wonderful because he was the first eye doctor to say that if I was feeling pain there must be something wrong, even if the prescription seemed to be correct. He was also the eye doctor on Sesame Street. He got me involved with vision therapy, which was great. Along the way I bought so many pairs of glasses and tried so many prescriptions that looking back I'm astonished I did it all without any sort of functioning health insurance.

It was during this period, when experimenting with reading prescriptions that were basically a slightly weaker version of my distance glasses, that I began losing my glasses. I lost a pair of steel-colored reading prescription glasses on the train, going from New York to New Haven, and discovered that the Metro North offices have boxes and boxes of missing glasses that you can paw through. I could have lied and said, "These are them!" and just put new lenses in. You easily could just go in and announce, "I lost a pair of glasses with black plastic frames" and you'd have your choice of about fifty pairs, arranged by month in old wooden boxes and bins that seem to have been used since the 1950s. There are boxes of cell phones, scarves, gloves, tons of stuff. I suppose that after a time they donate them to some good cause. I also lost a pair of pinkish-colored wire rims, distance glasses, on the train, ones I'd only had for a few months. Three hundred dollars down the drain. It's the kind of thing where you kick yourself for years because it's just so damn stupid of you.

The best pair of glasses I ever lost was a vintage frame of bright yellow cat's-eyes that I'd had fitted with sunglass lenses. I left them in a restaurant in Haiti, and although I doubt that anybody in Haiti has a prescription like mine, the glasses were gone. Haiti does not have the culture of the lost-and-found box.

My first pair of glasses bit the dust when the boy next door stepped on them or sat on them, I can't remember which. They were crushed, that's the main thing. Then in seventh grade, when my family was really broke, the parents of my best friend took me to get new glasses. They bought me a bunch of clothes too, all in an amazing act of generosity. God, those glasses, you look at them now and they were so ugly, although giant-lensed, tinted glasses are coming back into vogue. They made me look a bit like a frog with square eyes. It's kind of awful to admit how ugly those glasses were because the people who bought them for me were so very nice. That whole event—how complicated and tied in knots.

Their daughter, Cynthia, was my best friend at The Country School, where I went from sixth to eighth grade. Her family was well-to-do and they lived in this big colonial house that was from colonial times. Not a colonial-style house, but the real thing, build in the sixteen-somethings. They lived like Yankees, that is, with little to no winter heat, making their own applesauce and cooking waffles in the fireplace. They had a keeping room, hung round with mounted animal heads from safaris (her dad hunted and also collected guns), and Cynthia's mother had hand-embroidered the crewelwork drapes in there. Her father used to call me Elizabeth, when everyone else called me Betsy, and would sometimes brush my hair for me. They had a pond out front, one they'd made themselves with John Deere tractors. They also had a wonderfully trained German shorthair pointer that the dad took on field trials. They owned acres and acres of woods that sometimes us kids would explore while wearing loud colors during hunting season so we wouldn't be mistaken for deer. There were three sisters. Cynthia was the eldest, then came Nancy, and then Diane. I sometimes think that Nancy and I would have been really good friends if we'd ever tried.

I can't really remember how it all happened, but one day, Cynthia's mother decided they were going to take me shopping for new school clothes and a new pair of glasses. Maybe I'd said something to Cynthia, maybe I'd even said something to them. But I can't imagine what I would have said, since mostly what I remember is being very guarded with people, especially from school, rarely letting them know exactly how broke we were. Still, it must have been pretty obvious that we didn't have a phone a lot of the time and why. Most of my clothes were coming from Goodwill or my cousin's hand-me-downs, and I'd learned not to talk about that, especially when other girls in the class were talking about the pros and cons of Viyella and cashmere and wearing Bonnie Doon argyle socks and planning to go to boarding schools like Rosemary Hall or Exeter after eighth grade.

It was an odd thing to feel really grateful, and therefore cautious, about the shopping trip and to feel really excited and sort of free at the same time.

I remember trying things on and being asked if I liked them and not really wanting to say. I remember, too, that Cynthia and I got a couple of things that matched, the same style in different colors, as a kind of gesture of sisterhood that real sisters probably would avoid most of the time. A blue corduroy Levi's vest, a couple of pairs of pants. We wore pants all the time then.

I haven't seen Cynthia or any of her family for about twenty-five years. But sometimes I think it would be nice to write them a note and tell them how much those glasses still mean to me, how much their generosity made a difference when my life was rough, how much it still makes a difference now, somehow, that so long ago they did something to help me without asking for anything in return. Just because it seemed like a good thing to do.

CURING RUG LUST

My godparents gave me my first real rug. I still don't know exactly where I found the balls to ask them for an Oriental rug. Mostly out of my never-ending sense of everybody-has-so-much-and-I-don't, I think I just hauled up and asked them one day. A while later they gave me one.

My godparents have so very many Oriental rugs. They have so many that some are in storage and they've forgotten about them. Since my godparents are always broke, I continually wonder how they afford these rugs. True, some are inherited, but others they bought. It has gotten to the point where I covet them so voraciously that I will be at their house and standing on a rug and staring at it as if maybe by the force of my sight I could somehow incorporate my body into being part of the rug. They have small rugs, they have runners, they have room-sized rugs. They are all handmade and beautiful. Some are old and worn, full of personality. Others are shimmering, lustrous wool, celadon and red. Sometimes my godparents are just trying out a rug and it stays for months on loan from the rug dealer whom they've known for as long as I can remember. He washes rugs and hangs them in the air on the roof atop his store to dry. Sometimes my godparents haul a rug out to the back yard and hose it down and it smells like a wet animal for a week or two.

On a recent visit a rug I had never seen before on was spread across the living room floor, an art deco Chinese rug in a minty green with a big medallion of a white dragon in the middle of it. For months I'd been trolling the web, looking at sites selling art deco Chinese rugs. I first saw them when watching the Style Channel, part of a Betsey Johnson runway presentation where she had hauled out her collection of Nichols rugs and lined the runway with them, finishing the presentation by cartwheeling along them like a grade-school girl.

Nichols rugs were made in China during the 1920s and 1930s for export to the United States. They have a sort of art deco–meets-Orientalism feel. The main reason I love them is that they are often screaming with wild colors, hot raspberry pink, bright lime green, mustardy yellow, colors all thrown together. Green with purple. Gold with pink. Aqua with lavender. This is not a Protestant approach to color. The rugs I love the very best are the bright pink ones or the green ones or the ones that are wildly loud, a celebration of vivid hues that sing and shout their way around the room. I have fallen head over heels in love with those rugs. Like the way some people have perfect pitch, I have a color memory and I can conjure their images in my head. I ache for them. I ache, I do.

The first Nichols rug I saw was in the faculty club of Occidental College, and from the first time I saw it, my passion for the rug was so overwhelming I often felt the need to physically restrain myself from throwing my body on it and just being with it. Later the building was converted to the college president's residence and the rug was removed. Not knowing then a thing about the rug or its worth, I tried to track it down and even offered to buy it. It is currently in a storage facility in Arizona. I worry that it is lonely and needs me. I think about jumping into my car and going to liberate it.

I've been achingly in love with these rugs, in the kind of desperate and pathetic way a teenage girl is in love with a pin-up boy in *Tiger Beat* magazine (for me that was Leif Garrett and then, when I was cooler, Lou Reed, whose groceries I once packed when working at Balducci's, an upscale grocery store in New York). Pantingly in love. Love sick. Love drowned. Several times a week for months and months, I was visiting the website Cyberrug .com and scanning their offerings, wondering whether I really had the guts to just charge a three-thousand-dollar rug on my credit card, knowing that I already had racked up more debt than I cared to acknowledge. It was like a new kind of window shopping, relaxing and enervating at the same time. I basked in the transporting beauty of these rugs. Looking at them made me happy. It still does. And if just looking at them online could make me feel happy—and this in the depths of a clinical depression—I was pretty sure owning one, lolling around on it, vacuuming it, lying on it to read, playing pickup sticks on it, smelling it, digging my toes into the pile, or watching out for the worn spots would make me damn near euphoric.

So when I walked into my godparents' house and there was one of those rugs, one of *my* rugs on the floor, it was as if one of the ice queen's slivers of glass had lodged in my heart. It made me angry. I was going to say it made me inexplicably angry, but my anger was hardly inexplicable. I just felt ripped off. And I felt stupid for feeling ripped off. I spent the whole visit this close, *this close!* to making some really horrible, self-indulgent off-the-cuff comment about how they should give the rug to me. Part of it was the shock of it all. This particular rug had belonged to my godmother's mother, who died after a very long time being sick and sicker. My godmother cared for her, and her hard work made it possible for Grace not to have to end her days in an old folks' home. I had never seen this rug before (it was probably in storage and somebody forgot about it!), and I like to think that if I'd only been a little bit prepared, my response to the rug wouldn't have been nearly half as ugly and would have left me only a little ashamed of myself instead of a lot. It was almost like the shock of coming home and finding some new sibling I didn't know about had moved into my room. I mean, I love my godparents. I love them a lot. And I find myself really revolted by myself when I sit in their house and want their stuff. Sure, there's a psychological angle to it—wanting their stuff is about wanting things like security and love and all that. But a big part of it is just about wanting nice stuff.

My edges felt hot and lacy like an egg frying in oil. I crackled when I was near the rug and had to walk around it. I tried not to look at it because when I did, I just filled up with envy. I was an emotional blister. Somehow, I kept it to myself, I think, or at least I hope I did, and didn't ruin the entire trip being caught up in the growing tide of atavistic jealousy that sucked at me every time I got near the rug.

About six weeks later I was visiting friends in Chicago, and one of them who is way more stuff-obsessed than I am—he's an art historian—showed me a couple of rugs he was willing to sell me. We talked rugs for a while and being a historian he knew much more about these lovely gaudy beauties than I did. He had decided to get rid of them because of the awful labor conditions under which they were made. Self-deprecatingly, he said he'd decided on Peking rugs, which are older, in the hope that they were somewhat less the product of human misery. I was, of course, in basic agreement with him, but at the time, I held to myself the thought that maybe, just maybe, it wasn't really that bad. I could still think about getting one of those rugs.

Both rugs he's willing to sell are really old, from around 1910 or so, and are even worn out in spots (he called them "holey"), which I don't mind.

That bit of life on them, it's OK. It's deep and character-filled. One is dark blue, and I prefer that one, but our living room tends to be dark and I worry it would drive me crazy, having the dark rug in the dark room. The other is white but much more worn out . . . What to do? He assures me the rugs are just sitting in a closet not really getting used and just to let him know. I wonder whether I'm thinking about buying them just because I can. Do I really like them or are they just available? He warns me that the white one, while nice, has no resale value.

But here's the cure for rug lust that makes you hate your godparents. At least it was a cure for me. Even after looking at Stephen's rugs and thinking about buying them—and I'm still thinking about buying them—I was trolling the web with a vengeance. As I was searching further afield one day, I came across an old photograph showing rows of young Chinese boys, stripped to the waist, sitting before these enormous rugs. Even worse, a white guy in a white suit and hat hovers over them, watching them work. Their backs are so straight. Their shoulders are so thin. And here we are, face to face with all that Marx said gets sieved out of the commodity by social action: the stark labor through which objects of immense beauty can be created. I had two terrifying thoughts here: one is that it would be too awful to have such a rug in my home. After seeing these pictures, how can I not feel the immense horror of those factories measuring every knot tied by small and dexterous fingers? How can my comfort and joy and sense of deliciousness be resting on that history? No, the connection is just too plain, too obvious, too right-there for me to fetishize the rugs any longer. Or is it? (At this writing I have another Nichols [or Nichols-type] rug sitting in Stephen's garage. I found it on eBay and bought it for less than two hundred bucks, but it was "local pickup only," so I talked Stephen—well, really his wife, my friend Mary—into picking it up for me. That was well over a year ago, and I haven't had the chance to pick it up myself yet. I may never.) The terrifying thing is that I'm still occasionally making my online visits, and it seems to me that every visit is a step closer to being willing, even eager, to bask in the luxury afforded by child labor.

Of course I can't. I mean, for God's sake, I study children in the other part of my anthropological life. Even more than that, I study kids who are marginalized and exploited, and when I've got my cape on, I charge through the world trying to awaken people to the basic humanity of children. How on earth can I ever buy, or own, or enjoy one of those rugs? And what else is in my house that is just as tainted, just as terrible?

As I looked at those pictures it was like something just turned off, a little switch for this particular desire, or maybe it was more like a fuse being blown. May it never be replaced. Still, the beauty of these rugs has me by the throat. My new plan is this: paint the cracked linoleum of my kitchen floor using the colors and motifs I find in these raucous rugs. To pour my own labor into bringing the birds and flowers to life and to bring some of that giddy, colorful joy into my home in a way that leaves life cresting upon it. Or so I hope, anyway.

WINDOW SHOPPING ONLINE

I have three primary different modes of window shopping. There's the focused one, where I'm trying to find something specific and am trying to get the best price, features, and quality of item X. Second is the long-term consideration, and this usually involves eBay. Right now there are a changing set of things I'm interested in on eBay—Vivienne Tam clothing, and (surprise!) rugs—Chinese art deco, Kazak, or Caucasian. Window shopping on eBay involves varying levels of fantasy and self-control. I might initiate an eBay daily delivery of new items in my selected category, and each morning check the items while I'm drinking my coffee. This gives me something to read now that I've stopped getting the paper delivered. However, the problem with the daily delivery is the constant temptation to buy. The advantage is that it lets me get a very good sense of the range of items and their prices before I actually do decide to buy anything. Like the fantastic deal I saw only yesterday, a lilac-colored Chinese art deco rug with yummy-colored flowers, a full nine by twelve feet, for only seven hundred dollars Buy It Now. I talked myself out of it not only because of the child labor thing but also because it would have made my living room much too unabashedly girly. Today I have didn't-buy-it remorse since the seller seems to have realized the rug was worth much more and repriced it to $2,900. Shoot, I should have bought it just so I could sell it again and make a couple thousand dollars off it. Of course that didn't occur to me at the time. What I miss, though, is that effortless window shopping that used to happen in New York on the way from this place to that one. I miss that a lot. eBay window shopping is entirely different so I wouldn't even call it any sort of substitute for window shopping in the city, but it does have its own dangers and pleasures.

The third, most fun and least dangerous way to window shop is what I call "let's take a trip through the Internet," where I start off with something I just realized actually might exist, like dominatrix Pilates classes, and I look for them. As I start looking, I'll usually think of something else along the way that would be fun to look up, so I start looking for that and along the way get taken somewhere else and on and on. Half the fun is seeing where I end up and where I went along the way. This involves opening lots of tabs, so that different pieces can get put together—the dominatrix Pilates classes might lead to Pilates machines leading to workout clothes leading to looking up the address of Danny's Discount Warehouse, where all dance gear is only ten dollars, then to whatever dance classes might be on in Culver City around the time I might go down to Danny's if I decide to go, oh and whatever happened to that woman who used to teach those Cuban classes? I'll Google her and see what comes up, which reminds me there were some articles I wanted to find so I'll jump onto ProQuest while I'm on the net anyway . . . and so a few hours go by.

The more you make the more you spend and as the Marx's fortunes improved, their spending increased apace; they were always in debt, although they were no longer poor. In 1856, Jenny received a small inheritance from an uncle, and this enabled the Marx family to get out of their Soho rooms and rent a home on Grafton Terrace. Just four months after the move, they were awash in bills again. In the early 1860s, Marx's mother passed away, leaving him an inheritance, and shortly after that, a good friend left him money as well. The two sums together were an enormous windfall, allowing the family to move up and out again, this time to a good-sized home in the tony Maitland Park area.

Though the Marxes always seemed to have lived beyond their means, during this period they were maintaining an especially lavish appearance of bourgeois respectability, mostly because they were desperately trying to get their girls into a position that would allow them to marry well. Throughout the mid-1860s, Marx borrowed shamelessly from Engels, in one case using his funds to throw a fancy ball while failing to pay the rent and then going on to borrow more!

Dear Engels,

As you may have suspected, the reasons for my prolonged silence are not the most pleasant.

For two months I have been living solely on the pawnshop, which means that a queue of creditors has been hammering on my door, becoming more and more unendurable every day. This fact won't come as any surprise to you when you consider: 1. that I have been unable to earn a farthing the whole time and 2. that merely paying off the debts and furnishing the house cost me something like £500. I have kept accounts (as to this item) pence for pence, as I myself found it unbelievable how the money disappeared. To top that, I have been sent every conceivable, antediluvian IOU from Germany where God knows what rumours had been circulated.[31]

Marx never did anything by halves, and this included a tendency to spend, spend, spend whenever he had the opportunity. Here he admits to Engels that in recent months he has spent what in today's dollars would amount to over fifty thousand dollars paying debts and furnishing the new home he and his family had moved to in March.[32] I find myself asking a whole lot of questions. How much of that money paid off debts, and how much went for furnishings? What happened to their old furniture? Was there any old furniture? How much did furniture cost then? Their previous home had been quite generous though not like their new one, a mansion with over ten rooms. The rent on this home was £65 per year—this in a time when £150 was considered quite an adequate yearly income for a lower-middle-class family with three children. Did they have the rule then that your rent ought to come to no more than one-third your yearly income?[33]

In response to this letter, Engels, ever reliable, sent £50, the equivalent of about £4,000 today.[34] On August 18, 1865, Marx again wrote to Engels again saying he owed the butcher £10 (quite a hefty sum: it would be about $1,000 today), and explained rather obliquely that much of the money sent earlier had been taken in taxes by the English government. Oh, and the landlord was being troublesome too, presumably because he was still unpaid. A few months after this letter, in the fall of 1865, the Marx family hosted a fancy ball for their daughters Jenny and Eleanor. Yet in November, Marx wrote to Engels again that the landlord remained unpaid and that an additional £15 Engels had sent had been used to settle other debts. Marx's financial shenanigans make my own experience with juggling maxed-out credit cards seem like child's play. There's more to it than that, though, and as Marx himself so famously observed in his Eighteenth Brumaire of Napoleon Bonaparte, "Man makes his own history, but he does not make it out of whole cloth."[35] As Marx explains to Engels, they were living so far beyond their means not for themselves, but for the girls. He writes:

It is true my house is beyond my means, and we have, moreover, lived better this year than was the case before. But it is the only way for the children to establish themselves socially with a view to securing their future, quite apart from everything they have suffered and for which they have at least been compensated for a brief while. I believe you yourself will be of the opinion that, even from a merely commercial point of view, to run a purely proletarian household would not be appropriate in the circumstances, although that would be quite all right, if my wife and I were by ourselves or if the girls were boys.[36]

Sometimes when I read this passage I think, "Man up, Karl! Take some responsibility rather than blaming it on the girls!" After all, if they need to establish themselves socially, how does he think it is going to happen? Magic? Certainly not. He turns to Engels to put the situation right, rather than shouldering that responsibility on his own and this strikes me as a touch craven, to be honest. I am touched, though, by his sensitivity to the burdens that his own work and ambitions have placed on his family, and his awareness of how his daughters in particular have suffered at his expense. Having had a father myself who in many ways was rather more like Marx than not in the pursuing his life's work at all costs department, and who made little financial contribution to my upbringing, maybe thinking about this makes me madder than it would otherwise.

CATALOGS

Of all the struggles I face in my life, the one I feel most acutely and most often (these days at least) is the war of my contradictory desires. On the one hand, I want everything: a well-trained dog; really lovely clothes and private school for my child; a big-screen TV with premium cable; not having to worry about money.

Yet on the other hand, what I want is less, much less—in fact, nothing at all: to throw the TV away; grow my own vegetables and stop continually imagining my house as pieces of rooms seen in magazines, torn out, and saved in a file; to remove "shopper" from my identity profile and eliminate buying stuff from my range of pleasures. I'm not talking here about joining the simplicity movement, though I admit it has its attractions. I do somewhat envy these people that I occasionally read or hear about—one guy who lives in Brooklyn and claims to produce as throw-away garbage one mere shopping bag per month, and he has a live-in girlfriend; or those black-belt tightwads who somehow can raise a family of five on a salary of thirty thousand dollars a year and still save significant amounts toward college or houses or both. The strict discipline of such people seems to me to be about as attractive as wearing a hair shirt or a belt of nails—it smacks of mortification of the flesh. Then I think, it's sick that living without all that crap seems like the mortification of the flesh to me.

The photographs that were buried with Marx after he died were a pretty new technology. It was a new idea, taking photographic portraits, and the informal family photo of the kid blowing out the candles on the birthday cake had yet to be invented. Photographs were more like paintings in the way their subjects posed, and in the overall composition of the photograph. As photography became more of an everyday thing, the stiff formality of the pictures like Marx had changed too. As technology changes, so do we, that's not much of a new idea, and we have activities today that Marx could hardly have dreamed up if he tried. Take catalog browsing, for instance. For me, this is a ritualistic form of relaxation. There are the good catalogs and the bad ones. Things like Coach and Tiffany have limited appeal for me because the fantasy that I might actually buy anything from them is distant and faint. I do draw the line at purposefully ordering catalogs and instead make do with whatever happens to come in the mail. It's fall, and catalog season is at its height. The catalogs I like best are the ones where I can spend a certain amount of time deciding what I might buy. The food catalogs I'm not crazy about; cheesecakes and summer sausage don't launch me into contemplation the way scarves and Christmas tree ornaments do. As I get older, and since I've become a homeowner, the gardening stuff has more appeal, and I look at stepping stones and cement fairies and bronze frogs and Victorian gazing balls, whereas in college all that stuff left me cold. I hardly ever buy anything at all but can spend hours (yes, hours) thumbing through a catalog and even filling out the forms, all in a game of pretend purchase and possession.

In the mid-afternoon, when the mail arrives, what I want more than anything is to spend half an hour immersed in those pictures. But I have my rules. I don't catalog-dream late at night in the tub while everyone's asleep, or on the toilet (or not when I first get the catalog anyway, the bathroom is for later in the catalog's life). I also won't settle my child in front of a TV in order to read, partly because I do have a stick up my ass about parking my kid in front of videos. However, I have ignored her while she did just about anything, including, say, sticking her entire face in the dog bowl and drinking three-day-old water, while I entered my catalog world. A little dog saliva and algae never hurt a kid anyway, right?

Good catalogs: the Museum of Fine Arts, Boston. The Metropolitan Museum of Art. These are classy catalogues that have plenty of items I could think about buying, or think about asking someone to get me as a birthday present. On the other hand, I also adore the Oriental Trading Company catalog, which is just bursting with loads of cheap crafty stuff, great to use at birthday parties, or just to have hanging around the house for rainy-day activities.

When I was in graduate school, my archeologist boyfriend used to work in really remote places much of the time—St. Catherine's Island off the coast of Georgia, for instance, where there were no real roads, no stores. The groceries had to be bought on the mainland and brought in by boat. The island's one gas pump was unmanned and could be used anytime by anybody; there were only about two cars on the island anyway. I used to pack Joe off to St. Catherine's, or coastal Peru, with an armload of catalogs, circling things he was authorized to purchase for my birthday or Christmas or whatever event was coming up. Every once in a while I got a great, preapproved package in the mail.

But back to the museum catalogs. I love them and also hate them in a way, especially because they stand for what I really hate about museums these days: museum as gift shop. The snob in me also feels that unique originals are much better than museum reproductions, and I actually make a kind of hierarchy in thinking about the items in the catalog. Reproductions of actual things are low on my list. Items in the Museum of Fine Arts or Met catalogs are rarely, if ever, outright tacky (at which point I find them desirable again). What I often like is the jewelry or clothing that's based on an item in the museum's collection. Inspiration: a pair of faux-pearl earrings based on those worn by a young girl in an old Dutch painting, or a pin with a motif taken from pre-Columbian weavings. These are actual items I have wanted but never got. One of the favorite such things that I do have, courtesy of the ex-boyfriend who followed directions, is a reproduction of a pair of Victorian earrings that were themselves reproductions of Roman earrings. Hall of mirrors.

Catalogs must be read from back to front, preferably with a hot cup of coffee that sits atop another catalog or two being used as a makeshift trivet so as not to leave white rings on the finish of the table. Since our dining room table is a hand-me-down from Ikea that already has white rings on it, this habit is nothing except an attempt to instill in myself (at least) good habits for when we have furniture where white rings would really matter. A lot of my life is about trying to have the habits of the upper middle class, to treat my stuff like it's an antique and precious, when in fact, my stuff consists of Ikea hand-me-downs. The seats of the chairs in our dining room are woven (by me) with Shaker tape in sage green and neutral. Once my un-toilet-trained two-year-old daughter, standing on one of the chairs stark naked, peed about half a gallon onto it. I mopped it up, let it dry, good to go. I'm sitting on it now. The woven seats are part of the stuff-upgrade plan. You can have Ikea hand-me-downs, but you can make them into much more: you can improve them, the way going to Barnard improves a girl. You can give working-class stuff upper-class manners. Or you can choose working-class stuff for its working-class charm and celebrate it—with an educated air, of course. If you're Martha Stewart, you market the stuff right back to the working class at K-mart so they can feel "classy," that is, middle class, or even some version of rich. I say "you," but really I mean "me." I'm one of those people, and I'm not sure whether I'm proud, or ashamed.

OTHER PEOPLE'S LABOR

You need it, my friends tell me. You deserve it. Here's her phone number. The number of a nice Mexican lady, maybe an illegal immigrant, who surely will charge far too little to clean my home. But I deserve it. Somehow this is the last frontier for me, to have someone in my home (to my chagrin, I've already got underpaid Mexicans cutting my grass) to dust and mop and swab the toilets and do all that other stuff that I can never get to but that still drives me crazy. Besides, I'm living with two grown men (my husband and my godson, Kyshawn) who do things like nail good sheets over the window when they want an instant curtain.

How on earth, though, can one person deserve the labor of another? I mean, my child deserves my labor on her behalf, but does my PhD earn me the right to have someone do the dirty jobs in my home? And why is it so different even to have guys working outside in the yard? I can't imagine how I'll deal with it. I think I'll have to run out of the house so that I don't witness this person doing what I think I should be doing, that is, cleaning up the family mess, rounding up the dust bunnies, spritzing handprints off the walls and toothpaste spray off the mirrors. It's much too intimate, and a lot of what makes me uncomfortable is actually important to me: I don't want to lose my discomfort with the idea. At the same time, I want my house to be cleaner than I can get it unless I spend a lot of time doing it myself. Maybe caring less about all those little details would be the answer. But think: I'll come home and the house will be magically clean. Maybe if only I didn't have to deal with and get to know a real person I'd feel less guilty, maybe if I went with some big, corporate rent-a-maid service it would feel less exploitative. But if I'm going to do it, I feel obligated to have a personal relationship, to force myself to witness and acknowledge what is happening, and to also have my daughter see the realness of it as well. Because if she grows up thinking that other people are supposed to do housework for her, I'll want to kill her. I once heard a story that a kid saw a little Mexican girl and said, "Look, a girl maid!" I'm afraid of my kid ending up like that, thinking that brown people (and she's one too) are on this world to perform menial labor for people who deserve it.

It's a little bit like the way I feel about eating meat. Basically, if I'm willing to watch it die, I'll eat it. Not in every single instance, but I've seen chickens and fish being killed, I've seen entire cows being butchered, and I think it's a really important thing to see—there's life attached to that thing on the plate, and it has to be acknowledged. Same thing with work: people do it, don't pretend it's not the case. If you can't handle how the magic happens, don't get invested in the magic. At McCall's, the high-end butcher-fishmonger in Los Feliz, the owner had to stop carrying live shrimp because the customers didn't like seeing them wiggling around.

Now I'm already purchasing labor from other people all the time: Benin is in preschool, and that certainly costs money, and frees me up to spend many hours in the office. They care for her, but it's not the same. There's all that indirect stuff, interactions with cashiers, for instance, but it doesn't have that aspect of making me feel, well, guilty.

Benin was just in the hospital with pneumonia, and I was grateful to pay doctors and radiologists to figure out how sick she was, to dose her up with expensive Albuterol treatments and steroids, to attach her to an oxygen flow. Why is paying a doctor so different from paying a maid? The power differential is clear: when you're a patient, the doctor has the power. With a maid, you have the power.

I know I'll be too nice and too apologetic and that I won't really point it out when things aren't the way I want them. I'll be a sucker, maybe, or a sap. When I was younger, I used to sometimes pay a teenage neighbor to help me clean up. That way I didn't have to do all the work, plus she made some money and I had company. Then we'd make a big mess by doing a bunch of baking when we were done. That's the ideal way to do it, if you ask me.

When I was a teenager, I had a job cleaning the house of friends of my mother's. The husband was an agoraphobic who hadn't left the house for a long time. Down in the basement I'd do the laundry, do the shirts up on the hangers just the right way. Vacuum the stairs, dust, dust, dust. Can't remember what else I did, but I do remember that after about the third time I was unbearably bored by the whole thing. Vacuuming the damn stairs again. She fired me when I got done with all the appointed chores but I hadn't taken the initiative to clean the coffeepot. She told me I wasn't mature. Really? I was born a forty-year-old in too many ways. I was plenty mature. But I was so bored. These days I don't find housework as awfully boring as I did then. There's actually something a little restful about it, at least the usual stuff. But what just sends me are all the messes my husband and godson leave around even after they think they've cleaned up—the dried dribbles of pee on the underside of the toilet seat, the splatters of spaghetti sauce behind the stove.

So I stomp around cursing and feeling put-upon, cleaning and dusting and vacuuming and washing floors and wiping up spills that seem to be invisible to everyone else, convinced if I didn't intervene we'd be living in an absolute shithole. It's like swimming against the tide of indifference. I'm yearning to live in a lovely setting, with everything just so—a warm and inviting jumble of color and texture that's homey and nice—AND CLEAN, but I don't think they care about it at all. So while they're in their socks and sweats eating chips and watching the game on TV, I'm scrubbing mildew out of grout, putting stuff down the pipes so the drains won't clog, and trying to decide what color to paint Benin's room. They would never do these things and sometimes I hate them for it. I really hate the way that they feel entitled to leisure and I don't, which is clearly my own big problem, but there's the mildew and the dust bunnies and all that.

Maybe that's part of what I'm thinking about buying—someone else who cares for and cares about my living space. I won't be alone anymore. I can complain to her and roll my eyes about them. She can go "tsk tsk tsk" and put on the gloves and whip out the Comet and maybe I'll feel happy and free.

Running a household in Marx's time required servants, whose relationship to their employers was much more intensely personal than it is today. The basic conditions of household work—the laundering and washing, the cooking and shopping—all required huge amounts of time in the era before "labor-saving" devices like the washing machine and vacuum cleaner. When Jenny and Karl married, Jenny's mother sent Helene Demuth to the young couple, and Helene remained with them till the end of their lives, at which time she went to live with and work for Friedrich Engels. Karl was against wage slavery, but not so much that the offer of someone else's maid put his nose out of joint. Helene, lovingly known as Lenchen, did as she was told, and was certainly devoted to the family, not that she had much choice in the matter. We know little of the wages that may or may not have been paid to Helene, though those wages were surely inconsistent, given that she stayed with them all through the most trying times, when the entire family was in debt and eating little aside from potatoes and bread. She cared for the six children to whom Jenny gave birth, and nursed three of them as they died. When needed in other family households, she was sent to help. Helene was thus centrally important for the Marx family but of unequal status—with lesser rights to self-determination, certainly—and there is some evidence that she was viewed as being fundamentally less capable of such self-determination, primarily because of her unequal status. As with fondly remembered mammies, the love and connection the Marx family felt with Helene was powerful, real, and terribly complicated. Marx himself (somewhat predictably) fathered a child with Helene; somewhat less predictably, she continued in her intimate servitude with the family after the boy, named Freddy Demuth, was born and then sent away to be raised by a working-class family in London. Saving the day yet again, Engels claimed paternity, a move that mostly saved Marx from stigma and left Helene in the lurch. One wonders how much of this was Helene's own choice, sending her baby away so she could continue her daily chores caring for the Marx household and its children.

This level of intimacy is no longer typical of middle-class families and their servants. We hesitate to call our servants "servants"—they do not serve us; such an idea makes us uncomfortable. They do not live in—that's for the wealthy. We employ them, like pieceworkers, to perform certain tasks for us, at appointed times. The cleaning lady comes on Thursday. The yard man comes on Tuesday. They are independent, mysterious even, and because at least here in Southern California many, many of them are illegal immigrants, we do not want to ask too many questions (there's a joke that every day at 9 a.m. Beverly Hills becomes a Latino neighborhood). The more impersonal the interchange remains, the better. At the same time, the very depersonalization of domestic labor has made us incredibly uncomfortable with negotiating relationships with those who work for us in our homes, because unlike the relationships we have with most other commodities we encounter, the hand that does the labor for us in this case is much too manifest to ignore. We cannot reconcile the humanness of those hands with the intimacy of our toilets, our dirty sheets, the mold growing in the refrigerator.

MAKING ROOTS / MAKING ROUTES

Realizations are funny. Once you make them, what was once so obscure, so mysterious, becomes obvious. Ridiculously so. What happens in our mind and our souls when we open the window or pull the curtain aside? Is it being ready to see ourselves? And why, oh why, do some realizations take so long to make?

Especially since they are, as I said, usually so obvious.

This is why I have a "thing" for old stuff, old silver, worn-out-looking rugs, thrift store clothes from decades past, little pictures in frames—baby photos of other peoples' babies, wedding photos of other peoples' weddings (yes, I actually have a set of someone else's wedding photos from the 1920s in black and white, framed and on my mantel.). I've never really wanted or liked new stuff. If it's new, I want it to look old. But if it only looks old, I feel like it's fake. New to me I don't mind so much, it's unavoidable really, but I like my things heavy with history, embedded with the feelings of someone's life, of meaning and pleasure and use through the years. There are limits, too. For instance, I'm not fond of other peoples' bloodstains, or the slobber circles on old bed pillows.

I realized what it's all about the other day when Benin had gone through my jewelry box, and I couldn't find the match to a pair of earrings that my godmother had given me. I said to her, wailingly and meanly, "You know, if you go through my stuff and lose it I won't be able to give it to you when you grow up!" Ah, that's it! It's about passing things down. Not much got passed to me, really. A lot sure got lost between one thing and another. Most of the things I obsess about temporarily (or permanently) are really versions of heirloomy items that I wished I had because they eluded me somehow, or things I wished I had because that would mean my life would have been different. That second category of things I wish for is less about the objects themselves than about the life they signify—a life without the gaps and wounds I try to fill with thrift store finds and eBay purchases. It's not exactly that I wish I'd grown up rich. I mean, hell, I wouldn't have minded. But it's less about the material things than the solidity and continuity they describe. They have staying power. Maybe if all the stuff around me is solid, rooted, it will hold me in place too.

Nearly every single large purchase I've made in the past couple of years is something old or something with the aura of oldness. My first Internet purchase was of an old gold and jade ring, something of a replacement for a lost ring that my Chinese grandparents had once given me. I spent months visiting that ring online before I purchased it. When it arrived at the college mailroom, I ran right into the nearby bathroom to rip the package open and try the ring on. It's almost like part of my hand now. It is something to be passed down someday.

Then there is the lavender and green jade bangle I got for thirty-five dollars from Gim's store in Los Angeles' old Chinatown. Gim's store shrinks every now and then, just like Gim himself, shrinking and shriveling with age. Well, maybe he's not shriveling, that doesn't sound very nice, but he's just getting tinier and tinier and will someday be as small as the miniature bearded men fishing off the itty-bitty bridges in the glass cases in his shop. Occasionally my dad, Benin, and I meet up in Chinatown to grab a coffee and hot chocolate and watch people walk by. We usually stroll over to Gim's—which is really called Fong's—and I buy her a little something for the dollhouse. That's another incipient tradition I'm trying to hammer into her—remember this, I telegraph to her, this is going to be an important and happy memory for you, goddammit, I'm trying to give you lots of them and you'll look back and think, remember how we used to go down to Gim's and you'd buy me little tiny things for the dollhouse? (Next on my list is the teeny little cleaver and chopping board made of real wood.) The last time we went I got myself a bracelet too because it made me feel Chinese to have one and even though I already had one, that one was too big, though supremely important because it is one of the only things I have from my Chinese grandmother. With my skinny arms I could wear it around my biceps. Benin's arms are less teensy than mine, and someday that bracelet will fit her perfectly.

In the Chinese vein I've also bought an antique Chinese bench, my first antique purchase, that we now use as a coffee table. What I love about it is that it looks so used, it has saw marks cut right into it, ridges worn into it from some sort of everyday work, and while this object sits in my living room, I imagine that maybe it spent most of its life in some dusty outdoor market, covered in wares, lugged around and getting daily bumps and insults. The owners sanded it down and oiled it before packing it off to Los Angeles. I wish they hadn't. I would have loved to have found a crust of original dirt on it somewhere, evidence of former lives. While old stuff appeals to me, I don't like stuff that's fancy and fussy. In fact, rugs that are worn and holey are just fine with me. That down-at-the-heels thing is somehow comforting. Maybe it's a kind of leftover thing about preppy lack of ostentation, but that's not quite it. I was never really preppy, even though I went to school with plenty of people who wore those wool Fair Isle sweaters and plaid kilts with the big metal safety pin in them. I remember how hard my friends at school used to work to get their Adidas cross-country's, the white ones with the green stripes, really ratty and disgusting. The point with those shoes was to get the leather to the cracking point, get the creases just pounded in there, the laces frayed, and the backs mushed down, since tying and untying the shoes was unacceptable. Maybe whole houses fit into that this-cost-a-bunch-of-money-but-I'm-not-going-to-get-caught-up-in-keeping-it-nice-and-new thing.

There are so many versions of wanting, so many reasons for wanting. They're not all impulses reducible to vanity or emptiness or low motivations. When there's some sort of major gap between what you want and what you can get, that's when things get tricky. I want too much, always have. Then again, I've wanted too little much of the time, but unfortunately even that was too much. Each new, carefully chosen thing in my home is a piece of a puzzle, a step toward a certain wholeness. They help make my home *my home*. It's not the money. There's the bargain hunter satisfaction of not having paid a ton, and luckily for me I don't mind the odd worn spot, or a big seam down the middle of something that's really supposed to be a single piece. To me each flaw adds charm, a kind of healing, a scar that can be cherished. I like putting things back together. Roving around each room in my home, someone who knew me could tell the story of my life, most of its secrets. They are all included there, if you look closely, and they all create the fiction of a solid past, shored up by my fantasy that older generations made sure I was provided for so I could live within an unbroken chain of inheritance.

MY CLOSET(S)

There are three clothes closets in my house, and I have clothes in all three of them. I also have a storage closet in the garage, and that's full too. Many people have admitted to me in private moments that they would like to roam through my closets. I suppose these spaces must seem mysterious and endless. I also have two chests of drawers and rotating storage for stuff like sweaters or summer wear, but not shorts, because I don't wear shorts. Well, I have two pairs of shorts but I only wear them in the house on extremely hot days. I also don't wear jeans, except when I'm in Haiti. Or at least I hardly ever wear jeans and never wear them to work, and always buy them at the thrift store.

A huge amount of my wardrobe has always come from the thrift store. When I was young this was out of necessity, and it was something I hid and felt ashamed about, even as the clothes themselves didn't bother me at all: I liked them. As I got older I just never could bring myself to pay department store prices for clothes I knew I could get for a lot less at the Goodwill . . . and now with eBay, in addition to having snooped out my favorite thrift stores, I can wear all sorts of designer duds that I could never afford otherwise. Who cares whether they're new? I wear Jil Sander and Vivienne Tam and Betsey Johnson and have never paid more than forty dollars for one of those designer garments and usually pay much less, like five dollars, which is what a blouse or skirt costs at my local Goodwill, and yes, I've found Vivienne Tam for five dollars at Out of the Closet, the thrift store chain that supports AIDS-related work. An Eileen Fisher sweater, spanking new, in a wonderful celery color, for $3.99, and a Diane Von Furstenburg original for $6.99, Adrienne Vittadini, pristine, $8.99.

I've always loved clothes. Not brands and not necessarily styles, but clothes. I especially love fabrics and good design in clothes—fancy little details like those extra buttons sewn into the seam of a blouse in case you lose one, or details with pintucks or fancy seaming. As someone who sews, I appreciate well-made clothes and in fact used to make most of my clothes or at least the ones that didn't come from the thrift store, but nowadays I haven't the time or, lately, the imagination it takes to sew well. I remember once when I'd first moved to New York for school (I'd moved there basically without a plan as to how I would live, pay tuition, or anything) I was trying to get a job using one of the few skills I had, which was sewing. Somehow some friend of my dad's knew someone who knew someone and I ended up having a phone conversation where she informed me that the designer she worked for only hired little old Italian ladies to do very fine sewing. I'm sure she imagined that my idea of sewing was getting a Simplicity pattern and making a little calico sundress—which *was* my very first sewing project—but I had quickly self-taught myself into a whole range of pretty refined handwork. I was so pissed at the way she dismissed me that I went out and bought some cotton batiste and spent the next week hand-sewing a blouse, complete with drawn threadwork and hand-crocheted lace around the collar. Today the blouse would pass for an antique. That showed her, didn't it?

I did finally end up getting a sewing job, helping a relatively insane designer who had a little boutique on Madison Avenue and never did any work as far as I could tell. I would gather up the scraps from the shop and eventually took them home to make a duvet cover. One morning, as I was walking on Thirty-Fourth Street to the shop, past the Empire State Building, I heard this loud bang, like a cannon going off or a rifle being shot—not that I had heard either of those sounds in real life. It was one of those moments where the brain tries to make sense out of something that isn't making sense. Where had the sound come from? (Today, of course, one would first assume: terrorist bomb!) I looked around and didn't see people running as if someone had been shot, but then a little way in front of me I saw a bus backing up, and there was something furry-looking lying on the curb. "Oh," I thought to myself calmly, "somebody shot their dog." (As if people did that occasionally in New York.) I kept walking. As I got closer I noticed that what was lying on the curb was not a dog but the body of an extraordinarily hairy man, and then I looked down on the sidewalk and saw that there were tiny pieces of meat from his body strewn across the sidewalk. He had jumped from the Empire State Building, and when he landed, he'd split open like a sack of rice.[37] For some reason, I just kept walking. That was my first summer in New York, and I lived in the city for eleven years without ever walking that block of Thirty-Fourth Street again.

I didn't much enjoy working for the insane designer woman, whose son also hung around all day in a sort of jejune funk that was accentuated by his pointy black cowboy boots. She later farmed me out to a friend of hers who was busy knocking off some other designer's work, and the two of them would lurk around the dimly lit Seventh Avenue loft space, leaning over the cutting table and swilling highball glasses full of ice and scotch. Aside from it being a crap job, sewing clothes for other people is just something I shouldn't do. I've learned over the years that some of the things most important to me—sewing and dancing—are things I shouldn't do for money. It just ruins it.

In New York, I really discovered thrift shops, in part because I went into therapy. There came a point when my anorectic behavior got out of control enough that I really thought I would die if I didn't turn myself around. I managed to get into therapy at the aptly named Bellevue Mental Hygiene Clinic. It was like a bad movie, but I was lucky to have a good therapist there. (I still keep a Bellevue Mental Hygiene Clinic sign-in slip in my college copy of Michel Foucault's Discipline and Punish; I never actually bought Madness and Civilization, which would have been a better home for that artifact.) In any case, inevitably my sessions would leave me stunned or blubbering or just sort of in a trance at the end of the hour, and I'd need something mindless and yet productive to do for another hour while somewhere at my subterranean level I processed whatever it was I'd dredged up that day. As luck would have it, there were several great thrift shops within a couple blocks of the clinic, so I headed off and almost always stopped in at one—or all—of these shops. I still have some of the best finds from those shops: a light blue beaded linen cocktail dress from I. Magnin, a tiny little three-quarter-sleeve jacket in the most amazing fabric that looks like hand-painted Moroccan tiles, a hoard of buttons from the 1930s. I still remember some of the fabulous things I didn't buy, especially a partially finished silk crazy quilt from the late 1800s. What I still have from those days are cocktail dresses from Bendel's and some fantastic jewelry.

I especially love what I think of as "old lady clothes"—vintage suits, beaded sweaters, embroidered slips, and silk scarves. I cannot pass up a good scarf and probably have about sixty of them stuffed into three drawers of my work desk at home. Well, they're not stuffed. They're carefully arranged. First, they are separated by material—silk, cotton, or synthetic—and then they are further arranged by color and design. They are folded, neatly. I have so many scarves because I spend about four to five months a year with a scarf tied around my neck. Mainly I have the scarf around my neck to keep warm—the downside of a very long neck like the one I've got is that it's one of the places where your whole body figures out if it's cold, so you've got to keep it warm. I like turtlenecks, but can't wear them every day because that would be boring, so for much of the time a scarf is part of my outfit, usually from October through March. Tragically, I regularly wear out my most favorite scarves just because I wear them a lot, and I don't wear them in that artfully-draped-Hermès-square way that women in Paris do; I wear them wrapped tight up against my neck so I won't freeze, so it's really a case of making a necessity into a fashion-forward statement.

Every year when the weather starts to turn cold, it's like coming back to a group of old friends. I keep remembering, "Oh yes, there's this one or that one" and half the time my outfit of the day starts with the scarf and not the other way around. A couple of my most special scarves were gifts from a former student who had had a full career in fashion before deciding to finish her undergrad. At thrift stores, scarves are always the deal of the century. Even at the Huntington Memorial Hospital Thrift shop, which I consider to be criminally overpriced when it comes to most of their stuff, scarves are usually two or three dollars. Even in some of the snotty little Santa Barbara vintage stores, scarves are a reasonably good deal unless they've been deemed "collectible," in which case I suppose you're supposed to keep them under glass or something. Brands do not matter to me in a scarf. I hate those designery scarves anyway. Flowery patterns, cool sixties-ish splashes of color, bold stripes—those make good scarves. As do those hand-rolled edges, though

I'd rather not think about who was doing that work. One of my best scarves is by Jean Patou, cream-colored with small black polka dots and a medium blue one-inch-wide border. The Jean Patou reminds me of my mom because the one perfume she used to have was Joy by Jean Patou.

Many of my clothes are archived. I don't wear them, or don't wear them much. The point is, I have them. There's the light blue chiffon cocktail dress that belonged to my mother's mother, and the kelly green polyester *Star Trek* pantsuit that is wickedly good-looking on, particularly with the $2.50 brown suede boots I got in the Santa Barbara Salvation Army store. The problem with the pantsuit is that the top is just a little too snug in the ribcage, and when I wear it I eventually start hyperventilating because I can't catch my breath.

Many people remember me because I tend to wear ankle-strap shoes with little socks. I recently ran into a woman I used to work with in New York more than twenty years ago, and just about the first thing she said to me was, "I remember your socks!" The socks, like the scarf around the neck thing, are more a matter of necessity than a fashion statement, or maybe it's a backwards fashion statement. I wear the socks mostly because I hate putting my bare feet into shoes. For years, I only wore little white cotton socks, Buster Brown brand, which could be gotten at Woolworth's for very little money. This was back when Woolworth's still existed on Broadway in the Village, and they still sold pillowcases with designs you could embroider on them, printed in a blue ink that washed away when you first laundered the item.

The summer after I graduated from NYU, I went off to field school for six weeks in southern Illinois. When our time in the field was done, I stopped off in Chicago to visit a college friend. While I was there, we called some other friends of ours, who, it turned out, were all working at an educational publishing firm. I had no job and about five dollars. "Do you think they need anybody else?" I asked. A week later I had a job earning fifteen dollars an hour, which was three times what I had been earning before. With my first paycheck, I decided to treat myself. I bought three pairs of socks. From Bloomingdale's. I remember it taking an extraordinarily long time to choose the socks, and it took even longer to allow myself to buy them, more than an hour at least, me standing there in the sock area, holding the socks, frozen, trying to get myself to go up to the cash register. It was the first purchase I had made in years that was just for the pleasure of it. It felt incredibly dangerous, like pulling the trigger of a gun.

If I remember correctly, the Bloomingdale's socks cost something like $2.50 a pair when I bought them. I still have one of the pairs, a black-and-white houndstooth that I only pull out on very special occasions. These days it is so much easier to buy socks because I make a lot more money than I did then, and because at Target there is always a giant variety of socks for $1.50. Nearly every time I go into Target I toss a few pairs into my basket. The patterns and colors change on a regular rotation, in sync with the current rhythms of fast fashion, and socks seem to fly in and out of the drawer with astonishing speed. One of my dogs eats socks whenever he gets the chance, and I have an ever-growing pile of single socks that I cannot quite bear to throw away.

Smells are a memory window, and for me, clothes are too. It's difficult to catalog, exactly, the ranges and delicacy of relationships between me and various pieces of clothing. Some just come and go relatively quickly but each has a story that I remember, usually at a minimum how much it cost and where I bought it. Sometimes I also remember where I wore it, which then can make wearing it again rather complicated because on the one hand I might want to preserve that particular memory and not impinge upon it by wearing it too much or, god forbid, running the risk of wearing it out and not being able to wear it at all. I still have some clothes from before I went to college: a cotton camisole my piano teacher bought me when I was perhaps thirteen years old; my mother's old high school sweatshirt; the outfit I was wearing the first time I met my husband. I have a pair of my dad's cutoff jeans stashed away somewhere—I nabbed them from him before his stroke, and used to wear them when I was doing home repair chores in hot weather. What would I be letting go of if I let those pieces go?

In Marx's life, clothing was only one of a household's items that served as a repository of wealth. In times of need, the family's linens and silver were also cycled repeatedly between home and pawnbroker. There was little credit available during that time, most people did not have bank accounts, and it was at pawn shops that the majority of people could get access to cash when they needed it. As Marx learned, however, this was not always an easy process. In London, when attempting to pawn a piece of Jenny's family silver, which bore the royal crest, he was nearly arrested as a thief.[38] Imagine a wild-haired, threadbare German walking into the pawnshop carrying a big silver soup tureen emblazoned with the royal crest.

For Marx most possessions of value were things that could move in and out of his home, because they also moved in and out of the market, as they shuttled between the linen closet and the pawnbroker.' He occasionally pawned his own overcoat, but only as a last resort. With his coat at the pawnbroker, Marx could not do his research at the British Library, since a coat was required for admission to the building.

During Marx's time it was not unusual for someone to pawn a particular garment like a good hat or coat every Monday and to redeem it each Friday. Possessions, then, operated in part as economic reserves that could be put to use at almost any time, and unlike most possessions today, the things people had retained their value over time. (Think of the advice about buying new cars: they lose about 10 percent of their value the minute you drive them off the lot!) With this sustained value, peoples' stuff was both theirs and also, potentially, a financial resource. The rise of Craigslist and eBay have revealed part of the abiding value our homely items still possess, but on Craigslist and eBay, people sell their things away. With pawn, there is a loan, secured by the worth of a particular item. Only if the loan is not repaid is the item forfeited; while it is held captive in the pawnbroker's vault, it still belongs to the owner.

One of the fancy words for what is at work in the world of pawn is "fungibility." What the idea of fungibility describes is the changeableness of, say, a coat that can be transformed into an amount of money. With pawn, unlike other kinds of market trans-actions, possessions have the aspect of fungibility; they can be changed into money for a time, then changed back. This is a pretty cool thing. Pawn retains a personal element, even an intimacy that can be seen as redeeming (no pun intended) on the one hand, and on the other is in some ways more like the exchanges people made before capitalism made things so abstract. Because it depends on specific possessions of value, pawn is deeply material in a way that banking is not. Often referred to as "the poor man's bank," pawn shops have been especially important for the poor and/or those without access to credit or banking, and remain so today.

To get a sense of the broad importance of the pawn industry in Marx's day, consider some numbers: in 1848/49 there were 1,837 licenses issued for pawn enterprise in En-gland, Wales, and Scotland; by 1869/70 that number had grown 79 percent, to 3,390. Given that in 1861 London's population was 2,803,989, and conservatively estimating that each of the 3,390 shops was taking in, say, 800 pledges a month, that is some-thing over 2.7 million pledges a month or nearly one item pawned for each inhabitant of London, making the pawn industry very much a part of many peoples' everyday lives.[39] Today we tend to draw rather stark lines between the safe and market-free domain of the home and the more conceptually evil realm of the market, and the idea of moving our household items in and out of the money world is pretty odd and uncomfortable. Either you get rid of it completely by selling it or giving it away, or you keep it. None of this fungibility business: coat, loan, redeem, coat.

There is something about the American consciousness that makes almost all of us convinced that we're poor while everyone else is living it up—except for poor people, who deserve to live like rats since they've screwed up so bad in life. *I don't even believe in those ideas and yet I have them some of the time.* Especially the everybody-is-living-better-than-me bit. I drive around Los Angeles (or wherever I'm driving), peering into people's yards, trying to imagine what it's like living in their houses or neighborhoods, sizing up the worth of their real estate, deciding in a self-serving way that though they might have more material wealth than me, their lives cannot possibly be as rich and reward-ing, since as Dickens always knew, being poor is basically so interesting. At the same time I'm yearning in the most awful way to have whatever it is that they've got: a river-rock Craftsman front porch. Smith and Hawken garden-ing tools. A space-foam bed. A live-in nanny. Trust funds.

I remember hearing someone on the radio once, describing the United States as the richest country in the world *and* at any time in history. In Haiti, they call rich people the MRE, which is short for the Morally Repugnant Elite. That's me. That's us. As a nation, we are the MRE of the entire world. And at any time in history.

I realize how rich I am every time that I go to the third world, which is the only place outside the United States that I've ever traveled (well, last summer I went to London, my first non–Third World foreign trip, and thought, this is why people get into tourism—it's so easy, you can just jump on a subway). This is what I am: rich. Not just privileged or not actively poor, but rich. It's a lesson that I appreciate, but it's a lesson that also leaves me extremely uncomfortable, in part because some of my psyche is truly dependent on viewing myself as deprived. To be an American in the Third World is to have the opportunity—even, perhaps, the obligation—to face up to some very big stuff about one's own wealth. Fundamental to this are the kinds of relationships that can exist between Americans and those who live in the Third World. Despite our ever-so-populist pretentions, it is impossible to get around the fact of our richness and their poverty. We want to somehow pretend that as the rich tourists we are, we can meet "them," just person to person—that our richness, which is invisible to us and which renders us in-sensible, shouldn't matter to "them" either. We're offended if we feel used. What if they don't like us for who we are but rather for our ability to waft in and out of their lives, leaving a trail of dollar bills for them to follow like Hansel's trail of breadcrumbs to our candyland of plenty?

I first realized that I was an agent of the MRE when I went to Haiti. In the United States the closest I have ever come to an American president was almost running into Bill Clinton when he was on his first campaign. I was going down the stairs at Grand Central Station and he was on his way up. Someone else stopped and talked to him. From twenty or so feet away I could feel Bill's charisma, a feeling that made me vote for him because all of a sudden, not a lie, I felt that I liked Bill. In Haiti, getting close to the president was so much easier than some almost-encounter on the stairs of the train station. Suddenly I could do things like go out to dinner with Fritz Mevs, one of the very richest men in Haiti. Perform in front of the president. Meet the minister of culture. Hang out with the man who is now the leader of the political opposition. Little old me from New Haven, Connecticut, and it wasn't because I was politically savvy or especially beautiful or anything like that (though having an especially beautiful friend who was the object of Fritz Mevs's lust was helpful). Being American, and knowing people who worked for NGOs and USAID, meant my automatic entrée into the highest rungs of society, at least to brush shoulders. It was slightly exciting, like walking into someone else's life by mistake. What was disorienting was to realize that this world of luxury and swimming pools, of wealthy disaffected playboy sons, of philandering wealthy husbands and of beautiful tough Creole mothers, Humvees and household servants, was somehow "my" world in Haiti, the one to which I "naturally" belonged (not that I could exactly be accepted that way, but where else were they going to put me?). I had to actively work my way down to the level of my closest friends in Haiti. How could this rich, self-indulgent world be my world? How could powerful political people be my friends? How could this be really my life and not some mistake?

When I go to Haiti, I usually stay with Pili Jean-Louis and her family. Pili is one of about seven people who can be considered Haiti's middle class. A particularly fierce woman in her forties from the island of La Gonave, Pili comes from a large family and seems, through her hard work, to support a network of about ten or twelve people. She's a dancer and choreographer, does community work, and works on and off for a Spanish NGO. Pili has just finished the first stages of building a house just outside of Petionville, and I've never seen it. Her old apartment in Petionville, which is often described as an upscale suburb of Port-au-Prince, had three small rooms and a bathroom in about five hundred square feet of space. Usually about seven people were living there at any one time. There was running water three times a week; it had to be collected in big barrels and any small container that was around. I tried to calculate one time and guessed that we had about two hundred gallons of water a week to use for our every bathing, toilet, and dishwashing need. I think that my family of three uses two or three times that much per day, and we don't even flush the toilet when we pee.

Intermittent electricity, a jerry-rigged refrigerator with a freezer at about fridge temperature and the fridge section somewhat lukewarm, and no land-line telephone. Today, most Haitians who can afford it just get a cell phone, because to get a phone line in your home takes several years and quite a few bribes, and even then, service is awful. Cell phones work pretty much all the time and are quite reliable. There were bucket baths in cool water. No air-conditioning. No fan. For most people in Haiti, this is living large.

When I'm there, I don't mind living that way. Amazingly, I find that I don't even really miss all my stuff: cable TV, built-in gas cooktop, washing machine and dryer. I like living without all the luxuries. There's something liberating about cutting ties to all my crap, even just for a few weeks. Some-how it makes me feel more human, more alive. But that's also a problem, isn't it? It's not the job of people living in the Third World to make me ap-preciate my life. Yet in a very big way, that is the biggest and longest-lasting impact of my time spent in Cuba, Haiti, Peru, wherever. The experience is fundamentally liberating: to go for a period of time with just a little bit of my normal complement of crap (one small suitcase) and to be perfectly happy. To skip television. To buy only what is needed today. In other words, to put normal consumer routines into a kind of magical suspension. To replace our hall of mirrors, our empty shopping-center existence, with the realness of living poor, because while we believe that poor people deserve to lie in those beds they've made for themselves, we also want to believe that their lives are actually better than ours in those ephemeral ways that really matter: they're poor but happy; they appreciate the little things.

Basically, when we're not blaming poor people for having created their own poverty, we like to romanticize them, to imagine that the apparent sim-plicity of being poor actually means that people are happier. Either way, we let ourselves off the hook. It's their own fault that they don't have much and suffer, or they really don't suffer because they don't have much. Of course, only relatively wealthy people could imagine that poverty is either a personal choice or a privilege. Still, when facing the flatness of ads for every kind of big and little thing that might grab our attention, when negotiating the mess of insecurities that just might be smoothed over by buying this or that thing or service, I can appreciate why it might seem like people who don't have to deal with all those choices are somehow better off. After all, if you haven't got the money to buy anything for your family's dinner, you don't have to worry about whether it's hip enough, nutritious enough, pretty enough, convenient enough, "green" enough, organic enough . . . all those things that threaten to crush us with their insistent pressures.

This is the thing that happens to Americans in Haiti: the commodity becomes us. As earnest Americans, we think that everybody just wants to be our friend. Once we figure out that our being rich has a lot to do with it, we feel, well, offended. We're not being treated like people. We are being treated like money. And money is valuable. Now there's no doubt that it can be frustrating to be treated like a walking dollar bill, but in a way, at least it's honest. I'm not saying that Pili treats me that way, because she really doesn't. Still, we are faced with the economic truth: in Haiti I'm rich, she's not, and I can give her lots of stuff because I'm feeling generous, and if we're good friends, she's the one I will decide to be generous with, not someone else. In my own day-to-day life, I've got friends up the food chain who choose to be generous to me, and I appreciate their generosity and like to think that I cultivate and value my friendship with them utterly apart from their ability to give me stuff, though when I really face up to it, maybe that's only partly true. So at Pili's, I arrive with a rather small duffel bag for me and a huge suitcase filled with all kinds of things for her. I get enormous pleasure out of being generous to her, spending money buying things for her and her family that I wouldn't get for myself. Maybe it's even a way of demonstrating my richness, my wealth, my privilege, my 1,350-square-foot home in LA with round-the-clock running water and electricity and closets filled with basically new clothes that I don't wear anymore.

This past March, I spent a week in Cuba studying folkloric dance. In Cuba we lived like kings and queens, princesses, infantas—twenty-five dollars a day for a converted convent room with Monet-blue ceilings and marble-tiled bathrooms. The nuns never had it so good, smoking Cohibas and sipping rum in the evenings, that all-Fidel-all-the-time channel soothing us from the television downstairs in the lobby. Pili has a daughter, Danielle, who is a student at Cuba's International School for Sports and Physical Education. Danielle gets one hundred pesos a month spending money, which is about four dollars. So in one night, I'm spending all the money she has for five months. Of course, the United States is a rich country and it's expensive to live here.

After all, what can you get in the United States for twenty-five bucks? Certainly not a charming room in an old convent where you feel transported, elated, and special. Breakfast included.

Some members of the MRE are closeted, like myself; others are open and unashamed. In Cuba, I took those people to be "people not like myself (of course)." They include a couple from Spain, eating in a posh courtyard open to the street with their backs to the passing public, a peacock striding past them; older men who have picked up what Cubans call *hinoteras*, which we gloss over as prostitutes, but really they're more like the Cuban version of people like the Marla who married Donald Trump—that is, gold diggers—but even then, it doesn't really capture the dynamic. These are women who cuddle up to nice, rich men so that they can live well. Dinners out in fancy restaurants, clubs, clothes, even some money; what's a little sex in exchange for that? My wish is for the men to be at least ashamed, but what they're buying in Cuba or Malaysia or Thailand or the Dominican Republic is the opportunity to indulge precisely without shame. And women do it too—remember *How Stella Got Her Groove Back*? In restaurants I look at them sideways and whisper to my neighbor, "See that!" I'm scandalized. And here I am, in the same tourist restaurant, feeling friendly and generous because I've invited my Cuban friend to join me and of course I'll pay, hell, it's only two dollars for the meal. But that's completely different. I don't want sex. I want a dance class.

Meanwhile, the group of us—fifteen students, two parents, Monique the sociologist, and I—are taking classes all day long from a folklore troupe, Ban Rra Rra. The entire troupe works just for us from nine in the morning till three in the afternoon. One student says to me breathlessly, I thought we'd be like sitting in the back of their regular classes! I tell her, it's like having the New York City Ballet all to ourselves. At lunchtime, the students, parents, Monique, and I go next door to a restaurant where they hand us plates heaped with shredded cabbage, lettuce, and tomatoes, and other plates with rice and black beans. Hot fried plantain chips. It's a dollar to eat there, two dollars if we want chicken, and since we're in a neighborhood that doesn't cater to tourists, negotiating how to pay in dollars and not national money is long and confusing. The members of Ban Rra Rra, though, spend lunch time in the hall where we've been dancing. They eat cold ham and cheese sandwiches and a soda. Lunch, I realize stupidly and late, is a segregated affair.

We arrive at our improvised dance studio each morning toting tall, cold liters of water, and gulp at them frequently. It's hot, it's humid, and after only about twenty minutes of dancing, most of us are drenched. So are the drummers and singers. We haven't noticed that they don't have water. We haven't thought about them being thirsty too. One member of our group, Brandy, arrives one day with a box full of sodas during the break for the group. Feeling guilty and awkward, I buy them a bunch of sodas the next day. When nobody wants the colas I've bought, I feel a strange mixture of snippiness and despair.

On the last day I was in Cuba, wandering through the streets of Havana with Monique, we met an old guy selling little lollipops, one peso each— about four cents. I looked at his hooded eyes and wispy, gray beard and said, "Do you have Chinese ancestry?" He looked at me and said, "Do you have Chinese ancestry?" Turns out he was half Mexican and half Korean, and I spent the rest of the day wondering how his parents had ended up in Cuba before the revolution, or maybe after it. Since I didn't ask, I'll never know unless I run into him in Havana on some other trip. "Let me give you a lollipop," he said, and Monique and I started digging in our purses. "No, don't give me any money," he ordered, "These are gifts for my friends from North America!" A mother was there with her child, a little girl who was looking up at the lollipops with hope. "Well, then, let me pay for hers," I insisted. "If you give me money, you will insult me," he answered with the greatest gravity. I'm thinking, "It's only four cents to me, I'd give you a *dollar!*" but he wouldn't take any money. There was no way not to take the candy and no way to pay for it. Checkmate. I took two lollipops, stowed them in the pocket of my backpack, and carried them back to Los Angeles, where my daughter found them and chewed them to bits.

Karl Marx was a bourgeois father who married above his station, and he, along with his wife, strove to maintain what one biographer calls "the nightmare of bourgeois respectability." None of Karl and Jenny's sons lived to adulthood, and as their daughters headed toward becoming women, marriage was viewed as an inevitable goal. Being a good wife meant mastering a number of skills, and family correspondence tells of lessons in art, riding, and music as well as detailed efforts at cooking. Too often his insistence on bourgeois living is taken as evidence that Marx was a fraud or a hypocrite, but if his daughters did not have the right upbringing, what other sort of life could they realistically expect to lead? Like us, Marx lived in his time and had to negotiate the necessities of the day and this certainly meant ensuring that his daughters had the knowledge and ability to be good, bourgeois householders, mothers, and wives. Perhaps more important, Marx was just as contradictory as any of us. When he went to a glassworks to talk to the workers and see the conditions under which they labored, he and Engels bought some pieces of glass as souvenirs. Souvenirs of what? Worker oppression?

FUN SHOPPING

Despite the utter unreality of money, we have to work hard to teach kids that it is real, that it imposes limits. That's what allowances are for, especially for middle-class people. I've already imagined how much allowance I'll give Benin and the kinds of talks I'll have with her about money. And the fights. Yesterday, after failing to convince Benin that buying milk would be fun and exciting, we had just such a fight. She wanted to ride in the shopping cart but would not sit down. We left the Trader Joe's without ever having made it past the parking lot. And I lived without the milk and the butter that I wanted, and lived without the shopping. Oddly, I also found myself chastising her in a way that made it seem like a punishment that we didn't get to have our fun shopping experience. Thinking about that now, I'm amazed at the ease with which, in the regular course of things, turning shopping into a reward was my response to our conflict. From her point of view, it wasn't about shopping, but about standing up in the shopping cart. She would have been happy to ride around in the cart in the parking lot without ever going into Trader Joe's at all.

PRESCHOOL BIRTHDAY PARTIES

There was a period for a while there where I had a kind of theoretical, anthropological interest in children's birthday parties. That was before I actually had a child. Now I dread them. I can't say why exactly, except that my idea about birthday parties, my sense of them, is that they are these horrible rituals that torture children and adults alike. They are also rituals of consumption. And yes, I know this isn't really a new idea.

The thought of a child's birthday party makes me want to run screaming. My own birthday parties as a kid were highly anticipated, and I remember really looking forward to them, though I was always convinced that my brother's birthday parties were better. You'd think that those memories might give me more sympathy, but they don't at all. One time, when we were living in a very modern two-story apartment in a converted brownstone that had two interior balconies overlooking the living room, my mother and stepfather hung doughnuts by strings from the balcony down to the floor below and kids lined up with their hands behind them to see who could eat the doughnut off the string the fastest. Odd, but cheap, fun, and memorable. I like that.

The worst part about children's birthday parties is the present opening, where the birthday child opens one by one a huge pile of presents while the other kids have to look on, ooohing and aaahing (and now, I realize, the parents also look on wondering whether the present they got was good enough or cheesy or cheap, or whether they overspent or gave the kid the third Twister game of the day . . .) and the kids are yelling out things like "I have that!" or "I wish I had one of those!" Or they're trying to help the birthday boy or girl open the presents because maybe she's a bit clumsy. And there are tears, so often. You don't open presents at weddings, but you do at birthday parties. I'd much rather see the birthday loot set out across a table, the way it is at some weddings, than have to sit through the present opening. There's something that seems so tacky to me about the public opening of presents.

It's the enforced jolliness, the enforced joy and fun that really gets to me. Even worse is when the whole thing takes place in some faux child space like Chuck E. Cheese or Gymboree or Travel Town. Recently my daughter got invited to a party at Chuck E. Cheese and I just knew I couldn't go. My husband had to take her. I RSVP'd on the last possible date. I refuse to go! I said to him. I'll take her, he said, amiably. Thank God.

My neighbors tend to have big family parties on a kid's birthday, and I like that much better—a bunch of picnic tables in the yard, balloons and streamers, maybe one of those jolly jumper castles or something, a big carne asada, beer and soda in tubs of ice, and loud music. But honestly, I'm way too lazy to organize something like that.

Meanwhile, the invites come rolling in for Benin. I find these little cards in the parent cubby pretty often, sometimes from kids I don't even know— and when I ask her about it, neither does she. The whole etiquette about birthday parties about who to invite I don't quite get either—some parents seem to want to leave no room for error and just invite all forty children from the preschool. On Benin's third birthday we only invited about three kids from the school, and it wasn't a party, exactly, it was just to meet us at the Bob Baker puppet theater. My husband did all the work, all the inviting. We didn't have a birthday cake or anything, not then. We had cake later at my dad's house, with candles and a rousing rendition of "Happy Birthday."

Most of the time, we just don't go to the parties that Benin gets invited to. I feel like such a, well, a party pooper, but just thinking about going to these things gives me a kind of sour feeling behind my teeth. Which is ridiculous. I know my antipathy is way out of scale here. Most of the people I know don't throw horrible all-out affairs, the ones where kids have twenty-dollar goodie bags and the whole party cost two thousand bucks. But it's the cycle of competition that I don't even want to dip my toe in, or Benin's little toe, either.

It's all unspoken, but there is a kind of calculus of present-party-participation that you just can't get around. Since I have no intention of spending even two hundred dollars on a party for Benin, I am not really thrilled about having to go out and buy these presents for her to take to other kids' parties. How little can I spend without being totally embarrassed? Plus, my usual MO in gift-giving is this very careful, very thoughtful process where I try really hard to match the gift to the person and try also to get something special, unusual, and preferably not mass-produced. None of this really applies for a kid's party, and especially for some kid I barely know. First of all, I wouldn't know what to get. Second, I'm mad about having to go to the party anyway, and don't want to put much effort into it. Then, I feel a little guilty about being mad. Why should I take my weird birthday party issues it out on some three-year-old kid? On the other hand, I figure any kid going to school with Benin has way too much crap anyway and doesn't need a thing, so getting some great gift when I could spend that money on something useful, like giving it to charity, seems somehow immoral. Maybe that last bit is over the top, but since my own approach with Benin is not to have her overwhelmed with tons of crap, I'm not really interested in being roped into other people's celebrations of "too muchness." My one exception is books. I have always allowed myself not to feel guilty, ever, about buying books, and Benin has lots of books—including a nearly complete set of Berenstain Bears that I lucked out finding at the local thrift store. Still, I'm a little embarrassed to be known as the mom who gives books and nothing but books. If I was a kid, I'd certainly feel just slightly ripped off.

This year, the solution to my birthday party squeamishness hit me as I shopped at Target two days after Christmas picking out a few half-price Christmas tree ornaments for the ongoing collection. (This included this totally funny glass ornament of a cucumber, complete with warts. What were they thinking? It looks utterly, um, obscene—like a shiny green dildo. Is there some traditional Christmas cucumber thing that I don't know about?[40] I bought two, one for me and one to send to my godmother, the Christmas ornament queen. She'll love it.) I was walking by the toy section and saw that there were lots of toys marked down quite a bit. So I decided to buy all the birthday presents I might need for the whole year, and to spend about five dollars a gift. But to buy things that, if they weren't on sale, would be ten dollars or more. That way, I figure, parents who go so far as to think about how much we've spent on the gift they will think I spent at least ten dollars when really I spent much less. So, whew, I don't really have to feel too guilty! And I broke one of my main cardinal rules of gift-giving: I bought several of the same thing. I got four Play-Doh sets in buckets. I got two little play houses. I bought five little velvet evening bags with beading and ribbons. For adults, I got sequined napkin holders and sequined votive candle holders. Yes, I felt guilty. I felt like a cheater. There was nothing carefully chosen and individual about it. It's entirely prefab. There's no sort of mediating social labor involved in these gifts that makes them personal, something between me and them. And I don't care.

The one exception is the set of Tinkertoys I bought for my friend Caro's son, because she told me he'd gotten some for Christmas, so I thought an addition would be nice at his birthday. During the last couple of years, Caro and I have become friends, and I did want my gift for her son to have that personal thought, even if the gift is just as store-bought and mass-produced as any other. And on sale, too, which she won't mind, since we're constantly comparing bargains we've landed. It's funny how the quality of thought that goes into a purchase can somehow blunt my sense of the larger problem with even making the purchase in the first place.

For the rest of the year, when we get invited to a birthday party, it will be easier to say yes. I'll just go into the garage, grab a little purse or Play-Doh bucket, wrap it up, and call it a present. I guess we'll get about five letters saying, "Dear Benin, Thanks for the Play-Doh" and five letters saying "Dear Benin, Thanks for the purse."

Now I can only pray the parents don't catch on and get offended. Will I get ostracized for being the mom who gave every kid this year either a Play-Doh bucket or a velvet purse? Or maybe Benin will just stop getting invited to parties because we're not doing our part by having some monster party and inviting all the kids. Luckily, Benin's birthday is in the summer. Maybe we'll just go out of town that week.

When I was in Haiti one August, I took a side trip to Santo Domingo with my friend and host, Sharon Bean. We brought our families along too, going to a UNICEF-sponsored session investigating the trafficking of children across the Haiti–Dominican Republic border. We stayed in a very lovely hotel along the Malecon, with a big pool, plush rooms, and a staff that was especially appreciative of my daughter, which of course made everything right in my world.

One night, I used the phone in my room to make a collect call home so that my then-husband could talk to Benin. The call lasted ten minutes.

A couple of months later we got a bill for a $64.86 phone call. Plus a $10 fee for something or other. Along with a special, automated note on our bill indicating that I should read special message 12345 on the reverse of the bill, which read, basically, that we were expected to pay all charges or else.

The call had been handled by an outfit called International Satellite Communications. And the bill had their phone number on it. That number, by the way, is 888–657–1959.

Now when it comes to asking for things like, say a raise, I'm a total wimp. I feel all wilted and iffy, unable to speak up for myself with any confidence. But on this matter, it was like I was riding the crest of a wave. I felt, first of all, completely self-righteous. Sixty-four dollars and eighty-six cents for a ten-minute phone call? Are you people out of your minds? My approach was to pretend I was someone else, rather than my wimpy self. My approach was also to avoid yelling and remain tensely, tersely calm. Cool, direct, to the point, and not interested in being nice.

Pretending to be someone else, I calmly asked for the supervisor, got his name, threatened to write letters, and got the bill reduced by 60 percent. It was like being on a theme park ride, one of the ones where you feel like you're an explorer in the jungle—it was an adventure, and it was *fun!* Throughout those conversations, I was observing myself, thinking, who is this person who can be so demanding, throw her weight around, and not care if she pisses people off? I want to be more like her!

In his professional life, Marx had only one intellectual collaborator, Friedrich Engels. The son of a wealthy textile mill owner, Engels supported the Marx family by regularly sending them money. But throughout their association, Marx and his family also con-

tinually received gifts from Engels, and there was a big difference between money that Engels sent because Marx needed it and gifts Engels sent because he wanted to, even if the gift was one of money. Gifts are something that have probably existed since humans have (and even before), and part of what is interesting about them is that, like stuff, gifts are things with special qualities—qualities that we give to them through our own imaginative intervention. Like commodities, gifts create relationships between people, but rather than tearing down humanity, gifts build it up. Even more complicated, now of course things can do all of it at once, between one thing and another. My godparents might someday give me the rug I lust for, and that would be a gift between us, but in its history, woven in those knots, the hard labor of long dead children still remains. The work of those children was bought and paid for, and eventually the rug was bought from a dealer or a store, passed down within my godparents' family.

Gifts are exchanged between people, and built into gifts are ever-expanding ripples of human obligation. Unlike in capitalism, where everything is bought and paid for in interactions that cut off human relationships, gifts build up human relationships. Don't get me wrong—this might not always be a pleasant experience, in part because to be the recipient of a gift generally means that you are then indebted to the giver until you give them a gift in return. In the space between getting and giving, you are tied together by the unfulfilled obligation. Think about the calculations people often make in buying wedding presents. One rule of thumb is that you ought to buy a present that approximates the amount spent on the wedding that represents your portion of its cost; a lavish wedding needs an equally lavish present. The worth of a gift is often also an indication of your "investment" in the relationship. A shoddy present is evidence that you don't care much. In the potlatch tradition among the Pacific Northwest Native tribes, gift-giving often had an aggressive element. Potlatches were feast events where one group would invite another, and heap gifts upon them. The recipients were then obligated to reciprocate with an even more lavish display of gift-giving. In the decades after contact, when Native economies began to radically change, potlatches became so lavish and so extreme that they took to burning huge piles of Hudson's Bay blankets to show how little they cared for stuff. At these events, the point was to humiliate: to provoke the indebtedness of the giftees and to demonstrate the generosity, and hence the great power, of the givers.

The rules for gifts are that the giver should give them, unasked. Marx regularly broke this rule and often demanded or begged things off Engels, and the fact that Marx did this, together with Engel's continuing tolerance of this behavior, says a lot about the nature of their friendship. At Christmastime, Engels sent baskets of wine and food; these arrived in proper fashion, unasked for, although I would guess, much anticipated, and even more appreciated. Still, the baskets of treats were very unlike the cut-in-half banknotes he sent when Marx needed money. Once Marx had received the first half of the bills, Engels would post the other half so they could be made whole again and used to pay the rent or buy the bread. At least that is what Marx said he was going to do with the money. Often as not, he did something else with it, since his letters continually seem to complain of unpaid rent and angry landlords.

What Marx offered Engels, in return for these monetary gifts, was the countergift of intellectual partnership. "It is truly soul-destroying to be dependent for half one's life," Marx wrote to Engels in an 1865 letter asking money. "The only thought that sustains me in all of this is the thought that the two of us form a partnership together, in which I spend my time on the theoretical and party side of the business."[41] It is a partnership that Marx, famously dismissive of the intellectual work of countless others, conferred solely upon Engels. The value of this partnership was powerful indeed to have survived so much. Gift and countergift managed to maintain an uneasy balance most of the time.

I LOVE YOUR NAIL POLISH

Two hundred fifty-five characters. That's the limit. See, I wanted to write Revlon a love letter, but on their website they ask you to limit your comments to 255 characters. They want to hear from us consumers, but within specified limits. For the first time in my life, I'm pretty much in love with a beauty product. Revlon now makes this new kind of nail polish that comes in two little vials, the color and an overcoat together. It really really works. It sticks right on and doesn't chip chip chip, at least not nearly as easily as others I've tried. It dries fast too, and it has become one of those little luxuries that I've been enjoying. It makes me feel pretty to have nice-looking nails, if you can get past the fact that I gnaw at the sides of my fingers like a little gerbil when I'm tense. To get a clear sense of exactly how short 255 characters is, with that previous period I hit 590 characters. My task here is to write a love letter in 255 characters, a love letter about nail polish. Maybe it ought to be a series of haikus. I guess Revlon doesn't want to hear endless rants or raves and there's something interesting about this constraint. Clearly wasting words like "I love your nail polish" is definitely out, and with endless space I'm sure I would have said something like that.

This nail polish falls into the category of things in my life that make me feel rich. Though feeling rich, per se, isn't quite the point, neither is it about a feeling of abundance or luxury either. Still, having "done" nails says something about having time, having resources, and it doesn't matter to me much whether I do my own nails or get them done. Actually, I'd almost rather do them myself because I'm so squeamish about having people service me in such a direct way—and yes, once again, I know that's my problem. I love those moments, those few minutes of enforced idleness while I have to sit around with my fingers outspread, gently waving them in the air, gingerly turning book pages or pushing up my glasses.

Love Letter Number 1
Nails spread in a fan
Hard Beetlewing color shines
Bottled luxury

Love Letter Number 2
Sleeping family
Nails wave in the air to dry
Queen greeting silence

Love Letter Number 3
I'm never complete
But with finished copper nails
At least I look done

The above, including titles, total 220 characters. At my computer I press the send button.

The Revlon Consumer Information Center has received your comments from our website. Thank you for taking the time to contact us. Our response time to your inquiry may be several days. We appreciate your patience and understanding.

Your reference number is 001248758A.

Please do not respond to this acknowledgement, but if you have a question concerning your email, please contact us at our toll free number 1-800-473-8566.

Sincerely,
Rachel Evans
Sr. Consumer Services Representative
Revlon Consumer Information

Here's another haiku try, over the limit at 274 characters, 316 if you include the spaces. I guess I'll have to divide it into two messages.

I love your nail polish and this is why:
Never believe ads
But this told it true—faith
saved and manicured

it works it works and
the surprise, joy! enamelled
for ten days or more

I'll feel rich this week
Amethyst nails or copper
Fingertip wealthy

Now a shorter one at 237 characters including title and spaces

I really love your nail polish more than a person should
Acrylic beauty
Fast dry diamond sparkling
Flashing spirit gift

Alienate this
These nails are mine I bought them
Happiness adheres

dizzy fume love file
ragged everyday feeling
smoothed polished nails gleam

Or maybe it's better with the last two stanzas like this

emery files down
ragged everyday feeling
dizzy fume love: polish

rest for now and dry
fingers spread from open palm
secrets unfurling

It is not much of a surprise that I never heard a thing from Revlon. It was an experiment after all, one of the several that I found myself undertaking. In some ways it was liberating—I could pretend to be someone else, some other sort of consumer, and do things just to see what would happen. Even now, I occasionally find myself pretending to be someone else entirely and doing something that I myself would never do: waltzing into Louis Vuitton and spending forty-five minutes being shown bags I have no intention of buying or buying something knowing I will return it the next day; going into See's chocolates just to get the free piece of candy, and oh, can you give one to my daughter too? It's actually me who goes into See's for the free piece of candy but what I do is buy maybe one or two pieces and get the free ones, it's just one of those things you *have* to do, and no, you're not cheating. They just give it away.

LITTLE BENCHES

Sometimes I imagine that the spirits of all those whose hands made and shipped and wrapped the things in my home are there with me, and that the rooms of my home are crowded with the lives they have led. It's their hands I think of most, hands that people—those cruel capitalists, as Jamaica Kincaid calls them—have zeroed in on most powerfully and painfully through time. Small, nimble fingers. One time, in Haiti, I was talking with an Israeli man who had a manufacturing center in Port-au-Prince. We were at an expat bar called Bolero, sitting on stools next to a Norwegian guy drinking himself to death in a good-natured way. The Israeli was talking about his other ventures in Asia. I asked him, "Why Asia?" and he reached across the table, picked up my hand in his, and said, "This is why." My hands are dexterous, it's true. I sew with fine and even stitches. I used to play the piano, and I type really fast and accurately, but my hands are not small. So I end up wondering: which of the things in my house was built on that idea—that someone's small and dexterous hands were needed to make it just so? That painted bowl? That upholstered chair?

These things are reminders of my privilege. They speak to me and say, remember that you are lucky. Remember that you are rich. Remember that you do not suffer as many others do. My little benches say these things to me every day. Sometimes I have to put them in the garage so their voices will be muffled. I brought them back from Haiti in 2003. Ever since my first trip to Latin America in the late 1980s, I've been haunted by little benches, and I think it's their devastating simplicity that touches me most. Small and homemade, little benches are thrown together out of scrap wood, perhaps seven or eight inches high and a foot long. They're a plain little household item, seemingly innocuous. Sometimes they're painted, sometimes not. They have a kind of gravitational beauty, the kind of thing nobody notices, because it's so simple, so everyday, but when you really look there's a kind of perfection in them. It's not quite so easy to say little benches are bad, or romantic or naif or pure. In the end, they are what they are—products of hard lives and need and few resources.

This is what little benches are for: small people can stand on them to be tall enough to reach the sink and do the dishes. The small person might be a full-grown woman who just isn't very tall. (Wondering why the woman isn't so tall could lead you to ask about her hunger as a child, perhaps, and that hunger might have something to do with her never having spent much time in school.) Very often though, the small person is a barefooted child of six or seven or however old, boy or girl, it doesn't matter, they all do dishes. They carry water, too. Little benches are also for sitting on. In Haiti, an adult might take a little bench outside in the cool evening and squat on it to have a smoke, a little drink of clairin—cane liquor—and to gingerly handle hot barbecued corn, thumbing the chewy blackened kernels off into the palm and popping them into his or her mouth, talking with friends, laughing, listening to the other families and dogs nearby. The little benches I brought back from Haiti had crusts of red dirt on their bottoms from just such an evening. Little benches can also be for children to sit on while eating. If the child is a *restavek*—roughly, a child domestic slave—the bench might be too much of a luxury for using for a meal, whether as a table or a seat. But maybe not. The boy or girl, maybe eight years old, might take a bench outside and sit on it while cleaning shoes. This is a daily task especially when it's wet outside and shoes are splattered and encrusted in sticky mud. One August, when I was in Haiti with thirteen students, seven of us arrived at Pili's house to spend the night, after having trudged her unpaved road for half a mile in darkness lit up by lightning flashes, our feet sploshing into puddles and sliding into squishy ditches. In the clear morning, softly pink and blue, our shoes were lined up in tidy rows, washed clean not by rain or god's mercy, but by Paul's ashy hands. Paul, an eight-year-old boy who lives with Pili, is not quite a *restavek* but is lowest in the household's hierarchy of affection and food and everything else. Our shoes were touched and cleansed by those hands. He sat on a bench to do that work, while we slept.

Paul has the pointy shoulders of a kid who could stand to eat a little more, or a little more often. One afternoon, when he and a bunch of other people were over at the house where I was staying, I pulled him aside into the kitchen, alone. "Have this," I said to him, giving him a cold container of a sweet chocolaty drink. "Mesi," he said gravely, as Haitian children do (why can't I get my own daughter to behave so nicely?), and then stood there, almost rooted to the spot, drinking it down until the container was empty. It was as if I had ordered him to stand there and drink it until it was gone. I had imagined maybe that he would take his time. There was no way to tell if he had even enjoyed it. Was this a gift? I'm not sure. But I didn't know what else to give him, anything that I could be sure would just be his alone and not taken or lent or ruined. If he could *eat it*, I thought, he could really have it.

I wonder how many times Paul has sat on the yellow-painted benches that now sit in my living room. What work did he do with his sharp haunches perched on them? What laughter, what games? Who stood on this bench with bare feet to clean meat and chop vegetables? How many bowls of steaming rice were placed on it in readiness for the table because the counter was full?

In my house, the benches acquire a gentler history. I pull one up to the comfy armchair and place my feet on it, my daughter snuggled into my lap, fluffy comforters around us, and read picture books. She drags one into the kitchen and balances atop it as we make Sunday morning pancakes. My own girl, her calluses are from the monkey bars, where she has learned to hang upside down, arms crossed across her chest in imitation of a little bat. The Southern California sun streams in through the windows, the dog waits with her berry-black eyes trained on us hoping to lick the bowl, and in this world where I ought to feel content and whole, there is also this bench and its sister benches on that faraway island—benches that, when strung together, form a long unbroken chain, and standing on each one, a small person with two small hands.

Marx's commitment to not becoming a money-earning machine meant that a significant—even crushing—amount of work was thereby transferred to Jenny. That Jenny took this work upon herself willingly does not seem to be in doubt; theirs was a celebrated partnership in part because she was one of the few who could actually read his handwriting. On top of all the household work and child-raising, she hand-copied legible manuscripts of his work for publishers. (Can you imagine hand writing The Communist Manifesto *from beginning to end?) The pressures of her responsibilities were enormous and at times she seemed most alone when she needed her husband most profoundly. The family often went hungry and Jenny's letters reveal a round of household labors that included continual cadging of small funds wherever she could get them. Perhaps the most awful moment came when, after falling sick, their fifth child, only a year old, died. Jenny writes that none of their close friends could help them. Engels was at work for his father in Manchester, and others, though sympathetic, had no money to give.*

In the anguish of my heart I went to a French refugee who lived near, and who had sometimes visited us. I told him our sore need. At once with the friendliest kindness he gave me 2 [pounds]. With that we paid for the little coffin in which the poor child now sleeps peacefully. I had no cradle for her when she was born, and even the last small resting place was being denied her.

One could argue that the little coffin where Jenny placed her child's body was a blank, cold, bought thing like any other. I doubt, however, that Marx lived his own theories so thoroughly that he would have found that coffin abhorrent because it was the product of some poor soul's alienated labor. More likely, he laid his cheek on it before the box went into the ground, and mourned his small child's death.

THE KISS

Benin was about five or six years old, I think. Even then, she never asked for much when we went shopping. She had learned to keep quiet, I guess, after the time I had hustled her out of a supermarket leaving behind a full cart of shopping because she was having a temper tantrum. But this day, we were in a local market and she asked me to buy her a bag of chocolates. Just the kind of thing I always say no to without skipping a beat. She stood there, very quietly, holding the bag in her hands, and said, "Mommy, I have to ask you something." For some reason, rather than just saying no, and walking off, I stood there and let her ask. "Do you think you could buy this for me?" And for some reason, I said yes. I still don't really know why. For the record, I am not a complete antisugar fanatic, unlike the mothers at her school at the time, who were making me crazy in what I called "the lunch-box wars." This clique of moms (of course dads never seemed to be involved in these take-no-prisoners events) wanted all children at school to follow very specific rules: no sugar, no red dye, no food-sharing. As someone who bakes brownies and cookies on a regular basis and sees no problem at all in tossing one into my kid's lunch, I was feeling a little intruded upon. Why not teach your precious kids not to eat food from other children's lunches? And if your kids *want* the sugar, they're going to have to learn that some people do actually eat sugar, and that's the way the cookie crumbles! My kid shouldn't have to suffer because you, Mom, are a control freak. The lunchbox wars started me dreaming up the most un-nutritious lunches I could think of: fluffernutters on white bread, Cheetos, and strawberry milk;

American cheese on top of barbecue-flavored potato chips. Why not just a thermos full of Karo syrup?

This was the context in which I guess I was seeing that chocolate, and to spite those other moms, I told my girl I'd buy it for her. She stood quietly and eyed me, then lifted a finger and crooked it at me, saying, "Come here." I bent in closer to her, and she gave me the sweetest, softest, dearest kiss. "Thank you," she said, solemnly. For that kiss, I'd buy her anything she wanted.

ARE THERE MALLS IN HAITI?

One evening, while giving an informal presentation to the Black Students' Alliance about Haiti, one girl raised her hand and asked: "Are there malls in Haiti?" At the time it seemed a vapid and pointless question. The answer, by the way, is no. There are no malls in Haiti. In the wake of the 2010 earthquake, all the thinking I had done over the years about consumption in Haiti struck me as both utterly beside the point and deeply necessary. It was obvious to me that most of the reporters on the scene had no idea what they were looking at half the time.

For instance, on about the third day after the quake, there was a lot of reporting from the center of Port-au-Prince, near the iron market, where stores and stalls lined the streets. Nothing was open but people were hungry. Not only that, but the peasants were coming down out of the mountains with food to sell. There was no money either. All the banks had to stay closed not only because of disorder but because there was no electricity—and thus no working computer system. People started sifting through the rubble, going into stores, and taking out things of value. Reporters were chastising the "looters" for taking things that had no survival value, as if these well-fed interlopers from First World media outfits knew a whole lot about survival.

People had to get stuff out because they could trade it for the carrots, for the mangoes, for the radishes and onions arriving from the hillside towns of Kenskoff and Fermathe. They weren't looting exactly, although they were taking stuff that wasn't theirs and they weren't paying for it. Contrary to the judgments of reporters, this was precisely about survival—something that Haitians have more experience with than almost anybody on the planet.

We are so steeped in our own culture of consumption that we really cannot understand a place like Haiti, a place where consumption works in ways so different from what we recognize as normal. No, there are no malls in Haiti. Before the earthquake, the largest store was the Caribbean Market, a U.S.-style supermarket owned by one of the Christian Syrian families that used to dominate the supermarket business in Haiti. It had six cash registers and four armed guards and aisles lined with an assortment of goods catering to the international-aid-worker contingent and rich Haitians: boxes of breakfast cereal, soy sauce, French wine, macaroni and cheese.

Since my first trip to Haiti I have been continually fascinated with how shopping works there. For me it's a conundrum. First of all, everybody is impeccably dressed. Even in the earthquake, look at the pictures carefully—the Haitians are in ironed clothes, utterly clean, utterly presentable. It's the Westerners who look like they have been through the wringer, and I mean everybody: doctors, reporters, aid workers, you name it, they're scruffy, wrinkly, smudged. Not the Haitians. Where on earth do people get the energy to find clean clothes when their whole world has fallen to pieces? A bigger question in Haiti, where there are not only no malls but virtually no places to purchase new clothes, is where people find the things they wear. For instance, all those people you see on their way to church or to a Vodou ceremony, wreathed in spanking white from head to toe, whether it's Jesus or Damballah they seek to celebrate, where do they get all those beautiful white clothes, and how do they keep them so pristine? Me, I don't even bother to buy white clothes because they stay clean for an hour at best.

My pictures from Haiti often feature shot after shot of what is called pèpè, a term Haitians use to describe secondhand everything. Clothes, cars, McDonald's toys, all sorts of pèpè are the mainstay of Haitian daily consumption. The stuff arrives on boats, bundled into bale-sized packages, bought dockside by pèpè dealers hoping there might be something extra good inside. Usually you know what you're buying in a general way: sheets, women's underwear, T-shirts. This is all stuff from the United States, donated to places like Goodwill and the Salvation Army, who skim off the best for their retail stores and then sell the rest (which is the majority) by the ton to secondhand dealers who sort it, ship it, and sell it worldwide. Some of it is bundled into packages the size of a small elephant, held together with massive crisscrossing straps.

So in a way, shopping in Haiti is a bit like working your way through a nation-sized thrift shop. Most vendors of pèpè have just a few things, a pile that can be carried to market and home again, laid out on a cloth, or perhaps displayed on a rack complete with hangers. People specialize. Out by the big intersection of the Route Nationale the sidewalks are lined with what seems like an acre of shoes. On market days around town people set up their stalls and jostle for space. What I always wonder is this: how do Haitians find nice things that are the right size and that also match? Somehow they do, because everybody's outfits are gorgeous.

Style, under these circumstances, is hardly about looking in magazines or watching music videos and emulating Eurotrash heiresses. People are proud and brittle, and looking good is important largely because the costs of looking bad are cutting. (Someone like me, who is utterly hopeless, gets a free pass because I'm MRE, and foreign, and at once considered moderately insane and marginally cognitively challenged.) On one visit, toward the end of our stay, my daughter carefully chose things of her own that she wanted to give as gifts to children in the neighborhood that we had gotten to know. I was touched by her desire to give something of herself, and I had already spent several hundred dollars buying backpacks and school supplies for all of them, so I figured this would just be a little added something to the loot they'd already gotten. The day after she distributed the gifts, a neighbor stopped by, the grandmother of one of the children. "*Rete aveugle*," she counseled through the security door, "Be blind," she said, meaning "Don't pay any attention." People were complaining about being given secondhand things, insulted that the items had not been new. On the one hand, I understood. On the other, I had no patience. "If they don't like it they can give it back or give it away," I said, feeling ready to go home, where I understood the rules better and where I could avoid the mall as a matter of principle and still have plenty of choices for finding what I wanted, whether a flower pot or a beaded sweater. "Next time," I thought ungenerously and self-servingly, "I won't bring anything at all." As if that might solve anything.

BABY NUMBER TWO
TURNED ME INTO ECONOMIC MAN

Finding out I was pregnant with a second baby was a bit of a surprise, though as I've been telling people, grown-up adults like me and my husband certainly know what can happen when you have relations without using birth control. It's exciting, but it's different than the first time, since Benin was the result of much careful planning and anticipation.

It made me want to buy myself a present. Reason number one: because I just got my body back and now I'm going to get big again and I deserve something to make me look forward to that. Reason number two: to celebrate. Reason number three: because we're going to really have to tighten our belts later, so this is the last hurrah. Reason number three will probably lead me to decide that really I shouldn't get myself anything unless it's something either cheap or practical.

There's the question of what an appropriate present to myself under these circumstances might be. I've been wanting a new pair of glasses quite a lot. Something really off the wall and funky. Then there's the other thing I've kind of been wanting lately—a backyard chicken. To eat the slugs and the snails, because I'm too wimpy to kill them with beer traps or just to step on them, or to douse them in salt and watch their insides ooze out of their skins. But who gives themselves a chicken as an "I got pregnant" present?

The chicken would also need a coop, of course, and that's where things get complicated. I used to have a neighbor, an architect who worked for Frank Gehry. He got chickens a couple of years ago and put up the chicken coop, the chicken coop to beat all chicken coops, painted a light springy green and elegant as can be. I'm not particularly handy with power tools, and my husband even less so, so I don't see this happening for us. On the web you can buy chicken condos and hen spas ready-made, anywhere from $199 to $1,500.

My other big response, aside from wanting to indulge in eyeglasses and chickens and chicken coops, is to look at the house and think, my god, there's so much to do. When I had Benin, that was the impetus to go out and buy a house. We called it the nesting instinct. Now that we basically have a nest, baby number two urges me to make all those improvements we've been procrastinating on. Installing a dishwasher, for instance.

What I seem to be finding lately is that as much as I hate and abhor the idea of "economic man," I seem to be constantly performing rudimentary cost/benefit analyses: chicken versus dishwasher, new kitchen chairs versus improved attic ventilation, plants for the garden versus some slightly expensive food item like Marcona almonds or local hand-roasted coffee. I bought a ceiling fan for Benin's room, the room she will share with the new baby. That is, she will share it if we can ever get her to start going to bed without having a forty-minute screaming fit that involves throwing up three or four times. I sit here in the evenings, trying to tune out her wails, hoping the neighbors aren't convinced we're abusing her, and I can feel my blood pressure zinging round my eardrums. The other night she was screeching "Mommy, I want to poop," since she knows that poop in her diaper is one of the only things that will bring me into her room after it's bedtime.

My most economic manly decision: to work part-time for three years after the baby is born. I'm not sure quite how I'm going to pull this off or make it happen, but it's got to happen, because with two kids in my life, at the rate I'm going it just won't be possible for me to keep it all together, the teaching and mentoring and parenting and gardening and cooking and shopping and cleaning and writing and research and being chair of this and being chair of that and trying to get grants. And I feel bad because I haven't done any sewing to speak of in years—and I just bought this amazing treasure trove of patterns from the '50s, '60s, and '70s and would love to stitch up a bunch of those dresses. I'd been toying with the idea of working part-time anyway, but not seriously. It seemed kind of self-indulgent, and again I didn't want to deal with the financial implications of less than full-time work.

The manners we have in this society about money are, it has often been pointed out, far more occult and straitjacketed than for sex. Personally, I think everybody where I work ought to wear a black T-shirt that has their salary written across the chest in big white letters. When I worked at Occidental College I used to tell everybody my salary because it was so astonishingly low. As my stepmother often pointed out to me, I would have made more money working in Room 7, which is her funny way of saying that public school teachers like herself make more than college professors like myself, which goes to show you the beauty of unions. When I originally wrote this entry I actually couldn't quite remember my salary and had convinced myself it was $57,000; in actuality it was $55,000, and that was in about 2002. Notice I am not spouting off about my current salary but I will say that it is under six figures. Compared to most people in the United States I make lots of money, plenty for the whole family, so what am I complaining about? Maybe if I didn't live in one of the most expensive housing markets in the country my salary might give me more solace. And then there's the wall that I think I just hit: no matter how much money I make, it isn't worth it to be spending so much time at work away from my family.

It's not that I'm an antifeminist, women-should-stay-at-home ideologue. It's just that I cannot get by on less than eight hours of sleep, and if something doesn't get ratcheted down, my sleep is going to get eaten into. I hate to do anything badly, and I know myself well enough to know that if I keep trying to do everything, something's going to go badly. But being a bad parent, what could be worse than that? I just don't see the point of having kids if I don't make as much time for them as I can without resenting them. I like working. I probably like it too much. It's not the money that I like; it's the validation. Teaching is easier than parenting, but it offers the easy reward of making you feel that you made a difference in someone's life, at least sometimes.

Being a girl, I'll probably just keep trying to do everything. Or maybe I'll ask for the time off, but shyly, expecting nothing. But in my teaching myself the art of economic manliness, I'm learning about asking for stuff, and doing it boldly. And doing it selfishly. I am not bothering to think about what's fair in the larger circle, only what's fair to me and what makes my life more livable and a lot of that boils down this: less work but with as little of a pay cut as possible.

Do I think like economic man because that's just how people think? Or do I think like economic man because I was taught to? The humanist in me, the anthropologist, believes it's the latter. If I didn't live in a society that made all of these decisions so hard and so fraught, I wouldn't be lying around at night doing this endless series of calculations. I don't mean that I wish I were a hunter-gatherer who didn't need a job. In Germany, one of the least generous of the European countries, women get thirty-three weeks of paid maternity leave. Of course, I'm really lucky because at my college I'll get a semester off with pay, which amounts to about the same thing. Still lots of other colleges only give women one course off. They then have to buy themselves out of the rest of their classes to get a free semester. What a deal.

PICTURES OF THE RICE GRAIN

On Saturday, at a party, at a lovely modernist house in Altadena where every object was carefully chosen and made me feel like my own life was sort of ramshackle and tatty, I went to the bathroom and saw pink in the water. It was such a nice party, and I didn't want to ruin things, and not knowing what to do anyway I went out and stood against my car and cried. I had just spent the entire week telling everyone in my universe that I'm pregnant. My friends Susan and Catherine found me and helped me pull myself together enough to make an abrupt and probably somewhat incomprehensible goodbye, gather up my kid, call my husband, and try not to speed home and run stop signs. I was shaking.

We dropped Benin off at my dad's and went to the Kaiser urgent care, a place that I've visited more times than I'd like, the first time having been, as they say, one time too many. Throughout their shift, workers see people rushing in, convinced their worlds are about to come crashing down, each patient with their own earth-shattering personal emergency. But to the people behind the various desks, or in the scrubs, or wearing the lab coats, so much crisis ultimately becomes so much banality. So when I walk in there with blood dotting my panties, it's not some terribly important event to them, but just another miscarriage, another night, another shift, another sheaf of paperwork to complete.

Their indifference is different from what's going on with my husband, who hasn't a clue about what to do and hides behind a newly purchased Esquire magazine in the waiting room. He doesn't come back with me when I'm called to see the doctor. He's scared, he's confused. The people who work here aren't scared—they're just doing a job.

The first woman I deal with is a middle-aged black nurse, very business-like, who makes no eye contact. She takes my temperature and my blood pressure, which is as high as I've ever seen it, at 185/90. When it comes time to describe my problems, I'm numb and scared. At least I'm not crying, which is good, because it's clear that if I needed, say, comforting, the most I'd get is a box of Kleenex coming into view, proffered with her head turned the other way because she's really busy doing something else. I try to be really good-natured and calm, even making weak jokes, to show her that I won't be one of those drive-you-crazy demanding patients, which in my mind will trigger her to be nice to me. It doesn't work.

"You can go into Room 17," she says, and waves vaguely down the hall. I go in there and wait awhile. Then she comes in and tells me to go to a different room. Obedient, I follow. This one has an exam table with stir-rups and a sonogram machine, and she tells me to undress from the waist down and cover myself with the sheet. I don't have socks on, and I have athletic tape around one of my big toes where a callus has ripped off. The doctor comes in, a white guy with white hair. He reminds me a bit of Steve Martin and I almost say something. But then I'm thinking, why do I want to joke around and make nice to these people? It's a way of breaking through. I can understand professional demeanor, but these people are like Easter Island monoliths. He does take a moment to run the stainless steel spec-ulum under warm water before he puts it in and cranks me open to look at my cervix.

The sonogram machine works like this: it has a long wand, with a gray sensor at the end. They put some jelly in a condom and put that over the wand and then put that in you to look at your uterus and your ovaries or whatever else they want to look at in there and can get a view of with a good poke and a twist. On the screen, the image is gray and white and black, fuzzy, snowy. There is a dark oval with a lighter spot in the middle. "That's the . . ." The doctor had some kind of clinical term for that oval, I can't remember exactly what it was, the something sac, he never said anything remotely like fetus or baby or anything like that. Of course. He used the computer to mark the two ends of it with little crosses that were connected with a dotted line, to measure it. Printed out two copies and gave me one. A picture of my little not-yet-a-fetus thing. He tells me to keep it so that when I visit a doctor again they can see it, to see if it has grown. Being still obedient, I put it in my purse, but I really don't want it. "If you got pregnant when you think you did," he tells me, "then it's not doing very well." I'm supposed to get another lab test in a few days, and also to make a doctor appointment. Normally, I think I would be able to understand what he's telling me—how many days I should wait for the second test, when to get the doctor appointment, but my brain isn't working right. "I'm sorry," I say to him, "Could you write that all down for me? I'm having a hard time right now." With bland patience, he begins writing it all down. The Easter Island nurse gives me a Kleenex to wipe the jelly off from between my legs, I get dressed, and I have to stop at the nurses' desk to get orders for the first blood test.

There are jobs where you really have to engage with people's emotions and feelings and appear warm and caring, like a therapist. Then there is the nurses' desk at Kaiser. It's as if I'm interrupting group break time. I'm an invader, and an inconvenient one. They ignore me for a full three minutes while they talk among themselves. I'm smiling, pathetically, like a sick puppy who thinks that being cute might get her some attention. Another nurse with her hair in braids is slumped in a chair. "My two-year-old has trouble some-times," she says. "Does he eat apples?" says Easter Island. "Yeah, he eats all that stuff, apples, bananas." Another nurse, a blond-haired Latina, jumps in: "But those things are binding—rice, bananas, they just make it worse." "Re-ally?" "Yeah," Blondie says, continuing, "Here's what you should give him: prunes, carrots, stuff like that. You know, my sister-in-law's sister, when she just looks at a cucumber, she runs to the bathroom." Easter Island has taken my paperwork. "She likes cucumbers?" she says vaguely, confused. "No, I was saying that all she has to do is look at the cucumber and she runs to the bathroom." As she starts typing in the computer, Easter Island says, "I wish I could find something like that to work for me."

The whole thing is, it's not their job to give a shit that I'm standing in front of them "losing the pregnancy," as the doctor said to me. (You fucker, I think. I didn't lose anything.) But I can't help wishing they would. Standing there listening to this inane discussion about cucumbers and shit and bananas, it just hits me so hard that they don't care at all about my little problem because they just don't have to. They're not paid to do that. I start to wonder how many relationships in our lives are drawn and quartered around the limits of what we're paid or allowed to do. How much of our human interaction is circumscribed by contracts and union rules and OSHA regulations? Would I really feel better if they were forced, or required, to utter some sympathetic line so as to avoid a bad performance review? Right now I think, yes, I probably would feel better with some mandated sympathy. That would be better than listening to a bunch of women talk about how frequently their kids defecate.

Suddenly I realize that the only way I can assert myself before them is as a paying customer. The only way I can reach them is to think about writing some letter to some administrator complaining about poor service. I can't say, "You should care because it's the morally right thing to do!" or "You should be nice because that's what people do when other people are suffering!" My power in this situation, or any hope of attaining any power, comes from being not a human being with feelings and needs, but a customer who deserves good service. I'll probably get one of those surveys in the mail in a few weeks, as I often do after a visit to Kaiser, asking me to rate the quality of service and "care" that I received. Usually I throw them away. Though I know it will make no difference, no difference at all, I will demonstrate that I am an unhappy customer if I get my survey. I will exercise my power as a consumer. I begin to imagine the comments I will write on the form.

I get my blood test, walk through a maze of doors that are propped open with towels and pieces of tape, and find my husband in the waiting room. "Could you get my magazine back from that lady?" he asks as he heads out toward the car. Right.

So in my purse I now have this little picture. What's it really a picture of? We have similar pictures, taken of Benin, but she turned into a real live baby, a real person. I don't know what to call it, so I start thinking of it as "my rice grain." It's really bigger than a rice grain, about the size of a small bean and the shape of a piece of fat, stubby Arborio rice, not the long slim grains of jasmine rice we eat at home. Here's my problem: what am I supposed to do with this artifact, this evidence, this thing? Right this very minute, I'm pretty sure that the rice grain is still in my uterus, even though my cramps are getting worse and my bleeding has picked up. I know for sure at this point that the rice grain has no future to speak of. So what I've got in my purse is certainly not a baby picture. It's not that kind of keepsake. It's almost an antikeepsake, the dark twin of the kind of stuff that we push into scrapbooks and baby books and memory books. Marketers certainly have no use for something like this. Still, it's a picture of something that, for a couple of weeks, was going to be part of my life for a really long time. How do you deal with a picture of your baby that wasn't? Maybe I'll just kind of forget about it in my purse for a really long time and it will crumple up and disintegrate or get peanut butter and jelly on it and become just a mess and unintelligible and I'll just sort of throw it away without noticing. Or I could do as my friend Mary said and burn it. Susan and Catherine have offered to keep it for me as long as I want so that I neither have to have it in my own home nor make any kind of big decision. As far as I can tell, the actual rice grain is probably just going to land on a sanitary pad, or in the toilet, or perhaps be sucked out in a D&C procedure, and I highly doubt I'll get the chance to bury it in the backyard beneath a new flowering plant.

Somehow it would be easier to get rid of the sonograms of Benin than to discard the rice-grain picture. After we got home, I dreamed that the miscarriage was over and I was pregnant again and happy. But right now, I'm crampy and bleeding and there's nobody on the phone and my husband is asleep. And I wish there was somebody out there whose job description read, "Comfort her," and even if it wasn't real, I think it would help, just for a little while.

PANTING IN IKEA

There's no denying that one of the ways I have coped with the miscarriage was by going shopping. I think the whole experience will be indelibly linked in my mind alongside key shopping moments. However, it would be simplistic to say that shopping was some sort of easy escape. It didn't exactly ease the pain. It didn't exactly distract me. Much of the shopping that I did was really about life, about moving into life as one life was moving out of my own body.

I was looking at my credit card activity online today, and I could see the different lines and purchases on there as a kind of document that chronicled the course of my miscarriage. There were the innocent purchases before the whole thing started: some gas, a couple of quarts of paint from Home Depot, groceries. There's no way to tell, of course, from looking at the list of purchases itself, when the miscarriage began. It made me think of those stupid (and yet terribly powerful) MasterCard commercials, where they list off the price of this and that and then it finishes with something like "The look on her face: priceless." Only looking at that list, my own commercial might be: "Chairs, $79 each; clock $23; table $39. Getting through a miscarriage: Priceless."

I was completely unprepared for how physically hard the miscarriage would be. In my experience, at least, miscarriages are only something people talk about once they've had them. So, going into this I didn't know anything about the process except that something happened. Somehow in my imagination I thought of a miscarriage as an event, something that happened rather quickly, like laying an egg. But mine took place over about five days, at least the main part of it. The first shopping I did during my miscarriage was on a lovely sunny day, when my friend Caro took me out to lunch. She had her first baby, Aled, around the time that Benin was born, and we'd already figured out that this time we'd gotten pregnant within a couple of weeks of each other. So it was pretty sad when she found out that I wasn't going to be having a baby with her for a second time. We'd decided to go walking around in South Pasadena, and went into a place called The Ultimate Outlet, where I mooned over piles of elaborate beaded bracelets but bought a white linen skirt, top, and pants for fourteen dollars each. In the midst of this awful event, it seems I'd decided to dress like an off-the-rack angel. That night, the rice grain dropped out onto a piece of toilet paper, and not quite knowing what else to do, I wrapped it up and hid it away, planning to bury it in the garden. It was dark red, but smooth, and already showing a slim, twisted stem of an umbilicus, cut and shiny, tiny as two entwined wires.

The doctor I visited for a gynecological check was someone I'd never seen before (and for a Kaiser HMO patient, that's hardly unusual), an older German man who brings in his old magazines for patients to read as they wait in the cool examination rooms. He was matter-of-fact, asking me if tissue was coming out, telling me my uterus wasn't normal-sized yet. He sat me down in his office and said he was sorry, but that if I wanted I could try to get pregnant again anytime. Did I want to go on birth control pills for a month? I said why, and no thank you.

That afternoon, after picking Benin up from school, I needed to go to Target to buy her some underpants and hoped also to find some of the thin nylon socks with lace that are her favorite. These days I can't stand to take Benin shopping, since her idea of fun is to crawl under display tables and to hide among hanging clothes with the toes of her tattered Dorothy shoes peeking out from underneath racks of blue jeans. The only part of the store that held her attention was the shoe aisle. That day in Target, I kind of lost it. Not with Benin. What fell away from me were the restrictions I usually place on getting things for the house that I'd really like, but can, in a pinch, live without for now. I just couldn't see the point in not having reading lamps any longer in the living room. So I bought one. I couldn't see why I had to continue putting off getting a couple of chairs and a little table for that sweet and sunny corner in the kitchen, which is one of the nicest spots in the house but has been empty except for the occasional box of books since we moved in. I bought these two chairs that I'd seen at Target months ago. They were nearly eighty dollars each, retro-1950s-like, chrome and red sparkly vinyl. Benin likes the sparkles—she's a girl with a magpie sensibility like my own. It runs in the family.

I got home tired and worn out and had to ask Robert to take over while I just got in bed and put the covers over my head. My hormones must have been doing loop-de-loops. I woke up a little while later covered in a sweat that hugged my forehead like a swim cap. The cramping and bleeding came in waves, sometimes so bad I ached all the way down to my knees. The bleeding wasn't exactly steady; sometimes it was as if a little bucket had been tipped, overflowing the pads I had to change almost hourly.

The retro chairs needed a little table to sit between them, to make a spot where you could sit and sip coffee while reading or grading papers. But Target didn't have the right table, so I decided to make my very first trip to Ikea. I woke up the next morning feeling pretty good, so after taking Benin to school, I thought an Ikea adventure would be a little bit of fun and diversion. All I wanted was a little table. Nothing much. So I'd decided: I'll take it slow, enjoy the ride, it won't be serious, it's not like I need much or anything at all. Diversion, fun, relax. I guess people are always going through something in life, but it is a little weird to be having a miscarriage (and having it go on and on) and be out shopping. I kind of wanted to say to people: make way, I'm having a miscarriage here! That would mean it was a crisis of the moment, something that required calling an ambulance or something, and it wasn't like that at all. It was just happening, slowly, sort of like getting old, something you just can't stop and that doesn't quite stop you, just slows you down. I found just the right table, a small metal thing with three thin, bendy legs, for about forty dollars. Then I discovered the really cheap section of Ikea and got a few neat items like cotton roman shades for four dollars each, a big nubby wool throw for four dollars too, and an easel as a birthday present for Benin.

My cramps were picking up, and as I was paying for everything I started getting pretty limp. I had a feeling like I'd drunk too much, only I hadn't drunk a thing. It wasn't so much that I felt drunk, it was more like that feeling you have the next morning, when alcohol fumes seem to be coming out of your pores and you feel wrung out. As I pushed my cart toward the exit, I thought I was going to faint. I clung onto the cart and lowered myself onto a bench, facing the little food court by the exit door. I had to pant a little bit, it hurt so much. I tried not to cry. But I still felt really sorry for myself, sitting in the cavernous space, looking at Ikea employees on their break shooting the shit, watching people farther down, pushing loads of stuff into the return and exchange lanes. I was wondering whether I should just call someone to come get me, or whether I should ask someone who worked there to help me to my car, where I could just sit there until I felt better again. Unable to make a decision, I just sat on the bench, feeling very lonely and scared. I ate the half of a muffin I'd squirreled away in my purse. The dizziness and weakness, I thought, was because I hadn't really eaten anything that day (except the other half of the muffin) or even the day before. Part of me felt like it was my own damn fault. What the hell was I doing out at Ikea anyway, in the middle of a miscarriage? What was I thinking?

And that's the moment that will stick with me. Sitting on that bench, doubled over, panting and hanging onto an Ikea shopping cart. Isn't it silly, though, that it took that, it took losing a pregnancy, to push me to finally make a cozy corner for myself in my own home?

CAPITALISM MAKES ME SICK

OK, I've been crying for the past two days. I was sitting in a meeting with a student yesterday, tears just flowing out of my eyes and fake-coughing so that she would think I had a cold or something. I'd be talking to her, and then some tears would start to overflow, so I would fake-cough, and then wipe my eyes. We both were acting like this was normal and I wasn't just sitting there silently crying as we discussed her fellowship proposal. I called a colleague in tears, cancelled my classes, and went home to make dinner for my godson and his girlfriend and drank three Hello Kitty juice cups of wine. Took half a sleeping pill, tried not to keep my mind spiraling endlessly around stupid things I had done recently, and fell asleep next to my daughter, whose scent I would know anywhere, even in the dark, even in a cave, even if there were a thousand other children there.

Since my miscarriage, I have been suffering a depression so powerfully physical that I am sometimes convinced gravity's pull on my limbs has magnified itself tenfold. There are moments when lifting my arm seems like a commitment so great I can hardly imagine getting my hand off the table and up to my face. My head hurts all the time and I feel as if a fifty-pound weight rings my head like a doughnut. I'm slow. I'm crabby. The constant tension in my muscles creates chronic pain in my neck and back. Concentrating is a chore. Details escape me. The moment that most frightened me was when, one late night at the dining room table, it seemed to me that a cocktail of bleach and sleeping pills wasn't such a bad idea. This was no slobbery moment of self-hatred. It was a cold-eyed assessment of the realities of the situation. Emotionless and objective. That's when I knew things were seriously out of control.

I called the psychiatrist. Trying to lever myself out of this funk, I have recently, and for the first time, begun to take antidepressant medication. For the first few months I felt a lot better. I also began to lose weight at an alarming rate. At five feet eight inches, I'm now down to 120 pounds, which is what I weighed when I was a fierce and dedicated anorectic. My size 6 clothes are baggy on me. Even my dance teacher thinks I'm too thin. Losing the weight has been effortless. What scares me is, I kind of like it.

Why am I so desperately depressed? Why does everything seem so hard? How come being hungry and shaky makes me feel alive? And why am I such a good faker that most people haven't got a clue? If you ask me (and bear with me here), it's capitalism! Now this claim might indeed seem ridiculously ideological. After all, if the medication is working (but it doesn't really seem to be working right now), doesn't that just prove that the depression is biological? I don't think so. Down to my very bones, I'm sure that my state is caused by the poisonous brew of stress, obligation, ambition, and busywork that constitutes my work life. The stress is multiplied by an emotional commitment to personalizing my work so that being a good chair, colleague, academic adviser, teacher, and writer of scholarly papers is indistinguishable from what is most profoundly me. The strain I feel is deepened by an enlivening sense of human engagement with my students and with colleagues. I love them more tangibly than I love many other people who by rights deserve my love a great deal more. This is all exacerbated by the guilt I feel about dumping my child in daycare from 8 a.m. to 6 p.m., coughing up $705 per month for the privilege of barely ever seeing her, and being so tired when I get home that domestic chores—sweeping, cooking, gardening—are more mountains to climb. Not to mention the tattered state of my marriage. Since my husband and I barely have time to speak to each other, I can't be sure how bad it really is. And, of course, I'm afraid to find out.

What convinced me that this depression is really about things like managing money and work and not about my serotonin level was a week-long trip that my daughter and I recently took to the East Coast to visit family. We didn't do a thing. We barely left the house. She was beamingly, beautifully, profoundly happy and joyful during that week. I was happier too, though I don't think I ever got to the beaming state. All we did was hang around together with my mother, her husband, and my godparents. We didn't rush to get here or there on time. No hustle. No bustle. I heard on the radio today that we work harder and longer than medieval peasants did. Maybe what I need is a bumper sticker that reads "I'd rather be serfing!"

Every day, every single day, I find myself immobilized by the amount of work that I absolutely must get done. There is more work than I can do, and recently I've had to take the most desperate step of backing out of commitments, something I have never, ever done before. Every day I think, I can't live like this. This is killing me. And then I sit down at my computer, make appointments, write agendas, communicate with administrative assistants, plan programs, grade papers, write grant proposals, evaluate my junior colleagues for advancement, design departmental curricula, write scholarly articles, eat lunch at my desk, say yes to even more responsibilities, leave by six to pick up my child, throw her in front of a video so I can cook and decompress (so I won't scream at her), slap her in a bath, dunk myself in it too, and fall asleep in her bed while reading her a bedtime story. If I'm lucky, I walk the dog for fifteen minutes and take a piss while reading the editorial page. I try to notice and appreciate the sky, which this morning was dominated by an orange sun surrounded by a pool of milky orange haze that looked poisonous and deadly.

Ambition is bullshit. Though I believe this, it has in no way decreased my own ambitions to achieve in my field or at my institution. Working hard dehumanizes me. Though I believe this too, it has not stopped me from putting in ten-, twelve-, fourteen-hour days on a regular basis, much to the detriment of the fundamentally important relationships I ought to be having with my husband, child, dog, cat, and myself. Identifying myself as my job is dangerous. Though I believe this, I know that I have no idea who I am away from my desk. I am frightened to death to continue like this. I am frightened to death to step away. No wonder the bleach-and-sleeping-pills cocktail seems like it might be tasty enough to try. The impossible bind I find myself in is squeezing the life out of me.

Anacondas twine around their prey, and as their victims breathe, they squeeze tighter and tighter until they die. You have to breathe to live, but if there's an anaconda wrapped around you, breathing will kill you, too. That's what it feels like when I think about the circumstances of my life/work. Really. Don't you feel it too sometimes, and wonder how you bear it? My wish is that in a year from now, I might be in a really different place, one that does not involve having made peace with my insanely diligent work ethic. I know almost to a certainty that I will never find that place. My head might hate capitalism, but my heart is bound to it. Without my work ethic, what am I? A small voice inside me whispers back, "Nothing." Maybe my biology primes me to feel the pain of that loss-of-something-I-will-never-have more intensely than I otherwise might. By this I mean, my serotonin levels really *are* out of whack, but maybe they are out of whack because the demands of this kind of life are just wrong. The weight I feel wrapped around my head is that anaconda sitting there, feeling out my breaths, calculating how to give me just enough breathing room so that I can last until it's hungry enough to want to eat. The depression is an unveiling, an awakening to the suffocating grasp of the anaconda. I'm afraid. I'm afraid I will never be able to stuff down from the surface of my consciousness the feeling of this weight and know that if I somehow do not, the anaconda will only get me sooner. Maybe I can tempt it with sleeping pills and bleach.

By 1865 the Marx daughters were ripe for marriage. The family finances had settled down a bit and the family had moved into a large house, big enough for them to throw a ball for their girls. If the grand ball was the event of the season for the Marx household, there is little doubt that there must have been a substantial bill from the dressmaker, since a fancy ball required equally fancy clothing. During the late 1800s, clothing occupied a different position than it does now—a dress was not an off-the-rack item but something more like a pair of prescription glasses. Like glasses, a dress required a substantial financial investment and was custom-made to fit the individual who would wear it. A dress required about ten yards of fabric, and the cloth alone cost a bundle. Then there was underclothing in the form of petticoats, pantaloons, and chemises. As an experienced sewer myself, I have a pretty good idea of the amount of time and labor that would go into making the typical dress worn in Jenny's day, and this during an era when predrafted paper patterns were not yet being produced. Hand-sewing even a simple day dress—from designing and cutting to the finished garment—would be at least three full days of work for someone working very quickly, doing little else, and barely sleeping. For Jenny, who had plenty of other responsibilities, sewing a dress, even with help, probably took upwards of a week's steady labor, and likely a good deal longer. This, multiplied by the number of people in the family who regularly needed clothes, is more work than she could possibly handle. Depending on the garment and the event, Jenny must have made use at various times of dressmakers and seamstresses. She was well known for her own sewing abilities, and after her death it was her ever-present needle that one of her daughters remarked would be sorely missed.

It was not until the very late 1800s, with the invention of the sewing machine, that mass-produced ready-to-wear became widely available. Clothing was frequently "made over" to reflect changing styles and fashions. Moreover, only the well-to-do wore new clothing. Until the turn of the twentieth century it was the healthy trade in secondhand clothing that allowed servants, clerks, and others of lower social strata to purchase items that were well made and relatively stylish.[42] The rise in inexpensive, mass-produced clothing made new clothes available to nearly everyone, although ironically the quality of these clothes was arguably poorer than that of the secondhand goods purchased previously. It was not until the late 1800s, then, that purchasing secondhand clothes became stigmatized, and it became de rigueur for everyone of every social class to possess new clothing.

Perhaps even more important than marking status, in the mid- to late 1800s, clothing operated as a fungible form of wealth. The full-skirted silk and cotton dresses belonging to Marx's daughters and wife were, often as not, lodged at a pawnshop when they needed cash for rent, food, and other necessities. With their decent clothes in hock, however, the girls could not go out, at least not to many of the events and places—such as school or social gatherings—required of girls of their station. Being properly dressed, for women of the middle and upper classes, required separate garments for day, for promenade, for tea, for dinner. I suspect that Eleanor, the youngest daughter, was educated at home only in part because her family could not afford to pay for school. Her good clothes were in pawn during the bulk of her school-age years, the period when the Marx family experienced its greatest poverty. Perhaps she schooled at home because she did not have acceptable clothing to wear. In summer of 1867, for instance, when

Eleanor was thirteen years old, she and her sisters were invited to pass the summer in Bordeaux and Royan by the family of Laura's husband-to-be Paul LaFargue. In order to make the trip, they had to redeem their clothes, which were in the pawn shop along with numerous other possessions; they then paid for their travel to France using the rent money.[43]

At about the same time that the Marx family was "living at the pawn shop," the Navajo were quickly developing important pawn economies of their own, these based at trading posts. After having been held hostage for four years in Bosque Redondo, the eight thousand or so Navajo who had survived their incarceration negotiated a treaty, pledged not to fight the U.S. government (or the Pueblos or the Spanish), and were relocated to a reservation in the Four Corners area in 1868. Arriving back on their lands, the Navajo were destitute: their herds of sheep had been taken from them at Bosque Redondo, and they had to start from scratch. In addition to their abject poverty, the Navajo faced uneven cash flow, as do all herders and farmers: the economy revolved around the shearing season and the lamb season, and in between money was hard to come by. Then as now, the Four Corners area was remote, beautiful, and sparsely populated. Access to money and to such goods as textiles, flour, and guns came primarily through government handouts and the trading post. Trading posts themselves often dealt primarily in credit and pawn both to encourage (or force) clients to shop at their stores, and because cash was in short supply in the region, even for business owners. For the Navajo, then, the entire economy revolved around pawn in a way that it did not for Marx. Grey Moustache, a Navajo silversmith interviewed by John Adair, mentioned the shortage of money in "those days," explaining that the silver bridles he made were rarely paid for in cash: "I used to make many silver-mounted bridles. You don't see many of those today except on the pawn racks in the trading posts. . . . I used to pawn my bridle for eighty dollars in the trading post."[44] There was little actual money involved, and even the coins that Navajo got ahold of were often transformed into jewelry. Coins were hammered into rounded buttons worn up and down shirtsleeves and on moccasins, soldered into hollow beads, or melted down and used in necklaces and concho belts. Silver was wearable wealth, sometimes made of actual money, convertible to cash or credit when pawned. Adair noted in the mid-1940s that it was still common to receive as change coins that had once been used as buttons, with remains of soldered-on loops, or showing evidence of having been reshaped.[45] One of my favorite transformations of coins was the "mother-in-law bell," in which a quarter would be reshaped into a small bell which older women with married daughters would wear on their sashes. Traditionally, the Navajo practiced strict avoidance between a man and his mother-in-law; the bells announced the mother-in-law's approach so that nasty surprises could be avoided. The bells were perhaps a poetic comment on the costs of marriage.

During the Bosque Redondo years, Navajo women switched from wearing traditional handwoven "blanket dresses" to wearing the velvet blouses and long skirts that
still constitute traditional Navajo clothing today. This change in fashion freed women
weavers from spending their time weaving for family clothing to making articles that
could be sold. Enterprising traders encouraged them to move into producing rugs rather
than the blankets and serapes that had formed the bulk of their production previously.
In contrast to silverwork, an entirely new realm of artistic and economic production,
the shift to weaving items for the market was a medium for preserving long-standing
practices—weaving had likely been learned centuries ago from the Pueblo—while at
the same time producing financial resources. The Navajo rug, like Navajo silver, is a
relatively recent invention, an embodiment of the complex relationships contemporary
Navajo have to their traditions, to the imperatives of white cultures and markets, to
flexibility, and to abiding social and aesthetic values. Both the need for textiles and
the need for money fueled the growth in Navajo weaving and other crafts for which
the tribe has rightly become celebrated. The Navajo, like the Marx family, were not
buying ready-made clothes: they purchased yard goods and then cut and stitched the
things they wore. Navajo women no longer produced the fabric from which their clothes
were made, but they still had to make their own clothes while continuing their weaving
work. Meanwhile, it was the weaving that provided (in part) the money or credit women
needed to buy fabric, needles, thread, food, pots and pans, and so forth. As Wilkins notes
in her study of relations between weavers and traders, the economic transactions were
not clearly capitalist or precapitalist, involving, as they often did, complicated mixtures
of barter, credit, gift, personal relations, and money.[46]

Much more is known about the social relations of pawn among the Navajo than is
true for the pawnshops frequented by Marx. The oral histories of traders and other such
accounts bring the world of the trading post to life, and vividly. By contrast, we must
imagine the personal relationships that may have been developed between proprietors
and clients in Marx's milieu, and for Marx, at least, a lack of such relationships could
lead to trouble, as it had that time he had been mistaken for a thief when attempting to
pawn Jenny's family silver. Contentious as trader-Indian relationships may have been,
they were also clearly marked by interdependence, particularly early on, when trading
posts were isolated to the point of desolation and where, for traders, the prospect of failure or even death was not ever too far-fetched an outcome.

Trading post proprietors (usually men) and their wives also often operated as go-
betweens for their clients and the outside world. They wrote letters for parents who missed
their children now in residence at far-off government boarding schools, and read their
children's letters when they arrived; they butchered lambs and sheep; they sold wool
to middlemen and other buyers. Traders influenced and reshaped Navajo culture and

economy in other important ways, especially as they developed markets for Navajo crafts in the form of silver work and weaving. Lorenzo Hubbell was among the first, and most successful, of the traders in developing the production of and market for Navajo rugs and encouraged the use of "traditional" designs using a limited color palette, a strategy aimed to emphasize the Indianness of the objects. Hubbell's trading room was lined with paintings he had prepared, guides that weavers consulted as models for designs and colors. Meanwhile, many Navajo weavers were interested in design innovation and wanted to use the brightly colored aniline-dyed wools that were newly available. The result, at least in part, was that weavers had an authentic notion of Indianness thrust on their artistic production, at least if they wanted to sell to Hubbell, who was the largest trader in Navajo rugs and other artisanal items such as jewelry and leather work.

With multiple strands of dependency, friendship, and commerce binding traders to their clients, pawn on or near the reservation was rarely, if ever, the simple, impersonal transaction that it might have been in the urban areas of London where Marx lived. As many contemporary pawnbrokers continue to do, trading post operators often kept pawned items well past their due date, freezing interest and helping to keep families afloat without their having to permanently forfeit their most precious items. Most pawnbrokers pride themselves, in fact, on having low rates of lost pledges, since forfeited items can lead to frayed client relationships and a loss of what is the most lucrative part of their business: the cash loaned against the pledge. Trading post pawn was even sometimes borrowed back for a big event and then returned.[47]

Today's trading post pawn rooms are climate-controlled vaults, used in part as secure places to stow treasured possessions; some even have separate rooms for rugs, jewelry, and guns. In the end, though, some pledges just cannot be redeemed, some loans cannot be repaid, and the pawned item becomes the property of the trader or pawnbroker. Unredeemed pledges create what is called dead pawn. This resonant term captures the liveliness of the social relationship that continues between the parties as long as the loan and pledge are viable, a relationship sometimes kept on life support by pumping interest payments into a cash drawer, other times kept breathing by special favors granted by the proprietor. It is inevitably up to the proprietor to pull the plug, and to transform the pledge into an item of dead pawn. Dead pawn has been fully alienated from its past owner, removed from circulation within that person's life, and is now available to be purchased by someone new. When used with jewelry, the term "dead pawn" specifically refers to Native American items that have not been redeemed. This form of dead pawn is, to use a contemporary term, "highly collectible." It is a coveted form of jewelry, I suppose, because it has the added value of once having belonged to a real Indian, a quality that I find makes it creepy and repellent. Let me clarify: what is creepy and repellent is precisely that the object has not been fully alienated from its previous owner and that the essence of the previous owner somehow imbues the object with added aura. With some objects, this lingering aura would be a positive—with my grandmother's rings, for example, the aura is something I value and want to share. With a stranger, though, and with an object like dead pawn that speaks of another's desperation—particularly of Native American economic dispossession, with all its five-hundred-year-long history of being screwed to the wall—the aura is a dark shadow, not a halo. Dead pawn can be seen quite often on eBay and the items that fascinate me most are the ones with the pawn tickets still attached. Try an eBay search on "dead pawn" and see what you turn up. Sometimes I fantasize about buying dead pawn, tracking down the owners and returning it, a fantasy that is somewhat self-serving and paternalistic. I would get what I deserved, I think, if I turned up at someone's house feeling all proud of myself with something in hand, say, a string of coral beads, and the person looked at me and said, "Why would I want that crap back?" or, more likely, "Who are you to bring this back to me, and what do you want, anyway?"

Tempting as it may be to view pawn as a relic, what might be called a "survival," pawn's growing importance points to understandings of consumption—and economy—that pay a good deal more attention to the nuances in alienability of possessions and social relations among actors. With regard to contemporary Navajo weavers, for example, Wilkins writes that these weavers consider the objects they produce to be persons;[48] it is therefore something of an ethnocentric claim that such personification can be reduced to a Marxian form of the fetish: it is a conceptualization of person-in-object that comes from a rather different place than Marx's notion of the misplaced-personhood inherent to the alienation of the commodity.

MY GRANDMOTHER'S RINGS

The things in our lives connect to pieces of our histories; they hold stories together. There are so many things in my house or my office or in somebody else's house, or a particular corner, maybe a store, or a piece of sidewalk that I can look at (or it could just cross my mind), and that particular thing is a shorthand way of referring to a whole complicated chapter in my life. One moment of thought and a swath of feelings, a relationship, a particular embarrassing moment, or some everyday event (like opening a door) that could have happened a thousand times but it's that single one that I can recall many years later, and only when thinking on the thing that holds that memory in it for me. There are objects of mine that can spin relationships between themselves, forming webs in which I am suspended like a fat and careful spider, or maybe it's me who gets caught in them like a fat and careless fly. Anthropologist Clifford Geertz talked about culture itself as webs of meaning, but neglected to ask whether it is us who are caught in these webs, or whether we are the spiders that spin them.[49] I guess it's a little of both.

With some things, the stories are especially deep and long. My grandmother's rings came to me in a long and roundabout way, about twenty years after she'd died. I wear them on the pinky finger of my right hand. They're so small that I can't wear them on any of my other fingers. Maybe I'd wear them on my ring finger if my knuckles weren't so, well, knuckly. I have two friends who've tried the rings on, tiny women who can wear them on their ring fingers, and they look beautiful, but I don't want to make the changes it would require (a kind of jewelry surgery) to enlarge the rings enough for my hands. I want them the way they were when they were my grandmother's. They are old-fashioned rings. I've never had them appraised, though one time when I still lived in New Haven I inquired about the appraisal process with my rings in mind—but I guess they're worth a little bit. Not millions, but something. Both settings are platinum and have diamonds. The engagement ring has a relatively fancy setting with a finely worked design of geometrically stylized flowers, triangles, and teeny tiny diamonds on each side of the large-ish main stone. I don't know carats, but the main stone is maybe three-eighths of an inch in diameter at the top. (I didn't know a thing about diamonds till I got these rings. But people would ask me questions and make comments, so I started to learn. "Is it the old-style cut? That's worth more." "Does it have inclusions?") The other band has seven small diamonds in a row. One of them is broken and I wonder how that happened—it came to me that way. I imagine that maybe it broke when my grandmother died, hit by a drunk driver while she and my grandfather were heading somewhere in their Cadillac. Could the impact have been hard enough to break a diamond in her ring?

She died in 1974. When I go to San Francisco I always visit her crypt at the Chapel of the Chimes, a wonderfully ornate and unctuously pleasant place in Oakland filled with shelves of people stored in book-shaped crematory urns, and people interred in walls, stacked maybe eight high, behind slabs of marble, their names spelled out in brass letters. Pa-Pa and Gung-Gung, my dad's mother and father, are right at the bottom by the floor in a chamber that you reach by passing through several other plazas, going upstairs, winding through tiled paths. This is the most accessible I've ever found them. Most people in my family say, when Lilac died, that's when the family fell apart. Quiet music is always playing, fountains tinkle, and you can pull up a chair, talk to the departed, and wonder how life might have been if it hadn't happened quite that way.

I don't really remember her much. When she died, I was in fourth grade, living in Connecticut with my mom and brother and stepfather, and my grandparents were in San Francisco. My dad was out of the picture, had been since I was four, and that's another story, another very long story. Pa-Pa and Gung-Gung came to visit us once bringing a huge cardboard box divided into little compartments—sort of a Chinese version of a Hickory Farms gift pack, full of delicacies like smoked duck feet, jelly roll, sweet buns filled with barbecued pork. Is it awful to remember a jelly roll in better detail than your own grandmother? Till then, most of the Chinese food I'd had was mom's doctored-up Chungking cans from the supermarket, or occasional meals out at House of Chao, where they sold little Japanese dolls at the cash register. That was before there were enough Asian people (or Asian businesspeople, maybe) in New Haven to support the Asian groceries and traveling veggie vans that are in New Haven now. Before you could buy bok choy at the Stop 'n' Shop. Before most people would have realized that the dolls in the Chinese restaurant were Japanese, though I think I realized it and just chose to pretend I didn't notice or care. Just today, I went to the 99 Ranch market in San Gabriel with my dad, an enormous Asian supermarket, maybe 25,000 square feet of tofu, soy sauce, choy sum, gai lan, nuoc mam, sake, French bread, live lobsters and catfish, Courvoisier, and onion pancakes. A far cry from those Chungking days.

My grandparents were as strange and exotic to me as those duck feet, and I didn't know how to approach them. I do think that if my grandmother hadn't died when she did, if she'd lived longer, things would maybe have been very different. It's a spilt milk issue, though, I guess. No use crying.

See, everybody knew that my grandma had *sense*. She had people sense, she had business sense. Most people also thought she hadn't been using her sense when she married my grandpa. Though she kind of had to since she'd gotten pregnant with my dad. She was U.S.-born, fourth generation in America, growing up in Oakland in a Chinese ghetto. I have an old picture of her with her brothers and sisters and parents, the whole family serious and ancient, seated before a painted backdrop. Grandpa was this dashing handsome guy who styled himself a fox but was more like Wile E. Coyote. He thought he was smart and tricky, but on the big things he always got outsmarted. He'd come into the country from China in 1920, someone's paper son, faked identity, so our last name, Chin, isn't actually our name at all. It's

Chiu, or maybe Chew, not that any kind of phonetic rendering in English could be authoritative. I've seen the character for our last name, but can't really remember it. Sometimes when my grandpa would send me a birthday check, he'd write "Betsy Chew Chin" on the envelope to remind me.

Grandma had restaurants. She used to buy houses, fix them up, and sell them. When I visited them in San Francisco, they had a flat in a building at the top of Telegraph Hill that they'd bought with her sister, Violet, and Vi's husband George. Vi owns the building now. They used to own some other buildings, too, the kind that now would be worth millions of dollars, given what's happened to San Francisco real estate. Sometimes I think, maybe I could have inherited a house in San Francisco the way Vi's grandchildren will inherit the building on Union Street.

If Grandma had sense and restaurants and real estate, Grandpa had good looks, ambition, and a kind of froggy prince amphibian vanity and charm. He worked his way up in the family association, the homegrown version of the Chinese mafia, not the fancy Hong Kong Tongs that we hear more about now, nothing quite so glamorous. Most of what I know about it comes from the banquets Gung-Gung used to take me to sometimes, huge rooms full of old Chinese guys who would heap my plate with food, since I couldn't talk to them. Clear soups with jade greeny crescents of bitter melon and little bits of ground meat swirling around like constellations. Succulent pieces of steamed chicken to dip in salt followed by seven more courses, vegetables, beef, pork, a duck. I can't talk Chinese, but I learned the first rule of eating Chinese early: eat first, ask later. On the tables were always bottles of 7Up and bottles of Johnnie Walker Red plus bowls of ice—the old Chinese guys' version of a Classy Drink. There I felt like I did everything wrong, including being only half Chinese and only being able to eat, not talk. I had zits, my hair always felt greasy, and I wasn't interested in business, medicine, or law. Since I was a girl, it wasn't quite as bad, I think, that I was into theater and anthropology. I have an album full of Gung-Gung's pictures, a whole lifetime's worth of eight-by-ten photos of old Chinese guys sitting in rows on bleachers beneath hand-painted banners in Chinese. He rode in parades. The family association gave me scholarships to college a couple of times, for good grades, I guess. Nothing too big, but even $250 went pretty far in 1982. My grandpa would make me practice hearing my name said in Chinese, our real name the right way. I can't even say my name right. But I remember I stood up and got my check at just the right moment, making it look like I was used to hearing it like that, pretending I understood everything that was being said.

Like a lot of Chinese women, Grandma put a lot of her money into jewelry. She didn't wear any of it—it was like her bank account. When she died, it all disappeared. Everybody denied having it: Grandpa, her adopted daughter Liani, my father. Well, Dad didn't have to deny it. It's not something he would have messed with. It was just gone. I didn't think about it then, really. Pa-Pa and Gung-Gung had given me a few things made of nice soft yellow Chinese gold, the 24-carat stuff, none of which I have now. Some got stolen when our apartment was burglarized. I lost one precious bracelet, and it still makes me mad as spit when I think about that. I wore it to ballet class one day and took it off at the barre and left it on the windowsill. How dumb is that? To think of all the stuff of mine that I've lost makes me afraid to give my own kid jewelry. Now I hide it all around the house and I have all kinds of rules for myself about wearing it and taking it off so I won't lose things, but it still happens once in a while.

Just today, I found an old pin that I thought I'd lost. It had disappeared when we moved to this house more than a year ago. It was in a jar in the back of a closet, a repository of random hair thingies, cotton balls, and stuff from the bathroom in our old place that had all ended up together when I was doing last-minute packing up. I was so excited to find it not least because it gave me faith in my little system for keeping precious things.

Rules for Wearing Grandma's Rings
Do not leave the house without wearing them
If you do leave the house without wearing them, no matter how far away
you are, you must go back immediately and get them, when you realize
what you have done
Exception: When traveling to places like Cuba and Haiti, leave the rings
at home on purpose
Always leave them in the same place when you take them off
These include: hanging from the screw in the light fixture over the sink
in the bathroom
In the blue bowl above the sink in the kitchen
On the nail on the guest bathroom wall
All of these are out of reach of children, dogs, and husbands
Do not wear rings when gardening
When it's late at night and you're alone driving in the car
And you feel vulnerable
Take the rings off quietly at a red light

And put them in your sock
In case you get mugged
Try to make it look like you are adjusting the radio
(this also applies to late-night subway rides in New York when you
pretend you are itching your ankle)
Every now and then scrub rings with an old soft toothbrush
Sometimes take them to a jeweler to get really clean and checked for
looseness

I don't really remember ever seeing my grandmother wearing these rings, though she must have. The engagement ring is so thin on the inside, rubbed almost to nothing from all the work and movement she did. She was always cooking and knitting sweaters, but the jeweler told me that platinum can get even thinner before you have to worry. It's still strong.

It's nice that the rings are beautiful and that I often get compliments on them, because there are lots of times when I wish I had a substantial amount of lovely jewelry (though I guess I would, if I hadn't been so irresponsible when I was younger), but what makes them really precious to me is that I have so little from my grandmother. And I don't mean stuff, I mean her. Because she died when I was so young, she didn't really have a chance to feed me and boss me and buy me teddy bears. Grandpa couldn't figure out how to relate to me other than to take me to lunch and feed me prime rib and then give me a check on birthdays and Christmas. Maybe she would have been the same, but I don't think so. A few years ago her sister Vi gave me a bunch of clothes from the family, clothes from my great-grandmother (whose name I don't even know) and my grandmother. I have them all carefully packed away in acid-free paper. Sometimes I think I should donate them to the Metropolitan Museum of Art costume collection, but what if they said they weren't good enough? My grandmother's clothes are far too tiny for me to wear. Some of them have little food stains on them, as if they were just worn the other day and are waiting to go to the cleaners.

After the rings disappeared, the family fell apart like this: Grandpa and Dad could barely communicate (that was nothing new, but Grandma held them together just a little bit), and then Grandpa got married again to this former beauty queen named Mabel from Hong Kong who was a ballsy gold digger and whose lack of shame, pretense, or remorse was stunning and almost admirable. She had two daughters about my age, maybe a few years younger, and cemented her marriage to my grandpa by having twin sons when I was about thirteen. It might have been a little odd to have uncles thirteen years younger than me if I'd seen them more than once or twice. As it was, they were basically these two kids I saw in pictures, or who left drawings on my grandpa's walls. (That was in the period when Mabel had moved out and used to drop the twins off for my grandpa to babysit despite his two strokes and his absolute inability to relate to children.) As far as I can tell, she ground Grandpa down to a nub and took him for all he was worth. But it's not just that she was evil; he was dumb, too. So it's not really fair just to blame her.

Mabel certainly was a piece of work. Most days, my grandpa went into Chinatown to have lunch at the Jackson Café, an old Chinese American place full of stoopy, balding waiters in white jackets, red booths, and thick Syracuse China plates. This was where I got to eat prime rib, even during the periods when I was a vegetarian. Having discussions about vegetarianism with your Chinese grandpa who thinks anthropology is about feeling the bumps on people's heads is largely a waste of time. So, what's a little prime rib among family anyway? They served Chinese food, too, which I would much rather have eaten, but somehow my grandpa wanted to eat American, right down to the dessert which was as far as I could tell was a peculiarly Chinese American dessert: a cube of red Jell-O with milk poured over it. Even when we did have Chinese food, he made sure to eat with a fork.

One summer, I must have been fourteen, I was staying in San Francisco with my dad on Union Street and Grandpa was living a few blocks away on Green Street, and I stopped in at the Jackson Café to say hi, maybe eat a little something. He was there with Mabel. And I remember that when I said hi to her, she silently turned her face away. It was like getting slapped. I thought maybe she didn't hear me or something so I said hi again, and she sat there rigid and tight, head turned ninety degrees to the side so she looked a little like a Chinese American Barbie doll (this was before they'd even made those), with that black bubble hairdo of hers and that thick black eyeliner—you know how those dolls look when you turn their heads too far to the side and their bodies, with their pointy boobs, are still facing straight front. It was like she was trying to look at a spot on the Naugahyde behind her—a fascinating blob of beef grease, maybe.

It took me a long time to figure out that the thing I'd done to make her so mad, to make her dislike me, was simply to exist. I guess she thought I was competition for Grandpa's money. I have to admit that I wouldn't have minded inheriting a little bit of money because, damn, at one point he and my grandma were pretty flush and comfortable, and I wouldn't have minded a little fluff from them. But mostly, like any fourteen-year-old, I was just trying to figure out why I felt like I lived on a different planet than most people I was related to. Money wasn't the main issue at all.

In a nutshell, Mabel got control of everything, moved out, and bought more buildings in her own name, and Grandpa died of a massive stroke bankrupt and profoundly alone. I was in college in New York when he died, and my dad decided for me that I didn't need to go to the funeral. I was broke, paying for college by myself, and Dad wouldn't send me the money for a ticket. And as usual, Dad decided that the wacky drama that played itself out over Gung-Gung's funeral was all about him. He calls it "the movie about me."

Dad had a safety-deposit-box key that Gung-Gung had given him, only he didn't know what bank it was from. When Gung-Gung was in the hospital, Dad was running around San Francisco going to banks to see if the box was there, or there, or there. Finally, a day or two after Gung-Gung had died, he found the bank and found the box, only the box was empty. What had happened? "Mr. Chin opened the box yesterday," the bank manager said. The hell he did; he was dead yesterday. Dad demanded to see the security tapes, and lo and behold there was Mabel with her boyfriend posing as my grandpa. I wonder if he was wearing my grandpa's bad toupee to complete the disguise. The box was empty. Turns out the box had contained, among other things, my grandmother's jewelry that had been missing since her death.

People being how they are, the bank said we have more lawyers and more money and more time than you do, and if you take this to court we'll run you into the ground (even though it was obviously their fault). Long lists were submitted—pictures, even, of my grandmother wearing certain pieces which Mabel claimed had been given to her by my grandpa. As if she hadn't stolen enough. Finally, about five years later my father receives a little box with a pair of gold earrings, two jade bracelets, one "water bamboo" and gold bracelet, some earrings, two broken ceramic sculptures, and my grandmother's wedding and engagement rings.

My basic feeling was—*those rings are mine.* It was a primitive, atavistic, elemental feeling, fierce and uncompromising and ugly. It was selfish. It was absolute.

And I felt so fierce about it for so many reasons. Some of it was because, since Mabel could so freely steal so much, even someone else in the family who "deserved" the rings couldn't deserve them more than me, Lilac's first granddaughter. Plus, when my grandpa died, he'd left my dad some money. Now I understand that I wasn't entitled to any of that money, but there was this little complication. A year before Gung-Gung died, my dad and his wife had asked me, begged me, to let me have them claim me as a dependent on their income taxes, since they'd gotten married and had been hit with a higher tax bill. Not that they supported me financially—I was busy working two jobs to pay my way through NYU. I said yes, wanting, as usual, to be nice. But I warned them that my financial aid package might change, and Dad said they'd take care of it. They got the tax break, and I lost five thousand dollars in aid. When I told my dad, sitting in a café somewhere in New York, he said, "Take a year off." This was back in the days when I was way too polite to shout "Fuck you" in a public place. I think I could do it now. If he'd punched me it would have been less shocking. Bad enough that Mabel would help herself to Grandpa's houses and money and his life, but to have your own dad screw you out of five thousand dollars when you're nineteen years old and working your ass off? So when he inherited a bunch of money (not nearly as big a bunch as he should have, of course) and bought a house with it and didn't slip me over a dime to help pay for school, I felt, well, cheated. And the amazing thing is that I still do. I still feel, absolutely, that my dad and his wife owe me five thousand dollars. Plus twenty years' interest. I try not to think about it because it makes me feel like I'm chewing glass.

So when the jewelry showed up and Violet started talking about how it would be nice for my dad to let his wife have the rings, there was no way in hell I was going for that. Whether it was my place or not, whether it was nice or not, whether it was appropriate or not, I was getting those rings. That was it, that was it, that was it.

Mostly these days I feel very loving toward my dad and his wife and my half-brother. I'm glad they live so close, glad they're part of my everyday life. Only occasionally, late at night, I chew a little glass when maybe I've had a bad day or something.

And so I have my grandmother's rings. They are the world to me, the world I lost, the world I never knew, the world I have made for myself. My family is as imperfect and multifaceted and cracked as the diamonds in these rings, as precious and troublesome, bent, ancient, worn down, lost and found. Sometimes, when I make a particularly animated gesture with my hand, flinging it up or out in just the wrong way, the rings just slide up off my finger into the air. Maybe they're flying free, or escaping. It happened on my wedding day, I remember, and the ring is dented from falling down hard onto the sidewalk after it flew off my hand. It flew, but it couldn't roll away. And most of the time, now, I remember that I can't just throw myself around any old how, and I try not to, and the rings stay on.

One disease born of capitalism is anorexia, though not all would agree with that claim. Marx's daughter Eleanor suffered from it when she was in her early twenties, a period during which she seems to have subsisted on little else but hot tea. Perhaps her condition arose from the maddening combination of being her father's factotum but not his favorite (that was his daughter Jenny), being forced to give up her first love and engagement because the man she loved was both too radical and too poor, or being the only one of the three daughters to nurse both her parents through their deaths, and on top of all that, being very, very, very smart. What does that have to do with capitalism? Like so many bright middle-class girls with ambitious and exacting—and successful—parents, Eleanor had a lot to live up to and a lot to achieve. Not only that, but she had a lot to live up to as she dog-paddled through a poisonous cultural soup of entirely contradictory expectations having to do with all the things capital values: achievement, progress, success, femininity. Be a free intellectual but marry well; do rewarding work but be a good mother; be fearless but be a lady.

Eleanor watched her sister Laura lose three children early in their lives, while Jenny became mother to four, much of that time spent alone, with her husband seeking work elsewhere. Jenny writes:

> Those blessed babies, though really charming good-tempered little fellows, put such a strain upon my nervous system by day and night, that I often long for no matter what release from this ceaseless round of nursing. . . . I do believe that even the dull routine of factory work is not more killing than are the endless duties of the ménage.[50]

Though Jenny's descriptions of the demands of motherhood were written primarily to Laura and not to the young Eleanor, I imagine that Eleanor—who never herself had children—might have intuited at least some of the difficulty her sisters experienced. Meanwhile, with her sisters away and married, Eleanor was the primary nurse to both of her parents for many months in 1881. They were both bedridden, him with pleurisy and her with cancer. They could not even move between rooms to visit each other. Eleanor seems to have been able to keep her energy and focus throughout this period because she was needed, and because there was so much to do. Her mother died on December 2, and shortly after this, Eleanor accompanied her father to the Isle of Wight. It is here, on this trip, that Eleanor finally had some time to think about her own needs and desires, needs and desires that paradoxically (or, perhaps, predictably) took her away from the needs of the family.

I do not ever like to complain—and I hate to do so to Papa—he bitterly scolds me—as if I "indulged" in being ill at the expense of my family—or gets anxious, and that worries me most of all. What neither Papa nor the doctors nor anyone will understand is that it is chiefly my mental worry that affects me. . . . I should be more likely to "get strong" if I have some definite plan and work than to go on waiting and waiting. . . . It drives me half mad to sit here when perhaps my last chance of doing something is going.[51]

Having suffered from anorexia myself, I'm deeply drawn to Eleanor, and feel as well the overwhelming sense of responsibility she had for her family, who relied on her so heavily, even as they appear to have treated her like a baby, or taken her for granted. Meanwhile, her struggle to establish herself as an independent person, to work, to do her own work, was constantly being thwarted by her family's needs. It was she, after all, who had the primary responsibility for getting Capital together from her father's papers after he passed away, and she prepared the English version of Capital. She was determined to be independent, even as she took on the responsibility of finishing her father's work. In a letter describing her labors in sorting through Marx's papers, Eleanor writes to her sister Laura:

I know Engels is goodness itself and that I shall always have all I want, but I think you will understand that I am more anxious than ever now to earn my own living. In time I shall be able to get on quite well, I hope. The house we have for another twelve months—but if we can get a tenant sooner we may leave. For the next six months, however, I don't think I could leave—as the papers must be settled before I can do anything. I suppose Engels has told you that we have at least 500 pages of the 2nd vol. [of Capital]—probably the whole. That is good, isn't it?[52]

ANORECTIC ENERGY

I have transferred my anorectic energies from the realm of food to the world of things. I'm pretty sure I'm not as ill as I was at eighteen and nineteen, those years where I was puking six or seven times a day, working at Balducci's, and eating, say, half a grapefruit and half a bagel and a cup of coffee and calling it breakfast, lunch, and dinner rolled all into one. That sick, I don't think I am. But still.

My thoughts are dominated by things and money and saving and spending and buying nearly as powerfully as I used to be consumed by eating and puking and starving and chewing and tasting and refusing. It feels to me that I spend a considerable amount of time in reveries of potential buying and possessing the way I used to spend time wanting to eat, thinking about eating, eating, and not eating. Back then everything was about eating or not eating, simply everything. Recently, in November, I had this amazing experience. I was in Washington for the American Anthropological Association meetings, having dinner alone because I'd arrived in the evening and didn't know where any of my Anthro pals were. I walked along in the Adams Morgan neighborhood and found a little French restaurant called La Fourchette run by what looked like Algerians. I'd passed up Mexican, Japanese, and Thai because there's so much good eating of that kind in LA, and I'm sure there's good French food in LA too, but I never do go to French restaurants here. I ordered a glass of Merlot and some mussels Provençal that arrived drenched in butter and olive oil, garlic and parsley. For the first time since I can remember I ate with a feeling of pure, ecstatic pleasure. There was no guilt, no tension, no anxiety. Just a sense of love and pleasure in the act of eating and tasting. It was the opposite of the kind of passionate engagement with food that has dominated my adult life, eating good things out of a sense of discipline, like a nun, or in fits of anger or depression. What a moment. It was one of those excellently perfect experiences that I think I will remember always.

Shopping remains a guilty pleasure, tinged with "don't" and "shouldn't" and also shot through with a profound lack of satisfaction, in the act and in the remembering. Mostly, I tend to buy things in a kind of impulsive abandon, after what seem to me to be long periods of saying to myself no, no, no. Suddenly, for example, I have two new pairs of glasses, having taken my godson to the optometrist because his own glasses broke. Now, I can say that I did need a new pair of reading glasses. My old ones had somehow temporarily disappeared, and I'm just waiting for them to turn up behind the couch, in the closet, under the bed, somewhere. Until then I bought this "safety" set of distance glasses because they were pretty cheap and more comfortable than my old glasses, a big plus, since the old ones have worn dents into the flesh behind my ears.

Maybe it's destiny. Benin came into our room this morning, holding my new glasses, with one of the earpieces bent back so completely they were 180 degrees from where they belonged, facing straight front, rather than straight back. If ever there was a sign. I shouldn't have bought them, obviously. Broken after one week. So: back to the old glasses, themselves a fraught purchase, since unlike the new ones they were hideously expensive. Better get a few more years of use out of them.

I feel like an anorectic consumer. I fold down the corners of catalogs, even fill shopping baskets online with things for the house, or clothes, or garden paraphernalia. Yet at the same time I've been whittling my spending, putting more into the savings account, trying not to buy clothes except at the thrift store, cooking at home from scratch to save money (but also because I like to cook), and then, *boom,* I drop $350 on those new glasses. Not that I didn't need glasses, but did I have to spend that much? But then I wonder: why do I feel so guilty? Is it really that much money? How come I feel so down to the wire with my funds, so unable to spend, when my salary is nearly six figures a year? I guess, given the exaggerated level of my education, I could probably go out and get a job paying a whole lot more, but the thing is, I think I'd feel just as deprived then. Somehow knowing that even by myself I earn more than the average American family doesn't make me feel flush, or privileged, or give me a sense of abundance and possibility.

Suze Orman is that woman, unaccountably on public television, who somehow manages to apply Oprah principles to capitalism. I wonder what Marx would make of her, the spiritual guide to your inner entrepreneur. She urges us to think about how we feel about money and to look to our childhoods to understand our relationships to money. The depth and complexity of my emotional tie to money and to the stuff you can purchase with it disturbs me, so I start thinking, she's onto something, that Suze woman. Of course, since I've realized that my approach to money has become fundamentally anorexic, I'm appalled, but at the same time, having beaten anorexia in the food area, maybe I can pull it together in the money area. Get this, I've only once voluntarily weighed myself in the last two years! I remember feeling so overwhelmed at the difference between intellectually understanding things about the illness, and being able to think and live in some sort of accordance with that understanding. I remember wailing, "How can I stop wanting what I can't have?" How, indeed? I wanted my parents to have been more responsible when I was little. I wanted someone to help me pay for college. I wanted someone march me to the doctor when I felt like if I went on puking any longer I was sure to die. I wanted someone to slap me silly and then wrap me up in a big hug and tell me it would be OK.

Part of growing up is acquiring the power to give yourself what you need. Or what you think you need. We inherit so much from our families, for good or for ill, much of it utterly immaterial, ephemeral, yet heavy as an iron frying pan. So much of what we strive to acquire is something done in dynamic relationship with these inheritances, whether of loss or generosity, fear or fulfillment. Some of us want to re-create the life we had, or think we had, with every little piece of the puzzle; others want to invent something entirely new, beginning especially with themselves. Getting stuff is also so often about plugging holes in our hearts. Since we can't make the people around us be what we need, we gather together things that soothe the pain. The lastingness of things can be good, like the way monuments stay where they are, solid, standing up to time and assaults of weather. Life can be crazily changeable, but this table here is just what it always has been. Solid. Dependable.

The issues are much the same, growing up with such a strong sense of not enough. Of course, I know so many people who grew up poorer than me. Being a kid on welfare going to an elite private school with the kids of Yale professors is pretty freaky, though. My fears about money are the same ones I've had about food, and about emotions: once you start, you might never stop. Eating, spending, or feeling. So you ration it out, hold on to it, constantly assess: how much have I got? How much can I afford to indulge?

I realize now that even when I was really anorexic, it was tied up with money. I was always so broke in college. (These are my "I had to walk two miles barefoot through the snow" stories.) I remember taking the New Jersey PATH trains home from NYU to my apartment on Forty-Ninth Street; the trains stopped at Thirty-Fourth Street, didn't go any farther north. I'd walk the extra sixteen blocks because the ride was fifteen cents less than the New York City subway cost. I had a two-dollar-a-day budget. There. Was. No. Room. For. Error. Everything about my life was so intensely disciplined, in part from absolute necessity. There was one free hour a day to do nothing, or watch TV. Everything else was work, study, practice, ride the subway. Breakfast: half an apple, half a banana, three tablespoons nonfat yogurt. No exceptions. In French class, my grad student teacher called on me and asked what I ate for breakfast. He wanted me to say: eggs, toast, orange juice. In those days, orange juice cut my throat too badly for me to drink it. "What about something else?" he asked. "Broccoli?" I said. "We don't have a word for that," he answered.

I was working at Balducci's, that fabulous food mecca whose green and white shopping bags can be glimpsed in Woody Allen films. Because the Joffrey Ballet had its studios upstairs, Balducci's was full of anorectic cashiers— what an irony. I was earning $4.25 an hour, pulling double shifts so I'd have money to live on and pay my school bills. They had installed surveillance cameras downstairs in the basement where a lot of the food was stocked (big flat cardboard boxes full of Viniero's Italian cookies and vats of cannoli cream). The never caught us eating, of course not, but they did catch our manager Phil doing it with one of the Joffrey girls who had long, luxurious red hair.

At the end of the day, after the store closed, my coworker Andrea and I would count all the registers, putting our hands on enough cash to pay for our entire college educations, listening to sappy Muzak, seagulls going "Caw, caw" in the background. Other girls working there with us, girls from the Bronx who still lived at home, had graduated from high school and finished with their educations, spent all their money on makeup and buying presents for their boyfriends. Envy. We'd look up rich people's credit ratings for a laugh now and then—Lee Iacocca, Leona Helmsley. Daughter of the Balducci family marrying the son of one of the non-Balducci partners in the business, getting a house for their wedding present, daughters our age.

Rich people came into Balducci's, dropping three or four hundred dollars on a couple of truffles from Italy. The people who owned Izod would come in, amassing so many bags of groceries they had to be loaded on dollies and carted to the curb. Sometimes I'd steal a bar of Lindt chocolate. Once the store flew in huge, fragrant clusters of grapes from Belgium, in individual plastic boxes, and you could smell them all the way at the register. There were high points, like getting to pack Lou Reed's groceries, cracking a joke and making him laugh.

It was so painful to be surrounded by so much, and yet having not enough, not nearly enough. There was no rhyme or reason to it. The Balducci kids were not smart or talented or even especially hard working, they were just part of a family that had a ton of money, so they got houses as presents. The food thing, the money thing, the materialism thing, they're about too-much-ness, and our overwhelming desires for them clamp down on us with all their strength. When you're in college, at that transitional and tender time, getting distracted by all of this is certainly part of growing up, and certainly part of trying not to grow up at all. Anorectic thinking argues that discipline can cure some of the symptoms, but it fails to take into account that it can create its own problems as well. The underlying problem is this: to ease the pain, you have to learn to stop wanting in the first place or at least learn to want the right way. Hell if I know how to teach myself (or anyone else) how to do it, though.

Mi-Mi was my mother's mother. Born on the Whale Ranch in Ojai in the early part of the twentieth century, she used to ride her horse to school. The story is, she would decide she was too tired to ride home after school, and would call her dad, asking him to come get her in the car. "You do that one more time," he finally told her, "and I'm going to give your horse to your brother." She did it one more time. So he gave the horse to her brother.

She was in the first class at Scripps College, and married one of the college founders' sons. No doubt she thought she'd hit the jackpot, but my grandpa was the black sheep of the family, and while my grandfather's brother was founding the Los Angeles chapter of the ACLU and living in Hancock Park, my grandparents divorced and my grandmother pretty much raised her three kids on her own. I think she was disappointed that this happened and probably felt a huge resentment that the life she had looked forward to, expected, counted on, didn't happen. Not that she showed it one bit. Relying on determination, an iron will, and an amazing ability to keep up appearances, she and her children were always impeccably dressed; Mi-Mi was tremendously stylish and had been a department store model when she was young, and her devotion to fashion never waned. Every week she went to the beauty salon to have her hair washed and set. When I knew her, she worked at a store in Santa Barbara called Michel Levy, a place where they sold Pendleton plaid clothing and Étienne Aigner shoes. She knew I loved to draw, and would send me the cardboard that came out of the shirts that had been shipped to the store, an example of the thriftiness that had allowed her to survive.

I was the only piano-playing grandchild, so my grandmother told me that one day the Steinway upright in her living room would come to me. Like her house in Santa Barbara, bought for twenty-seven thousand dollars in the mid-1940s, the piano was fully paid for, and she was immensely proud of it even though she herself did not play. That piano helped make her home the "right kind of house." I hadn't asked for the piano, but the thought was a nice one, and occasionally I would look forward to someday having a Steinway to play.

During my years taking lessons, I never had a piano of my own. I took lessons at a place called the Neighborhood Music School. The building looked like a Soviet-era hulk of cement blocks inside and out, and it always had that cement-y smell, which I still find comforting today. Down in the basement there were practice rooms, and that's where I went every day to practice. I liked being alone in those rooms, just me, the piano, and the muffled sounds of whoever was practicing nearby. Down there I was alone, yet among others.

Later, when we had moved out of New Haven and up to the coast to a beach town called Madison, I would practice on a piano in the Congregational Church, where there was a red-haired boy in the choir whose voice was so sweet and heartbreaking that I had a crush on him just because of his voice. Practicing at the Congregational Church was not as comforting as practicing at the music school, mostly because it made me feel like the poor kid. When I knocked on the door, it just seemed to me that I was greeted with that "I'm-sorry-for-you-poor-kid" kind of look. Which I was, but it wasn't much fun to feel that way, particularly in an old-money New England town like Madison, where most people apparently thought that poverty was imaginary and certainly not something existing within the town's borders. Our next-door neighbors, a raucous family with six kids, also offered to let me practice at their house. This was a family that sat down to a full-cooked dinner every night and passed bowls full of peeled potatoes doused with butter and parsley. We did not have those kind of dinners, and sometimes, if Mom and my stepfather were away for some reason, I would have dinner with our neighbors at their house, feeling like a visitor from a foreign land. Often this would be a day when my whole family was at the hospital because my younger brother had had another terrifying asthma attack. Our neighbors would sit in their living room, watching TV, as I did my Schmidt finger exercises and scales and my Bach inventions, creating order for myself in the midst of the chaos that was my family life. I still think it was awfully generous of them to be willing to sit there listening to me plonking away on the keys while they were trying to watch TV. I was at their house when the news hit that Nixon had resigned. Arpeggios. Scales. Fingering. Phrasing.

In the context of all of that, the idea of having my own piano meant something. It connected me to the things I had done to keep it all together when things were starting to fall apart. Having my very own piano, especially one passed down to me from my grandmother, would be an affirmation that there was something solid at the core of my family and my life. It was to be the first—and only—thing I officially inherited from my family, something passed down specifically to me as a demonstration of belonging and continuity. So the day Mi-Mi announced offhandedly that she'd decided to leave the piano to an acquaintance of hers, I sat stunned, in a kind of shock. I mean, it's not like I'd done something that I remotely could imagine that might have pissed her off. Wasn't I the one who had hand-painted an apron for her with a design of pears, which she collected in every form? Wasn't it me who had found a set of very cute little clown candles for her to put in the circus room? Hadn't I been good about sending little notes, holiday cards, and thank-yous, knowing how much a certain kind of good manners were important to her? The thing was, she was getting on by then and had some issues with dementia, but in that moment, I utterly forgot that, and it seemed very, very personal. Now, though, I think it wasn't personal at all.

Some of the filterless moments she was having by then could be kind of funny, actually. Her issues were never the big scary ones, so we didn't have to worry about her wandering out of the house and getting lost. It was more like she just misplaced her politeness and would say any old thing she happened to be thinking, or repeated some oddball comment she had heard somewhere. Like many people who are aging, she became both more opinionated and less flexible. For instance, she decided the Episcopal Church, to which she had belonged all of her life, was too liberal, and one day announced that she had become a Methodist.

The discipline and simplicity of the Methodists was and was not a good fit for her. My grandmother had always lived by strict rules, and the strictures of Methodism suited her. On the other hand, aesthetic simplicity did not. Like nearly all the women on my mother's side of the family, my grandmother had an acquisitive streak. Like me, she bought most of her things secondhand (and unlike me she had also inherited some furniture). Her house was a testament to her ability to acquire and place an astounding number of items, all arranged by theme, memory, idea. It was like a ranch house art installation. Every room had a name. She had a room she called her "Opium Den" (Asian theme), where the TV was. Her bedroom was all done in a powder blue that was her signature color. I have an evening dress of hers in exactly that same shade, which matched her eyes. And then there was the Circus Room.

The Circus Room was down in the basement, and had at one time been an (illegal) rental unit that she used for a bit of extra income. It had two twin beds and was full of circus stuff: animals, carousels, and of course clowns. The idea behind the Circus Room was that it was a fun and delightful place for the grandchildren to stay when we visited. In truth, we all approached that room with a kind of dread that is highlighted in slasher films. Egad, that place was creepy! We all bonded on how horrifying we found it to spend time in there and would beg Mi-Mi to let us stay in the Garden Room instead, another room downstairs that was much more neutral in its decorating scheme and, with its wicker furniture, much less likely to provoke nightmares.

She lived in that house for close to fifty years, and for most of that time it was a little like her own personal version of the Winchester Mansion—that crazy house where the wife had been told that she had to continually be building on her house unless she wanted to die. My grandmother didn't build; she nested. She arranged. Down in the "Party Room," which was the main room on the lower floor of the house, a circle of dolls in high chairs were poised eternally in celebration, with tea sets and party favors. Little elements might continually be added or adjusted, and so I often sent her gifts that reminded me of one her rooms.

Suddenly, though, she decided she was done. She was perhaps about ninety years old then, and living on her own was proving to be more and more difficult. She could no longer drive, and with her typical uncompromising attitude, she would just set out walking toward the supermarket and take rides from strangers who saw her making her way along the road. We thought this might be a tad dicey as a transportation strategy, so eventually, she went to live with my aunt in Fresno. After all that time lavishing attention on every single detail of her home, my grandmother left it behind, and seemed happy to do so.

It fell to my aunt and her daughter to take on the Herculean task of cleaning out the house. Ivy had punched its way through the Garden Room wall. Newspaper clippings had colonized the Ping-Pong table at a depth of perhaps two feet. I still to this day cannot imagine how my aunt and cousin cleared it all out. Toward the end I went and helped out for a weekend or two, but my contribution was a drop in the bucket: by then nearly everything had been boxed up, sorted, carted off to secondhand stores or the dump.

I took from the house a few small pieces of furniture—a desk that sits in my daughter's room, a small chair that my mother remembers from her childhood. I don't have the piano, though. When my cousin delicately asked whether it might be OK for her to have the Steinway, saying yes was easy to do. For me, the piano had gone, and it could never belong to me, not really, not after it had been promised to someone else, even if we decided that the new promise my grandmother had made was a mistake, a slipping of the filter, a stray thought she never really meant to have. I held on to my sense of betrayal, I'm ashamed to say, because the thread of continuity had already been snapped and couldn't be repaired. I needed the piano to come from her, to be her gift to me to pass on to my own children.

By the time my grandmother was in the process of dying, she was stripped down to the bones of her essential self, and I came to realize that whatever obstacle had been built up in my heart around the incident of the piano needed to be negotiated. I am not sure I managed to entirely dismantle that obstacle, but in two key moments, I was able at least to get much closer toward tumbling it down. I was holding her foot, massaging lotion into her skin, which was so thin and translucent I could see into her body: she was almost the visible woman. Her skin was also terribly fragile, and even removing a Band-Aid brought with it the probability of a skin tear. She had always seemed so indomitable to me, and I had never once considered her someone who might be vulnerable to much of anything. I had never liked her much, I realized, and yet I saw that I loved her. Later we had a wonderful conversation, even after last words had been spoken. I was in her room with her, alone, and made a remark, one of those sounds we make, "Mmm hmm." She answered. "Mmmm?" So I answered back. We went back and forth like that, making increasingly silly statements out of these sounds, no words among them, and yet making perfect sense as we went along. It was one of the longest talks we had had with each other in all our lives.

Mi-Mi is buried up at the Methodist Church in Ojai, the town where she was born, her ashes interred in a small memorial garden on church grounds. I try to go there at least once a year. I bring my own small offerings: a bunch of flowers bought from a Mexican couple who have turned their front yard into a flower farm, a candle, some of the candied ginger she always loved. The view of the mountains from that spot is spectacular. And so is the thrift shopping. The weekend we interred her ashes, I drove past an Ojai estate sale, parked, and landed a Kenzo blouse for five bucks. Mi-Mi would have been thrilled. It's something I imagine us enjoying together. And whenever it is that I finally allow myself to truly experience that thread of continuity, one that remains unbroken, I will have finally received my grandmother's last gift, and the one that really matters. It's the gift of self-knowledge and self-acceptance, free of judgment, excised of what is petty and mean inside of us. When I think of that piano now, my heart doesn't hurt the way it once did for much too long.

Unlike her father, Eleanor was not much for social convention in terms of her own living situation. She was determined to work and to earn her own living, something her father insisted would take away from his more important intellectual labor. After both of her parents had passed away, Eleanor became involved with Edward Aveling, a married man. They lived together—a rather shocking choice in those times, but a choice they could at least feel righteous about because it represented their values and beliefs. This period of Eleanor's life seems also to have been satisfyingly domestic in interesting ways, with her rather charming complaints about whitewashing and housecleaning. In 1887 they rented a country cottage, where she writes of flagstone-covered kitchen floors and an abundant garden; in December of that year, in a description that sounds Martha Stewart–like in its details, she wrote:

> I believe I have a genius for house painting. We have a most splendid enamel here now (if you like I'll send you some pots) which I find invaluable. I enamel chairs, tables, floors, everything. If the climate only permitted I should enamel myself.[53]

What she loved was the theater. She was drawn to the theater but was not an especially good actress, although she was a galvanizing public speaker; she was especially taken with Ibsen's play A Doll's House, for reasons that are hardly obscure. She turned her talent for managing an audience into a great strength as an orator and public speaker. Eleanor was the daughter who, more than either of her sisters, followed in her father's footsteps as an intellectual and social activist. She did this while often working and writing together with Aveling. When he became ill, as she had so often before, Eleanor nursed him; he thanked her by going off and living with a twenty-two-year-old actress. When Eleanor inherited money from Engels, however, Aveling was back. After nursing him through a second major illness Eleanor learned from Aveling that he'd secretly married the woman that he'd left her for. This was, apparently, the last straw. Her suicide note to him reads: "My last word to you is the same that I have said during all these long, sad years—love."[54]

Anorexia is one of those diseases, like hysteria, that seems to have a particular genesis in a cultural moment and historical milieu. That Eleanor Marx should have suffered from this affliction is oddly appropriate—as a disease that is as wrapped up in consumption as her father's notion of the commodity is, it is one that embodies the killing contradictions of the consumer world. The deadly conflict between emotional needs and desires and being filled, or nourished, is contrasted by the material that is symbolically on offer when anorectics cannot eat because their spirits are too full of suffering. The suffering, for its part, is tied in many ways to the utterly conflicting demands that capitalism begins to impose on families, and women in particular, as it ramps up speed and intricacy. It speaks to the poverty of culture, to the emptiness of life dominated by priorities that have nothing or little to do with the human. This is not living, says the anorectic body, and Eleanor bore the brunt of that sort of nonliving throughout her life. Once she really found work that was invigorating, the anorexia seems to have abated, but the intensity of Eleanor's need for meaning and meaningfulness did not. Her punishing involvement with the weaselly Aveling seems transparently pathetic as a reliving of her relationship with her father: both men gave their best love to other women, but they still needed her to care for them because only she could give as much as they needed.

Eleanor's sister Laura also committed suicide, though under very different circumstances. She was in her sixties, and the rest of her family was long gone; in 1911 she and her husband, Paul LaFargue, did not want to become burdens on others, and so together they took their lives. Their graves are in Paris. Karl Marx is buried in London's Highgate Cemetery, interred together with the remains of his wife, his daughter Jenny, and Helene Demuth. Eleanor is the only member of her family who rests apart. Marx is survived by no known direct descendants.

DREAM-FILLED PRESCRIPTION

The Zoloft gave me amazing dreams. Being pregnant filled me with dreams too, intensely real and often shoving me into a wakefulness of deep sorrow and no clue as to what I was weeping about. Maybe just feeling too much of life. I'm still dreaming a lot and realizing that, medication or no, my last year or two was relatively dreamless when for most of my life dreams have been engrossing for me, something to sink into, often leaving me exhausted in the morning when I awoke, enwrapping my consciousness like a caul.

But, see, I wasn't really taking the meds to give me my dreams back. Then I wondered, why not? Why don't we see our dreams—not our daydreams and fantasies, the conscious desires—but our night dreams with their unpredictability and looping textures—why don't we see them as something we have a right to, the way we feel we have a right to happiness or lack of depression? We don't take meds to give us our dreams back, but maybe we should. Not that medication and the machine of corporate pharmaceuticals would necessarily be the place to find them, to provide them, to service our spirits in the way dreams do.

We get sold dreams, but not real dreams. We get sold dreams like "I want that car," or "I can get the perfect life," but those aren't the dreams I'm talking about. Night dreams, sleeping dreams, we have so little control over them, Carlos Castañeda's claims aside. Sure, you can look the monster that's about to eat you in the eye and fall into that eye and conquer that fear, or on waking dismiss the whole thing and feel your dreams shrink away from you. The corporate market hasn't hooked into those dreams, the real ones, since they can't figure out how to sell them to us. But when they do . . .

Nevertheless, I wonder what people's dreams were like two hundred years ago. Because one of the earliest dreams I remember was distinctly cartoonish. I don't mean it was silly. It was in cartoon. And the cartoon was Disney.

There were animals and trees with black outlines around them, and of course I was Snow White, running through the woods and tripping over a tree root. I could see my plump little black outlined arm, my hand held just so even in terror. I also have had nightmares about abandoned factories and large hotels. I have elevator dreams, subway dreams. People couldn't have had these dreams two hundred years ago, any more than they could have had dreams in a Disney-inspired cartoon-o-rama.

Films shape our real dreams, of course, though I have to say it's rare that a film version of a dream really manages to capture my experience of dreaming and shine it back to me. I love those clunky Freudian attempts by Hitchcock to show dreams and the subconscious, simultaneously creepy and right and yet overly intellectual too.

What's the question, what's the issue? To a certain degree, it's about how contemporary life, its commercialism, its marketability, becomes "dream-stuff," but not in the sense of betrayal, that is, a betrayal of true spirit being infiltrated by cold capital. It becomes something more, yet something less. Since dreaming is *outside the system*, that "dreamstuff," even if it's the stuff of the system—Nike shoes with wings, the Yellow Brick Road, or Aunt Jemima—it is usually used up, reshaped, reimagined, evaded, and of course fulfilled.

Disney can't come into my head at night and sue me for dreaming in cartoon, no matter what I get Snow White up to. I guess the same would be true of something I wrote and hid away in the chimney, or a fleeting thought, but it's not the same. Our dreams are our own. Though the word "own" is pretty dicey when it comes to dreams, since half the time they're evaporating or shape shifting from the first moment we begin to examine them with our eyes open.

You have the right to dream richly. Dreams should stick to you with a sweet graininess of old honey in the jar, or stick with the oldness of resin, the prehistoric depth of tar, or cling in the ends of a snarly thought like a foxtail grass seed in a fluffy sweater (did you know foxtails can enter a dog's paw and work their way all the way up right into the heart?), maybe pricking you here and there, an irritation or a cut. Dreams should make your waking somehow thicker: reality plus.

Capitalism sanctions rationality, and to me that is such a shame. So much gets reduced to what can be explained, demystified, quantified. These things have their uses, but so do things like magic and the unexplainable. Dreams sanction not the irrational, but the unrational. We need spaces for our spirits that are not ruled by the limits of what can be known through observation; we need room in our minds for thoughts that make no sense but remain nevertheless moving and beautiful. Irrationality opposes the rational, but the unrational is outside of it. The unrational, that which we move into as we dream, is neither antidote nor escape. Yet it cannot be explained away by talk of firing neurons, brain scans, or even psychoanalytic theory. All of these help us delve into the mystery of dreams, but they cannot really explain why the other worlds we visit in dreaming are worth the journey.

Objects can be deadened by the circumstances that gave rise to them, yet they can also be enlivened, and enlivened in a way very different from what Marx was thinking about when he saw tables standing on their heads. The magic, then, is not in the object itself, but in the context in which the object is made part of people's lives. In the famous Kula ring exchanges documented by Bronislaw Malinowski, ritual armbands and necklaces moved around an archipelago of islands, exchanged among men, and with each exchange, the necklace or armband gained more history, more life, much as a tree grows rings with each season marking its history. Take the armband out of the circle and put it in a museum case, and as with an insect caught in resin, the life is snuffed out, though it looks ever so lifelike. Even when we know the mechanics of life, the need for CO_2, beating hearts, and firing synapses, we cannot really explain what it is when something is animated with living spirit. Something that has been made purely for the purpose of making money is not the same as an otherwise identical object that has been made within the boundaries of continuities of sustaining human purpose. Such identical objects are, more often than not, entirely theoretical. Yet there is very much a difference between a thing you might possess that expands your humanness, and one that erodes it irrevocably. A big part of our specific problem is that we cannot tell the difference.

THE TURQUOISE ARROWHEAD

Once I saw sacred light coming out of a turquoise arrowhead, held in the palm of a man who was trying to identify a witch. This is a true story.

When I was seventeen, I left New Haven and went to go stay with my dad. It was summer, and my friend Beth and I took a series of Greyhound buses across the country. She was headed to family in Houston, Texas (where I remember her uncle taking us on a drunken Fourth of July drive, followed by a weird evening in a honky-tonk bar with her cousins), and I continued alone to New Mexico, where my dad was working with the Native American writer Leslie Marmon Silko on a film project. I carried my belongings in one of the white suitcases my mother had received for a European trip via ocean liner years earlier. Her initials, "S. T.," stood near the suitcase handle in small brass letters. The inside, predictably, was a light blue taffeta, my grandmother's favorite color. I was headed to Old Laguna Pueblo, and all I knew is what my dad had told me: "Tell them that's where you're going, and I'll meet you where the bus drops you off." I was traveling on a long ribbon of road, desert unfurling to each side, an hour or so out of Albuquerque, when the bus driver announced Old Laguna. As far as I could tell, there was nothing there, just a dusty, empty store by the side of the road. With all the itchy, sweaty self-consciousness of a seventeen-year-old who has made an entire busload of people stop in the middle of nowhere and wait while I bumped my suitcase along the aisle to the front of the bus, I pretended I knew exactly where I was going and stepped off, watching the bus grumble away into the distance. My dad was not there. Nobody was there. I'm not sure I even had any money on me.

He did show up, it felt like hours later but was probably fifteen minutes. He took me to where he was working on a crazy project that was a modern retelling of a traditional Pueblo tale about Estoyymut, the young hero, and his wife, who was secretly a gunnadyeh, a kind of soul-stealing witch. That's how I ended up lying on the floor in the high school gym, along with a bunch of young people auditioning for various roles in the film, surrounded by a group of tribal elders, playing the wildest theater game ever.

Estoyymut was like most heroes—young, virile, handsome—and he'd just married a beautiful woman. Oddly, every night after dinner he'd fall dead asleep. It turns out his wife was a gunnadyeh, a kind of witch who received a second heart from the devil and who could change herself into an animal at night. She was drugging his food so she could go off and meet with the other witches to do bad deeds—typical stuff, like carrying off babies and ruining crops. So Estoyymut gets advice from Spider Woman, then goes through a bunch of trials and close scrapes, and in the end manages to come out all right. This is the very, very short version of the story.

In the game, my dad wanted to bring the story to life, so he had the elders place the young guys who might in the film be Estoyymut in the center of a circle and give them the knowledge and training they needed to identify and fight gunnadyeh. Meanwhile, my dad took the young women and had them do a relaxation exercise where we turned ourselves into our witch/animal selves. The trick was this: only some of the women were really witches, and the

Estoyymut guys had to find and save the girls who weren't witches. At some point, one of those days, one of the elders came to the gym with a turquoise arrowhead. It was an object with great power, in part because these kinds of things were traditionally found by accident and revealed to their new owner, as it were, and then given a special blessing from a priest. The elder gave this object to one of the Estoyymuts to use in the theater game. The only thing was, nobody was playing. Suddenly it all became as serious as it gets.

The lights were off, the elders in a circle, sitting in chairs, quietly talking to the Estoyymuts, touching them at times, their talk a constant flow of knowledge and filled with a kind of quiet urgency I've never heard before or since. In retrospect I now think it was their chance to tell these men things they couldn't any other way. Over on the gym's stage, lying on the wooden floor, the young women were going down and under, taking on new powers and identities. At some point my dad said it was time to start: the witches got up and the Estoyymuts came to get them. I wasn't prepared for the violence of it. There were two or three Estoyymuts, big, strong, and handsome, and most of the young women were small, or smallish anyway, petite and lithe. The whole thing nearly instantly became incredibly physical: Estoyymuts were trying to grab or hold or pick up witches, and the witches, in turn, were fighting for their lives. They bit, they scratched, they launched themselves into the air. The big strong guys couldn't contain or control the witches, who were also at times masquerading as innocent girls to confuse them. "Save me," they would whisper, "I'm not one of them."

To kill the witch, you need to get her extra heart out. Estoyymut would get a witch and pound on her chest, to make the heart stop, or to put it out of order. The witch would writhe and scream. But after a certain point, Estoyymut was confused. He had four women lined up and couldn't tell which was a witch and which was not. This is when he pulled out the arrowhead. Until then, nobody but those in the circle knew he had it. He held it in his palm and then faced his hand, with the arrowhead cupped inside it, toward the women who he had lined up in front of him. One woman screamed and dropped to the floor. A light was beaming out from his palm. He placed the arrowhead on another woman's chest, and she clawed at the skin where it had touched her, crying she'd been burnt as if with hot embers. The light was beaming forth from the arrowhead. He found the girl who was not a witch and brought her to him, pushed her behind him, and moved on to the last witch.

Nobody had expected things to go the way they did, to become so real, to become so charged with life and death. Once we'd all calmed down, returned to ourselves, and turned on the lights, we saw that everyone was scratched and bruised, and some of those who had been witches had burn marks where the arrowhead had touched them. The Estoyymut who had carried the arrowhead looked at his own hand in wonder, thinking of how it had become the cradling site for such living power.

This is why I know that there are some things, some objects, that have powers both mysterious and real. I have seen it myself. I saw the light come from the arrowhead. But I wasn't a witch. That day, the arrowhead lay cool above my heart.

TURNING THE TABLES

A couple of years ago, Pili's daughter Danielle came to stay with me, along with her then four-year-old son. She wanted to come and study English, she said. I learned a lot while they were at my house, much of it not especially pretty, about the complexities and limits of friendship and expectation, and the way that whatever resources are at hand—space, food, money—create the shape of conflict and connection. By the end, I didn't like Danielle much, or her son. I liked myself even less. What a disaster.

Being a guest and being a host are totally different in Haiti and the United States. In Haiti, the guest is royalty. You give the guest your own bed, you wait on them hand and foot and attend to their every need. In the United States, one might give a very short-term guest the royal treatment, but for someone staying months and months, the expectation is that they will do their part, pull their weight, pitch in, and actually contribute to the household, since they are making demands on it. From the start, Danielle made it pretty clear I wasn't living up to her expectations as a host. I was proud of myself for spending a couple of days getting her room ready and making it nice. There was an extra TV in there, and fresh linens, and it was newly painted. "The TV doesn't work right," she pointed out to me, and showed me where faint lines fluttered across the screen. She didn't like the color of the paint. She didn't like the bookcase and unceremoniously emptied it, moved it into another room, and tossed the books back onto the shelves. "Oh, well," I thought, "she needs to take possession of this space for herself, to feel at home."

Like her mother always did for me, I got up to make breakfast. Unlike her mother, I did not prepare Haitian food. I love Haitian food, but I just don't know how to make it. To make a more honest admission, I do not relish eating spaghetti with hotdogs in the morning. Besides, when I'm in Haiti, I don't expect them to make American food, do I? Neither Danielle nor her son would eat much of anything I cooked. She would flounce into the kitchen and make something more to her taste, even if I was already working at the stove on a meal. So I stopped cooking. It's never a great idea to have two strong-willed, passive-aggressive women living together, and we were terrible housemates in part because we disagreed about most basic things but rarely ever talked about it, and we were sure that it was the other person who was wrong and inappropriate. The other thing that was never, ever spoken about was money. True, Danielle had given me three hundred dollars toward expenses when she first arrived, and I took it, in part to make her feel fully part of the household, and in part because I was pretty sure I'd need the money. But when I go to Haiti, I pay Pili much, much, more, in part because my research fund means that I can, and in part because it seems fair to me. I also feel that being served so dutifully by Pili in Haiti is somehow less out of whack when I've paid through the nose to stay there. Plus I still buy my own beer from Pili's store and pay for groceries too.

For Danielle, my unwillingness to shuttle her to her language school every day was an affront. "The bus stops three blocks away from the house," I told her. I was already driving her son to preschool every day—in the other direction—before taking my daughter to school. My morning drive had gone from twenty minutes to over an hour. I'm not a bus driver! She could save me a good twenty minutes in commute time every morning, just by taking the bus. That seemed entirely reasonable to me, but not to her. It must have been the beginning of her festering resentment, now that I look back. The beginning of mine, however, came when she approached me one day to complain about the state of the cleanliness of the house. She had been vacuuming, which I appreciated. "Look," she said, "I don't mind doing some of the cleaning, but we both need to do it," she said. What got missed, as far as I was concerned, was that her standard of cleanliness was ever so much higher than my own. I had long ago decided that housework had no place at the top of my daily "to do" list. If she wanted to sweep and vacuum every single day, that was her business. I was already grudgingly doing the bus driver act, so screw adding in daily house cleaning. The third time that she opened up the refrigerator, took a sniff, and remarked that it smelled bad, I growled, "Look, I'm in the middle of my semester, so I *might* get to it in December. If you want it clean now, you are going to have to do it yourself." Then she opened the dishwasher and complained that it smelled, too.

What I wanted to say, in my meaner and madder moments, was that life here in the United States is not probably what Danielle thought it might be or ought to be. I fantasy-ranted that I too would be able to keep my house sparkling if, like her in Haiti, I had a couple of live-in slave kids to do it for me. I remember talking with her once, before she'd come to stay, about the home she was renting on her own. "I have to do everything," she explained. "How do you manage?" I'd asked. "Well, I have Roulon," she said. "What's a Roulon?" I asked, thinking it might be a gadget or a kind of cleaning fluid. "He's a twelve-year-old boy," she'd answered.

Things got much, much worse. On a trip to Target, her son was overwhelmed by the place and went racing up and down the aisles full-tilt. She had gone off somewhere, and while he was trying to unwrap some toy that was definitely not going to get bought for him, I decided to scoop him up and deposit him with her. He began screaming at the top of his lungs, and I must have looked like a kidnapper, one on the verge of murder. "You need to control your child," I said to her in Kreyol. "He's just not used to it here," she said, brushing it off. I realized that neither he nor she had developed the skills they needed to be in Target without losing their minds. This meant that I was losing mine as well. I really hadn't signed on for all this, teaching them to control themselves in front of endless aisles of beckoning stuff, how to be surrounded by an abundance of things while not having enough human support, how to spend your days working, working, and working, and how to give short shrift to everything else. After all, that's life here in America.

By October, things had deteriorated so much we were barely speaking. We avoided each other as much as possible, her cooped up in her room with the door closed and the TV on, me skulking around the rest of the house as if I could even feel at home. She fried chicken the Haitian way and never cleaned the veil of greasy dots off the stove. By then our whole relationship was so misshapen there was no way to patch it together. When I learned she was talking to my students, who bought her sob story that I was a colonialist oppressor who wouldn't feed her, it was more than I could take. So I took a very deep breath and kicked her out. Her dad lived up north, in the Bay Area, and she decided to head there. I lent my car to the student who drove her up there. I'm sure she thought I was a selfish bitch, a slob of unbearable proportions, unkind, and so many other bad things. I certainly didn't like much of what I saw about her during that time. Still, I mourn the loss of that friendship and, along with it, the friendship of her mother. We have never spoken since. If I should ever run into any of them, here or in Haiti, I'm sure it will be all politeness and correctness. Yet as we turn away from each other, we will think to ourselves, "I know who you really are." Dust bunnies can do that to a friendship.

MINNIE MOUSE EARRING HOLDER

There's a piece of it in the kitchen drawer, I think. I just can't throw it away. I'm not entirely sure where the other pieces are—a bit of the ear, the bottom, the head. Earring holders are a thing for teenagers or "tweens," that new identity category created by marketers to exploit an even younger group of consumers. Earring holders are a lot of work to use. They're totally inconvenient and silly, especially ones like my Minnie Mouse earring holder. The Minnie Mouse earring holder is a metal figure with holes in it; you put the earrings into the holes. It takes way too much fine finger coordination to unclip the curly back that encloses the post, put the post through the hole in the holder, find the post on the back of the holder and, without being able to see what you are doing, put the curly back onto the post. And it's hard to find two good holes next to each other to hang the dangly earrings. But when you're younger, and especially if you didn't get your ears pierced until you were ten years old, like I did, all the organizing and displaying that you can do with your earrings is pleasurable labor.

Even though this earring holder has only one mismatched earring on it, even though it's broken and I don't have all the pieces, I can't throw it away. It's just too thick with memories. It's strange, since the memories are so unbearably painful and my mind, which has otherwise been so efficient at asphalting that part of my life over, still won't let me part with the one thing that distills the entire period for me.

My mother bought the Minnie Mouse earring holder in the gift shop of St. Raphael's hospital, the hospital where my childhood friend Sharon Weissman is now running the AIDS clinic. We always called it "St. Rafe's" because saying the whole word was just too long. St. Rafe's was stuck in the bad part of town, near a corner where even we kids knew ladies were out at night hustling—our big joke was saying "get thee to Chapel and Howe," an update of Hamlet's "get thee to a nunnery," which he said to the mad Ophelia. While I'm not Hamlet, being neither male nor a prince of Denmark, my mom has been my mad Ophelia just about all my life.

When I was thirteen, Mom had her second major breakdown. The three of us—my mother, me, and my brother, were living in an apartment in New Haven, owned by a Yale professor who was among the worst landlords I have ever experienced. When the neighbors upstairs flushed the toilet, which was directly above our toilet, it would rain on our heads if we happened to be atop the commode ourselves. We had a sweet, toothless old neighbor next door, a Polish woman who lived with her grown son and would talk to us across the chain-link fence, tend her garden, and say "God bless you." She and my mom would talk to each other nearly every day. Even now, my mom is good at making friends with people like that, the kind most others will pass by without a second thought. I learned that from her, how to acknowledge with love just about anybody who crosses your path.

At the time, Mom was working like crazy to keep it all together. We were on food stamps and she was working one crappy job after another—one at a liquor store for an impossible harpy who wore her nails six inches long and lacquered an off-black shade of berry, another as a ticket taker at a porn theater. Sometimes the electricity wasn't on. Sometimes there was no phone. I didn't invite my private school classmates home. Too weird. The one time I did have my friends over for a birthday sleepover, someone broke into our apartment, came in the bathroom window, and stole all my mom's jewelry, walking past us as we slept.

Mom's room was in the front of the apartment, not entirely private, separated by paned glass French doors, and she shared her room with the piano and my brother's tuba, when he was making his attempt to be both musical and acoustically dominant. We fought over everything. If I started practicing piano, he'd come in and start oomph-ing away on his tuba, each of us trying to assert our basic right to exist through volume and meter. My brother and I hated each other all through our childhoods, a particular sort of hatred that was stitched together out of fear, competitiveness, anger, immaturity, and cussed stubborn pride. We still approach each other in a gingerly way, prickly and unsure. I retreated into being perfect. I provided and anticipated. My silence was so strong, so ingrained, it was physical. It wasn't a silence like Maya Angelou's, a dramatic political gesture that was as much an act of will as it was a kind of civil disobedience. First of all, mine was a silence that allowed for speech. I just couldn't talk about anything I actually felt. Absolutely could not. I could think it, sort of. But I could not say it. And I am sure that from the time I was thirteen until the time I was in my early twenties, I could count on one hand the number of times I shed emotional tears of any sort. It was that sort of silence. Desperate and resolute. The kind that tightened around me, keeping me upright, yet suffocating me in equal measure.

Nighttime. Mom in her bed, the heat is off, and she's crying. "Would you sleep with me tonight?" she asks me, sounding desperate and sad. "No," I say, feeling slimy and mean and feeling, too, that if she leans on my any harder I will break in two myself, or sink into a pool of quicksand or something equally inescapable. I want to help her, but shit, I'm thirteen years old. Since I don't cry, she doesn't have the chance to hold me when I'm feeling blue and need comfort. I can't do it for her; it's too heavy a load. "No," I say, and the guilt slides around behind the skin on my belly.

God, that was a crazy time—and mom and stepfather, Brad, had broken up. Brad had just finished his book about Bobby Fischer, called *Bobby Fischer vs. the Rest of the World*, and Bobby wanted to sue him for eight million dollars. Everybody knew that Bobby was a nut. I guess Brad was living in New York by then—he certainly wasn't living with us—but one day there was this knock at the door, and a guy stood there out on the porch with a big fat sheaf of papers in a blue cover. Honestly, I can't remember what he said exactly, but what I do remember is that he handed the papers to me and left. They were the legal papers from Bobby Fischer's suit. They'd been served to a twelve-year-old girl. My stepfather, who happened to be there at the time, flew into a rage, and I stood there thinking, how is this my fault? What do I know about lawsuits? I'm only twelve years old. I thought things like that a lot. Things like "I'm only twelve years old. Why do I have to figure this out while the kids I go to school with are doing things like learning to ride horses and having Christmas in St. Croix?"

Not long afterward, at my short-lived job cleaning house for one of Mom's friends, the woman comes to me after I've cleaned the coffeepot and dusted and vacuumed the stairs and washed the shirts and says, "I've had your mother committed." I'm sitting at the kitchen table, a round wooden table, and her husband is making a phone call. Absently, I start pushing the number buttons on the phone. "I'm on the phone," he says, gently, and they can see how shocked and scared I am.

My mother's friend Lou comes. She's Canadian and wears colored scarves over her hair and big hoop earrings and has a rich, no-nonsense voice and tells me to do things like wash the knives and forks. She mops the kitchen floor, ugly white tiles in a pattern meant to look like stone. She cooks. I suppose she gets us off to school; I can't remember. Lou used to be the babysitter for the Noon family, whose daughter Jennifer Noon got grabbed one day after school by some guy; later they found her body in the woods. That was the year all the parents got real careful about dropping off and picking up.

I had only seen my father once or twice since I was four years old. When his play was up at the American Place Theater in New York, I went to visit him in the city once, and took the train in by myself. He refused to meet me at Grand Central. "Just take the subway," he said, and I did, but not because I wanted to. I was only eleven at the time and didn't know where I was going. But I was so desperate to see him that I'd do anything. I don't know who called him after my mom got sick, but he appeared one day in our apartment, filled with rage and wanting to do something about the whole fucking mess. My dad has always had some sort of freakish attachment to authority, likes black-and-white answers, and has a fascination with armies and airplanes and guns. He stormed into the house and got really, really pissed. Scary pissed. Throwing things pissed. Screaming pissed. Hitting people pissed. Luckily he wasn't pissed at me, so I went in my room, changed my clothes, put a red bandanna (one like Lou wore) over my hair, and put on a blue denim shirt that I tied into a knot just above my jeans. I went out. I just wandered around, headed downtown. I didn't have any friend that I could go to in a situation like this, nobody I could call and explain to them what was going on. "Hi, Cynthia, my dad is going apeshit in my house. Can I come over?" I'm sure something like that didn't even cross my mind.

I went into Queen's Wigs on lower Chapel Street. Lower Chapel is and was the part of downtown that's downscale, or, to put it another way, where the black and brown people shop. Cut-rate stuff. Aisles full of hair relaxer and coconut grease and orange flower water. I was just walking up and down the aisles, trying to keep my head from buzzing, trying to figure out how long I could stay away by myself, looking, but not looking, at the packages of hairpins and vials of nail polish. I didn't have any money. At thirteen I still looked very young, very little girly. I didn't start my period until I was fourteen and a half, even fifteen. I'm not sure I'd even started to have boobs. As I stood in the aisle, trying to hold myself together, a man passed by me, and as he did, he stretched out his fingers and touched my stomach in the place where my shirt rode up above the top of my jeans. He was looking the other way, as if he wasn't doing what he was doing, but I could see his finger reaching for me, aiming for another point of contact with my belly after that first touch. Of course I never told anybody about it.

Mom was in the hospital for months. I went to live with my godparents in their big old house over in the East Rock neighborhood. I had my own room there and got to keep going to my old school. I hunkered down into that nest of safety and security, just hanging on. I had this way of pinching down my sense of unreality. I could just act normal in any situation. Still can. When my French teacher would ask, in front of my entire eighth-grade class, "How's your mother?" I would mutter, "Fine," and when my friends would ask what was wrong with her, I'd say vaguely, "Oh, she's sick, she's in the hospital." And march on to the next class, the next chapter, the next homework assignment. My grades? A, A, A.

My godmother would take me to visit my mom fairly often, and it was on one of those visits she gave me the Minnie Mouse earring holder. Another time she gave me a brown leather belt made in one of her art therapy sessions. I remember a doll, a Red Riding Hood doll, the kind where you flip the skirt up and there's another doll underneath, the grandmother whose cap gets pulled back and on the other side is the wolf. I loved and hated those gifts. She was trying so hard to mother me, even from within the walls of a locked ward, even next to a roommate with bandaged wrists that were still seeping pink fluid. The staff threatened the patients who acted out by telling them they'd send them to the state hospital. I'd go into the ward, with its visiting room full of cigarette smoke and spindly philodendrons, and the kitchen area, with cabinets full of snacks and juice. Mom would throw open the kitchen cabinet doors, offering me a drink, something to sustain and nourish me. "Want some cookies?" I took them, letting her be my mom, letting her give me something, because she was still my mom and it was still her job to do things like give me cookies from a cabinet even if they'd been put there by hospital staff and not hauled home from the grocery store by her in the back of our car, an old light yellow Mustang with the outlines of running horses pressed into the vinyl of the seats.

I guess she was allowed off the ward, because she could go down to the gift shop and buy me presents. It was a long time before she could leave the hospital, six months, something like that. Then she went to live in a halfway house for a few months before coming home. I cried when I had to go back and live with her again. I was so scared and lonely, and I wanted to stay where I was because I felt safe. I cried just once, in my room at my godparent's house, the room with the yellow gingham wallpaper. I never gave my keys back and still have them thirty years later, the very same ones. Just in case, I guess.

For a long time, I used to think my mother was weak. I was afraid she was breakable, fragile, and brittle. But she's alive and she's here. Bit by bit, I've begun to understand the shape of her strength. Even when some part of herself was trying to kill her, she always refused to die. Never once, not ever, has she given off even the faintest hint that she did not love me fiercely, even when she could not take care of me, she made sure I was taken care of. Having felt the painful need to die myself, I know how much strength it takes not to give in to that, to push it aside and continue breathing. She has had to do this too many times, and the suffering it has caused her is unimaginable to me. But her heart has only grown as a consequence, her compassion deepened, and she is blessed with a kind of grace very few people can hope to possess.

Through all these years and no matter where I've lived, the Minnie Mouse earring holder has come with me. It has broken into bits, cheap metal thing that it is. But I can't get rid of it. There's a piece of it standing on the shelf now above my kitchen sink in front of the window. It's just the bottom with Minnie's red feet, holes of light streaming through them, jagged across the top where it broke. I don't want to search for the missing pieces. I have no desire to piece it back together and make it whole.

As pieces have gone missing, so too the pain has abated. I can still look at Minnie's feet and be that twelve-year-old girl who expertly pretended that everything was just fine and dandy. Now, though, I can look at Minnie's feet and also feel compassion for that girl, for her mother, and be grateful for how far we both have come. Minnie's feet might be stuck in the past, in those dark days, but we are not. Like Marx's table, maybe Minnie will start dancing, tapping along, beating out a rhythm to which only I care to dance. I'm good at inventing steps.

Sometimes I think I wouldn't mind if it would just disappear one day. Then, breaking free from those memories, I might unfurl like a sheet flung upward on a breeze toward the sun, spread out bright and warm, smelling of nice things and plain gentle goodness, opening—unwrinkled and buoyant and ready to drift down over my family, those I love, to cover their heavy limbs as they sleep on the grass, and me touching them gently, lightly, with an easy generosity I have only ever imagined I might possess and share.

MAKE YOURSELF A BELOVED PERSON

Perhaps it is a surprise that Marx had something to say about love: "If you love without evoking love in return, i.e., if you are not able, by the manifestation of yourself as a loving person, to make yourself a beloved person, then your love is impotent and a misfortune."[55]

The active and dynamic love that Marx envisions, like his understanding of human and social potentials, assumes that capitalism inevitably diminishes and devours these potentials. Love, as he understands it, is hardly possible unless dancing tables are set to rights. For him love evokes engagement with others and is incomplete—*impotent and a misfortune*, he says—unless it animates the social body as well as one's own heart. So the question becomes this: how can we, through the manifestation of ourselves as loving persons, make ourselves beloved persons? Would it be possible to upend our upside-down world and suddenly find that everyone in it was both loving and beloved? These are questions that are as important for us as scholars as they are for us as lovers, parents, friends, for we are all of these together. To insist on the rigid separation of these spheres is perhaps to reanimate what were certainly painful realities in Marx's own life—his refusal to be a wage slave and the price it scraped from those closest to him: his wife's health broken, two daughters committing suicide, all his other children dying, sick, or too young. Before we can set his fabled table squarely on its feet, we must realize that we have already found a seat beside him, sitting at that very table. It's a hot seat, to be sure.

The call Marx made was for human connectedness, and in many of the current calls for understanding the interconnectedness of the global economy, the global circulation of goods and people, I often find an astonishing lack of attention being given to the ways people themselves are connected through contemporary consumption in ways both obvious and obscure. The hyperconsumption of disposable luxury that has come to typify the wealthy sectors of the world, while connected to global crises like greenhouse gases and the stripping of the rainforest, is less often understood to be part of the reason that people starve in Haiti and children labor in India. Moreover, we must fight these things not just on our own behalf, or for our own benefit, but also on behalf of others and even for the benefit of all humankind. This is precisely the sort of human immediacy that Marx sought to inject into people's consciousness: that their actions and pleasures take place in circuits of human interconnectedness, where the objects that move among us are often mistaken for being the glue that holds us together. Of course we should care about global warming, and all the living things affected by it (and other everyday events). If we add to this the Native understanding of *living things*, a notion that intrinsically includes every aspect of our world as having life, our sense of responsibility and commitment grows accordingly. This is something quite different from advocating that we love our cars and find emotional fulfillment in shopping, and it is nothing like the romanticist, primitivist notion about Indians that I see too often shorthanded into the nearly meaningless saying "The Indians loved the land."

When I was seventeen years old and in New Mexico, during the crazy theater-exercise trip, two additional memories still stand out for me. In the first, I was being taught the proper way to begin a meal. There was a small basket on the table, and before beginning to eat, each of us had to take a morsel of bread, breathe on it, and put it in the basket. This, I was told, was a way of giving thanks, a way of telling the world and the spirits that you appreciated what you had. Your breath identified you; it was how you would be recognized when the basket was placed outside. In the second, we were attending what was called "a throw." It was someone's name day, the day of the Catholic saint for which someone was named. The entire family was standing on the roof of their house, surrounded by plastic laundry baskets full of food and household goods: cans of soda, boxes of things to eat, soap, washcloths, things like that. The throw began, and everyone on the roof reached into the baskets and started tossing things to the people below. I think I caught a box of Nilla Wafers and a can of 7Up. It was almost, in a way, like a version of the Pacific Northwest Indian potlatch, but without the edge of aggressive competition. What I remember enjoying was the collectivity of it—the trading of this and that happening among the people gathered in front of the house, the hilarity of household items falling from the sky, and my own pleasure at being included although I knew virtually nobody there, I had no home to speak of, and my own family had fractured nearly irretrievably. In this community, one that embraced the living, including living things, I first felt the possibility of finding my own way.

If Marx could write *Capital* and the *Communist Manifesto* and still meditate on the fundamental importance of love, it must also be a task to which we can commit ourselves. This is not the only reason to think about love, surely, but I cannot shake the realization that his conception of love is as powerful and enduring as his description of a commodity. Why is it, then, that nobody (as far as I can tell) has made Marx's notion of love something to take seriously? Perhaps because, in the end, we don't take love seriously, not nearly seriously enough.

As I read it, this is what he is saying: in striving to be beloved, we seek engagement with others and are less focused on self-pleasure; in seeking to be loved, we must work to earn and secure the love of those around us; in choosing to bestow love, we strive to build in others the joy that animates the universe. All of this, he notes, is something we accomplish ourselves, on our own behalf, and through our own efforts. You must *manifest* yourself as a loving person. Yet this is not enough. You must go further than this—because it is not enough to *be* loving, to exist in one-way relationship. You must, in turn, make yourself a beloved person—that is, you must find ways to become beloved of others. To be loved by another is what makes a person fully and finally human, but only if that person is also a loving person as well. Love that finds itself unfettered by the complexities of being loved back is as good as no love at all. Worse, it is, as Marx says, impotent and a misfortune. And this, finally, is the problem with commodity fetishism: too often we love too much those things which cannot possibly love us back. As consumers, we may love our things endlessly and deeply, but locked in these relationships, we are certain never to evoke love in return.

Despite the messy, selfish, patriarchal, and conflicting details of Marx's personal and family life, his was a life replete with love. He loved widely and was himself much loved. His passionate scholarship was, I think, also a manifestation of his love for the world more broadly. The truth is, I don't want to be buried in stuff, taken over by it, enveloped by an attachment to nonliving things that cannot love me back. Lately, I've been developing a very sweet texting relationship with my daughter. She says things to me via text that she would not say in person. She's goofy and she's funny and open in texts in a way she sometimes cannot be when face-to-face. It's not particularly horrifying: I can hear her snickering in the other room as she crafts some silly retort to something I've sent, and we ramp the whole thing up until the texts, flying fast and furious, have us both in stitches. It's a new form of literacy, I say to myself, as if to justify it. One can never be too literate, after all. And then, because she's a committed cosleeper, she jumps into bed next to me, calls the dogs, and we all fall asleep on a bed big enough to hold our dreams. I bought that bed on Craigslist. I bought the sheets online. The mattress topper came from Target. I made the duvet cover. Those careful choices are perhaps one part of the way I manifest myself as a loving person to the sleeping bodies beside me. Thousands of choices pile up all around us, if I'm looking for them—thousands of things and relationships. The dogs snore. My daughter snuggles. I burrow deeper into their heavy warmth and try to slow my gerbil-wheel whirl of thoughts and worries about washing machines, burnt-out electric circuits, summer camp, new shoes, grocery shopping, paint colors, hair appointments.

Someday, I'll finish that baby quilt I started for her before she was born.

3

Writing as Practice and Process

In taking on a self-consciously autoethnographic stance, I did what made sense to me as an anthropologist and as an ethnographer: I treated my entries as field notes. For me, the writing of field notes is a laborious, time-consuming process, and an indispensable one. The field notes for my dissertation project are typed, single-spaced, and housed in three-inch-thick binders—four of them. Despite their bulk, I find it difficult to say exactly what the field notes themselves produced. In the early 1990s the coding programs available were both clunky and expensive. While I used one such program and dutifully coded my notes into a range of discrete categories, what I think ultimately emerged for me as the primary value of my field notes was the process itself of writing them—the long hours spent reflecting and reiterating what I had done, seen, thought during my time "in the field." The process, much like many other forms of practice and remembering, is one in which very specific capacities are exercised and thereby strengthened. In the case of writing field notes (at least for me), these capacities included the ability to participate in an event while at the same time mentally recording it, and, later, the discipline of taking the time to revisit, re-experience, and re-feel the event in order to write about it with the goal of recording as much as possible in a nonjudgmental way. Judgment, parsing, and the finding of meaning were purposefully deferred, as much as possible, until later.

Field notes become the fund from which ethnographers cull the material for the ethnography itself. In this project, my aim became to rigorously produce field notes in much the same way as I had during earlier projects. One of the key things about the writing of field notes is that writing toward a goal is not the point. The effort, for me at least, was to record in as much detail as I could, things I had seen and witnessed, while also noting my own responses, points of confusion, questions, and gaps. I was well aware throughout the process that my own point of view was limited and that the observations I produced were likely to suffer the effects of those limitations. My aim was to acknowledge and understand those limitations as best I could, recognizing that any other researcher would, similarly, be caught up in a set of dilemmas and perspectival specificities that would produce their own points of clarity and confusion. Without a doubt, then, I am one of those social scientists who can embrace a notion of positionality that includes any variety of specificities of age, race, gender, generation, geography (and the list goes on), and value those positionalities for the truths they can produce. I have no expectation of identicality in those refractive, fractal, and endlessly detailed specificities, yet I do subscribe to the notion that when viewed from enough of a distance, patterns nevertheless emerge, and that these patterns are both beautiful and worthy of sustained attention. For me, field notes are an essential part of contributing to—and discovering—both those very important specificities and those undeniably present larger patterns.

Thinking specifically about process and writing, producing field notes is a fundamentally different sort of writing than that done by the novelist, who is moving a manuscript forward. With field notes there is no imperative to impose narrative, subtext, or other devices on the material. The task is simply to write, to talk about what happened, to record observations. If it was rainy that day, it was rainy. If I had lunch with the chief of police, that is what I wrote about. With its emphasis on recording the everyday on a regular basis, the writing of field notes does bear similarities to keeping a diary. Unlike a diary, field notes are a form of documentation, whose ultimate purpose is a larger comprehensive project aimed at a public audience; the purpose of the notes is to be the raw material from which an ethnographic account may be drawn. Yet field notes, like diaries, are understood (at least by me) to be deeply private. Anthropologists tend to select bits and pieces of our notes to incorporate whole into finished work, but to expose them outright is to throw one's self into public nakedness. Unless some of us want to openly acknowledge some very off-the-beaten-track desires and pleasures, such nakedness and all it implies is unseemly and uncomfortable. It's a bit like—

here I will quote a colleague of mine—"wearing assless chaps to a cocktail party." That is to say, inappropriate.

Not being the type to wear assless chaps to any occasion, public or private, I was extremely aware that in choosing to produce my field notes as intentionally public, it was very important to have them be neater and cleaner than field notes I would keep to myself. I also wanted to exercise some very specific forms of self-discipline, perhaps for self-exploration, and perhaps as writerly challenge. This is why I set myself the task of having the entries take the form of self-contained essays, written in a single sitting. These details aside, it seemed utterly obvious to me that a rigorous autoethnographic process would mirror any other ethnographic process: that is, the method of autoethnography, I thought, ought to be the same as ethnography itself: first take field notes, then analyze field notes, and finally write ethnography. It turns out I was wrong.

Autoethnography is practiced in a variety of disciplines, and at this point, perhaps the majority of autoethnography is produced outside anthropology. "When researchers do autoethnography," write Carolyn Ellis, Tony Adams, and Arthur Bochner, "they retrospectively and selectively write about epiphanies that stem from, or are made possible by, being part of a culture and/or by possessing a particular cultural identity. . . . Autoethnographers must use personal experience to illustrate cultural experience, and, in so doing, make characteristics of a culture familiar for insiders and outsiders."[1] For Ellis, Adams, and Bochner, the method of autoethnography applies primarily to the way the autoethnographer is written into the moment or narrative, and the use of analytical tools to render an individual experience relevant to broader ideas, instances, or patterns. With its emphasis on retrospection, selectivity, and epiphany, this approach to autoethnography draws on experiences analyzed through hindsight; the logic for choosing one instance over another, or the means through which moments have been accumulated, is idiosyncratic. It is a useful and powerful mode, but what I was after was a form of autoethnography that closely mirrored my own anthropological ethnographic practice.

The disciplined and rigorous production of field notes over an extended period of time was central to my practice. One of the key things about this discipline and rigor is the surprise and challenge it offers. Drawing selectively from memories, as so many autoethnographies do, strikes me as a strategy that provides too many opportunities to avoid confronting the unexpected. A reliance on hindsight skirts the problem of the editing process inherent in memory, where what we select to remember has already been siphoned, sieved, refashioned, and reshaped numerous times as it rises into our consciousness, or is retained at the forefront. This may be a process that makes bad experiences worse, or, as happens frequently to me, makes my own experience of shame or humiliation the centerpiece of an event when to be fair, nobody apart from myself even noticed my shame or humiliation. The truth or nontruth of such perception is of little consequence to me; the confrontation that is avoided in such memory-making is the requirement to record and consider the moment in its setting and context, to fix it through writing, to shape it later through analysis. Field notes themselves face similar challenges, but because they are written in the moment over long spans of time, they preserve and materialize thoughts and responses in a very different way than memory alone does. Existing outside memory, or perhaps in addition to it, field notes thus challenge memory, even as they constitute a form of memory-making. While memories can disappear without our seemingly knowing how or why, it takes physical work to make accumulated field notes go away, even if it is only the click of a button. One of the very personally painful experiences of taking field notes on and through my own experiences has been the realization of how fixing them in writing has changed, perhaps forever, the way in which my own sense of my past has been externalized. I read my field accounts of my own experiences and often do not recognize myself. My memories are no longer my own.

Coming as I do from a family of writers, I have always approached field notes in a writerly way, and this tendency was amplified throughout my engagement with the consumer diaries. Each entry was written in a single session, and each takes the form of a reflective essay. Normally my field notes do not take this kind of resolved form, so in that way they are unusual. I chose this approach in part because it made each entry contained and grounded, even as the terrain I explored was quite broad and unpredictable. I could feel "finished" at the end of an entry in a way that provided a sense of satisfaction, or at least doneness. The entries felt to me like a task: I would select a thing and the challenge was to describe and write about it with as much breadth and completeness as I could. My aim was to trace my own rabbit holes and dead ends, to attempt to be merciless in documenting how very wrapped up I can be in the world of consumption, thereby using myself as a case in point. There certainly was a choice of positioning and voice here. The version of me I put into the field notes was one where I would worry about proving my intellectual credentials some other time. Like any nerdy professor type who has spent her entire adult life in school, my reference points are often books, articles, and theories, but the point with this project was to be an everyday person while in the midst of these reflections. The roles of expert professor or lecturing anthropologist were not right for the entries. At the same time, I *am* those things, and writing often put me in a state of mind where such academic tactics as referring to authoritative literature or thinking about superstructure provided direction and comfort when I was attempting to capture my feelings about my childhood comfort object, Banky. In and of themselves, the authority the diary entries hold is that of *testimonio*, perhaps, with all the implied contradictions and difficulties inherent in that genre.[2]

Written over the course of several years, the entries capture my own life at different moments. It was only after I had accumulated a substantial number of entries that I began to think about how they might resolve into a coherent ethnographic narrative. This was the reflective and analytical stage of the project, and I was mired in it for an incredibly long time—nearly a decade. Ultimately, I was unable to wrestle the entries into something resembling a manuscript on my own, and it took the generous collaboration of my friend Susan Ruffins to bring key aspects of resolution to the project. Susan printed out everything, and laid it all out across her office floor, forcing me to sit and sort through piles; she read aloud bits and pieces to her family, and their own responses to what they had heard would filter back to me via her husband or children. She decisively and generously suggested leaving specific entries behind, and it was she who, through her own editorial and affective engagement with the work, identified the key themes that shape this book. After having been always a very solitary writer, I found Susan's gentle yet firm handling of me and my writing revelatory and not nearly as terrifying as I had imagined it would be. There is no doubt that her patience and kindness allowed me to bring this book to completion. Even as I was documenting my own consumer life, my marriage was ending; I experienced one spate of major depression at the onset of the project, and a second several years after having finished entry writing, as I struggled to produce the book. Neither the breakup nor the two depressive periods bore causal relation to the autoethnographic project, yet for me the project is bookended by these monumental events. I do not discuss them in any great detail as part of the autoethnography itself, however, and have made a concerted decision to leave out several key people in my life's events as I describe them. For some, this editing-out might constitute the creation of a fiction. On the contrary, I argue that it was ethically necessary, and though I describe some events at which key people were present as if those people did not even exist, the larger, true shape and feel of those events remains intact. These are strategies regularly used by ethnographers, in any case.

If my sense of this project is bookended by monumental events, it is bookended, too, by Susan's sustained and sustaining work, as much friend- and fellowship as it was editorial. I desperately needed all three, both as a writer and as a human being. The entries were an imagined dialogue between me and "people out there," and the ultimate shape of the book itself very much reflects a dialogue between me and Susan, together seeking to fashion a manuscript that speaks beyond our own conversations. Susan's involvement with this book is, then, nothing short of generative and crucial.

Many entries did not make the cut. They seemed repetitive, or beside the point. This type of selection is quite different, however, from the hindsight memory more commonly practiced in autoethnography. Choosing to keep entries whole, I worked to place and arrange them in a way that would allow key themes to flow. Thus the entries are not arranged chronologically in the text: in terms of ethnographic cohesion, this did not make sense. As a result, I had to struggle during the editing to be true to particular moments yet avoid being overly confusing. This comes through especially with regard to entries where my daughter appears; in some entries she is two years old, in others eight or nine, but her appearances do not follow the stream of time.

WRITING CULTURE (AND RACE) THROUGH AUTOETHNOGRAPHY

I am a product of *Writing Culture*—and in more ways than one. Published in 1986, the year I started graduate school, that landmark collection of essays has been hugely influential in anthropology.[3] Vincent Crapanzano, who contributed to the book, was one of my closest advisers in my graduate years, a postmodern theorist with a joint appointment in comparative literature and anthropology at the City University Graduate Center. A closer and more complicated way I am connected to *Writing Culture* is that my father, the writer Frank Chin, figures prominently in one of the book's essays. Because of these multiple connections, *Writing Culture* stands for me as a kind of shorthand reference to my own relationship to ethnography, writing, and writing ethnographically. The autoethnographic emphasis of this book extends into my discussion of writing. My experience of writing is shaped as much by my professional and scholarly training as it is by having grown up among writers—and, in particular, by being the daughter of a prominent writer known for his outspokenness on issues of race and racism.

In asserting that the writing of anthropology itself was an object to be analyzed, Writing Culture helped to establish the literary turn in anthropology as a force to be reckoned with, touching heated debates. As an important center of Marxist anthropology, the CUNY department was one where the Writing Culture wars raged with the kind of drama only achievable by New York working-class intellectuals. The fight, as I remember it, seemed to be about "the postmodernists" versus "the Marxists," and the two sides represented interpretive and critical approaches, on the one hand, and social-justice-oriented approaches, on the other. I remember June Nash saying during a talk about Bolivian tin miners that she "probably ought to be discussing hermeneutics," a word she pronounced with obvious distaste (is it my imagination that she took a sip of water afterward, as if to cleanse her mouth?); another day, in class, one student was screaming accusations at another of not being "one with the masses," because interrogating writing was elitist and lacked solidarity. I found all of this confusing. Wasn't it possible, I wondered, to be deeply committed to people but still engage in questions about the writing of ethnography? Wasn't Vincent Crapanzano an anthropologist with an incredibly strong streak of integrity and sense of justice? Eric Wolf, for his part, a founder of Marxist anthropology, was a gentle soul, a beautifully lucid writer, and an even more astonishing lecturer. Were we really poised on opposing sides of a war zone, the historical materialists versus the postmodernists, as the daily fights in the classrooms seemed to suggest? I certainly had no interest in choosing one over the other—I wanted to explore and embrace all of it. That was one way Writing Culture was part of my growing up in anthropology.

Michael J. Fischer's chapter in Writing Culture is titled "Ethnicity and the Post-Modern Arts of Memory."[4] In it he surveys a range of autobiographical accounts produced by what he calls "ethnic American writers," among them Maxine Hong Kingston and my father. My dad's inclusion is a bit ironic, since, to put it mildly, my father is not a fan of anthropology: when I told my father I was going to begin a PhD program he informed me in one of his twenty-page letters that anthropology is a racist, colonialist discipline and I had chosen to join the racists. When I dared to defend my choice in a twenty-page letter of my own, he was enraged. We did not speak for two years. Had I not broken our silence (I do not remember how or why I did it), I am certain we would never have spoken again. If my dad hates anthropology on principle, he really cannot abide Maxine Hong Kingston. Fischer's juxtaposition of her work with my father's is one he would certainly fail to appreciate.

Sometimes at home we entertain ourselves by saying the magic words, "Maxine Hong Kingston," and sit back to watch the show. The blood rushes to my dad's pockmarked face, his eyebrows lower, and he grits his teeth while managing to yell, "MAXINE HONG KINGSTON IS A WHITE RACIST!" He then proceeds into what for us is a well-worn rant about Maxine Hong Kingston, white racism, Chinese stories, Kwan Kung, and the heroic tradition of Chinese literature. If he ever read Fischer's article (which he would never do), I have no doubt he would go apoplectic. It would be a particular performance of apoplexy, though, one he has honed to a fine point over the decades, one my family and I tend to find both tiresome and amusing. There's a seriousness to it, certainly, and my father more than anyone recognizes his rage as a form of showmanship.[5]

Frank Chin has always been a writer's writer, the kind of guy who sacrifices nothing to his art, the kind of guy who leaves a trail behind him but carries little with him. For most of his adult life he has owned nothing but a car, a typewriter, a good pair of cowboy boots, and a change of socks. He would not appreciate his writing being appropriated by anthropology for its supposed ethnographic value. He would virulently oppose such appropriation. The first problem, of course, would be the way that he is compared with Kingston. While my dad is often assumed to be a chauvinist blowhard, his problem with Maxine Hong Kingston (or the other writers he criticizes) is not a gender problem. The problem he has chosen to highlight is that his project is fundamentally different from hers in terms of the audience he imagines and addresses. Objectively speaking (if I can even speak objectively on this question), his project is manifestly different from hers. To put it simply, my dad writes at and against white racism.[6] He names it for what it is, and he does not pull his punches. He is willing to be ugly, to be oppositional, and to throw things—word bombs, bottles of beer, punches—if that what it takes. Maxine is much less confrontational in her approach, and this is why my father brands her a "white racist"; he sees her as reaching out to white audiences in a supplicative or friendly gesture that he views as weak and self-hating. I do not need to go into the substance of the "Chin-Kingston debate" here,[7] but I feel certain that the significant differences in positioning with regard to white audiences fundamentally distinguish my father's project from that of Kingston's, and this is something Fischer does not identify when he discusses ethnicity and memory among Chinese Americans. To put it another way, Fischer's elision of Kingston and Chin's positions with regard to whiteness does violence to their individual projects.

In much of the literature on autoethnography—and Fischer's "ethnic arts of memory" treats ethnic literature much as if it is actually autoethnographic—there is a tendency to include ethnic and Native accounts as examples of an autoethnographic genre.[8] I find this exceptionally problematic, and not only because I can imagine how decisively and dramatically my father would reject, on many points, the legitimacy of being put in that position by a white anthropologist—or any anthropologist who by his definition would be (like Maxine Hong Kingston) a "white racist."[9] I certainly understand that Native accounts produce scads of material that is ethnographically useful to anthropologists, but I resist the appropriation of such material by our discipline because that is a racist move. First, such appropriation is practiced almost exclusively on "Native" accounts and texts; generically "American" (read white) accounts are not treated as ethnographic treasure troves because they constitute "history," not "ethnography." This pattern speaks both to the position of the anthropologists identifying material as ethnographic (white) and to those who have produced supposedly ethnographic material (not white). This strategy reaffirms anthropology itself as white public space in ways that still need to be effectively addressed.[10] For these reasons, I take the position that autoethnography is ethnographic only if the work was created with ethnographic intention; the Nativeness or non-Nativeness of the autoethnographer, particularly as a member of an indigenous or minority culture, does not create a subgenre of ethnographic production. Leave my dad out of it, for all our sakes.

My position on autoethnography and writing mixes the "down with the people" elements of my historical materialist affiliations with the "postmodern" concerns I have always had with ethnographic writing of any sort. As an anthropologist of color, I have had no choice but to struggle with the internal racial politics of my chosen discipline. My dad was right, I have come to realize, though I would never tell him so to his face.[11] Anthropology is racist. It is and continues to be so profoundly racist that I was asked by the president of the American Anthropological Association to sit on the "Committee to Address Racism within the Discipline" from 2011 to 2013. The forms of this racism are many, but for me they can be boiled down to the very problematic normative premise that white people study everybody, whereas people of color study themselves.[12] Thus I recognize that autoethnographic accounts by "Natives" (and by this I mean oppressed others, the abject, the marginalized) provide perspectives and accounts unrealizable by other means; the inherent political projects many of these examples represent are tremendously important. Such projects are so important that anthropology really needs to keep its paws off them. The tendency to normalize autoethnography along the lines of whiteness is one that ought to have been questioned long ago. The distinction is really much too similar to the notion of humanity, discussed in the introduction, as being inherently white, and simultaneously premised on the exclusion and effacement of blackness (and all others). How is it that we have one category called autoethnography and another category called "Native ethnography"? Are ethnically and racially unmarked autoethnographers without racial or ethnic identities that need interrogation? Are Native or indigenous ethnographers legitimated primarily by those identities? Why make race and identity the key for an entire class of people while negating it for others as having any relevance at all, and why do those cleavages fall along such racially predictable lines?

As I have already said, one reason my dad's work should not be considered ethnographic is that he himself would reject that label. My defense of the ethnographic is equally invested in claiming the value of my own training as an anthropologist. Given my very personal struggle with my dad along these very lines, you could say my feelings on the matter are Elektra-ish, complex. My father's goals in his writing are not anthropological, but mine are, and intentionality matters.[13] If in *Writing Culture* Frank Chin serves as a stand-in for any other ethnic or native writer who has produced personal accounts, self-servingly, I claim that my training ought to count for something, especially because my father thinks my chosen profession is bullshit. So to reiterate: being a thoughtful, critical observer of the world around you does not make you an autoethnographer. Being an *ethnographer* is a key part of being an *autoethnographer*. Lest I sound too elitist, I want to point out that becoming an ethnographer is not necessarily all that hard; I myself have taught ten-year-olds to be fantastic ethnographic researchers,[14] and there are any number of other projects in which the status of ethnographer (auto or otherwise) is rendered widely available to any who might be interested in developing the necessary skills.

Until he had a massive stroke at the end of 1999, my father wrote at night, every night, into the wee hours. After the stroke he changed: he asked me how I was doing, something he had never done before, and he started getting up at 4 a.m. rather than going to sleep at that time. But before the stroke, whenever I spent time with him, my lullaby was the sound of his manual Olivetti, later replaced by a Brother word processor, now replaced by an unbelievably aged Mac. On the other side of the country, my stepfather, with whom my mom, my brother, and I lived from when I was four until I was twelve years old, was a journalist—he wrote the first cover story for *People* magazine back when *People* magazine involved in-depth journalism, and specialized in doing profiles of the exceptionally famous.[15] My stepfather was an old-school hunt-and-pecker who never mastered touch typing. As deadlines loomed, he would work thirty-six hours in a row, stopping for ten-minute naps under the dining room table, atop which his towers of notes teetered, threatening to bury him permanently. My mother served as his typist, her red IBM Selectric buzzing and banging into the night as she typed her eighty-words-per-minute rhythm.

Writing, the way I had seen it growing up, was a huge amount of work, something to think about seriously in and of itself. I learned early that writing takes time, precision, and dedication. Perhaps this is one reason that the questions taken on by *Writing Culture* and the so-called postmodern turn struck me as only sensible. I knew all the editorial marks by the time I had finished grammar school. What was all the fuss about, I wondered. I have an uncle who is a writer much in the same mold as my dad: he is a guy who does it his way or not at all, and has the scars to show for it. An aunt is a linguist. My mother has a huge talent for writing and worked for many years as an editor in a printing house. In my family, writing is our culture. We all write; it comes naturally and without fanfare. We all view it as craft, hard work, a skill to be honed and practiced.

Much of the time I find writing a comforting process. I have control over it in a way I could never have control over conducting fieldwork. I like words, rhythms, phrases. I might have a taste of a passage in my mind, and there is a very specific form of physical pleasure and engagement that comes with transforming that taste into words on a page. To a significant degree I approached this project almost purely as a writing project rather than a scholarly one. At this point I can look back and situate the work in and among writing that has been produced about various relevant themes or issues that I take up, but as I was doing the work itself, I was not triangulating my efforts in relation to scholarship. Part of me would like to put this work out there as a writing project, end of story. On the other hand, the work becomes richer and more interesting through being put into dialogue with other peoples' thinking.

One of the ways this happens in the book is through research investigations that were sparked by objects and items I had decided to write about. This is the case, for instance, on my entry on napkins. Thinking about them sent me on a months-long inquiry into lace making and linen production in the late nineteenth century. Similarly, ruminating on thrift stores and secondhand clothes led me to pry into the long histories of markets in used clothing, and how they have shifted in the era of shipping containers and fast fashion. In this and other instances, I took the opportunity to move beyond in-the-moment musings, choosing to use a particular item as a window into an entire world of questions that usually began with "Who made it, and how?" In this way, objects became more than repositories of my own personal narratives and emotions, and I consciously attempted to see and feel their human origins and costs. Beyond this historical materialist approach, which was plainly aimed at dealienating the objects (insofar as that is even possible), these investigations had elements of delight and wonder. As I became increasingly obsessed with the world of pawn shops, I cajoled my family into spending one long winter road trip visiting Native American pawn locations in Arizona and New Mexico. This melding of adventure and research in learning about contemporary consumption is something undertaken early on by John Sherry and Russell Belk, who along with Melanie Wallendorf spent a summer tooling around in a van visiting yard sales.[16] These research forays were in themselves adventures, probes into rabbit holes that could have gone much, much deeper in every case. They gave me a sense, then, of the worlds within worlds populating my own daily life, should I care to recognize them. The particularity of each rabbit hole is less important than the recognition that there is an endless number of similar opportunities to go all the way down.

HAVING FUN

In a recent post for the anthropology blog *Savage Minds*, Ruth Behar gave the advice "Read more, write less." What she was getting at was the value of reading not for information, but reading to think about and experience the writing. Since learning how to read in first grade, I have always been a hungry and voracious reader. Most reading I divide up in my mind as being "for work" or "for fun." Fun reading, for me, is inevitably fiction, ranging from Man Booker Prize nominees to popular murder mysteries. The murder mysteries I plow through solely for plot, usually while on an airplane. I need two fat mysteries to get me through a cross-country flight. Work reading is anything scholarly or serious. Standing somewhere in between is *Anna Karenina*, a book I read through about every five years in a variety of translations, a touchstone text that I experience differently each time, each time reassessing myself as much as I do *Anna Karenina* itself. I must confess to doing a lot more fun reading than work reading if number of pages read is the measure.

I have long wished to be more creative on the writing side of things—while I love to read fiction, I find I do not have the imagination to write it. Though people tell me I am a good writer, I view myself as a very limited one. With this book I gave myself room to draw inspiration from beyond the world of scholarly conventions: I wanted to *play*. Thus the writing for this book was inspired by the playfulness of a number of things I had been reading and thinking about, ranging from a seventeenth-century Chinese erotic novel[17] to Todd Haynes's underground film *Superstar*.[18] In *The Carnal Prayer Mat* Li Yu plays with the forms and conventions of the day, when it was routine for Chinese scholars to provide commentary on each others' writings. What Yu does, to hilarious effect, is to provide his own commentary on his own writing as if he were someone else, taking on a serious voice to discuss events like penis implants (yes, in seventeenth-century China!) as a method for attaining enlightenment. Similarly, in *Superstar*, Haynes marries playfulness with seriousness, using Barbie dolls to tell a story about anorexia in a manner that is simple, chilling, and devastatingly effective. In many earlier versions of this manuscript I played around as well, experimenting with form and tone. Marta Savigliano's brave and brilliant performative writing has long had my total admiration, particularly because she performs theory on the page and on the stage in a way nobody else has even attempted.[19] At one point, I toyed with writing two books at once, much in the manner that John Jackson did in his wonderfully tricksterish essay "Ethnophysicality," where two essays ride along each other, one in the text, the other in the footnotes.[20] Unlike Jackson, I couldn't pull it off, and in the end a simple and even stripped-down structure was what worked best.

My father's novel *Gunga Din Highway* was described in many reviews as being a postmodern work.[21] My father was baffled, claiming he had no idea what postmodernism was. "I thought I was just writing," he said. Sly denials aside, I am pretty sure that my dad has no interest in literary theory, and yes, he has no idea what postmodernism is. It can seem like an evasion to claim that theory is not central to this book, but in terms of *how* I did the writing, particularly of the entries themselves, I wanted to be "just writing," approaching the writing as craft rather than argument, as expression rather than exegesis. Embedded in this resistance or rejection of typical scholarly format is a feminist challenge to patriarchal ways of knowing, along with a people-of-color rejection of Eurocentric standards as universally legitimate. The theory buoyed me, but this was never meant to be a demonstration of theory or an exercise in such. Artists are often advised to master technique and then to throw it away. I have tried to throw away theory as the scaffold for writing. For these reasons, I was not especially committed to the notion that creating a smoothly articulated narrative was important.

I began this book when I was in my early forties; now I am in my early fifties. Because I draw breath, I have earned the right to write in my own voice. It's a terrifying thing to try to actually do it.

4

This Never Happened

A   SURREAL   AUTOETHNOGRAPHY

OF   WHAT   MIGHT   HAVE   BEEN

This account is based on an unfinished diary written by Dr. ——, an anthropologist and longtime scholar of consumption. It is a merciless entry into the mazelike crevices of her consumer consciousness, and it is also a cautionary tale. Increasingly unable to separate her personal and professional obsessions, Dr. —— became a hoarder, unable to stop herself from amassing objects of every kind and description. She rolled, dragged, lugged, and lobbed anything she could afford, garbage-pick, or barter for and found a place for it in an organizational system that only she could understand and navigate. Like any hoarder, she had her caches of unused plastic bags, quivering towers of old *Sunset* and *Vogue* magazines, crisping newspapers. There is no doubt that in the end Dr. —— was crushed by consumption, overcome by it, and it consumed her utterly.

I came upon the diaries when I purchased the contents of several storage lockers at the U-Store-It facility on Mission Road in Los Angeles. While not worth much in my eBay store, the diaries possessed a power of their own, and once I began reading them, I felt I needed to learn more about Dr. —— and her life. Luckily, the materials I had purchased also included several boxes full of personal journals, and in the account that follows, I have pieced together the last years of Dr. ——'s life largely from these journals along with partially completed academic papers and other materials. I must admit a certain horror at what happened to Dr. ——. As someone who deals in stuff—I make my living, after all, by buying up the contents of abandoned storage rooms and then selling the contents in a variety of locations both material and virtual—I fear that what happened to her could be my fate as well. However, since my own involvement with stuff is not especially emotional and tends really toward the instrumental, it is not likely that I'll end up like her, that is, up to my neck in junk.

My chosen profession leaves me with large stretches of free time to devote to personal projects—gardening, quilting, house-flipping, whatever. So over the past several months I have been able to spend days and days at a time to poring over the diaries and the journals, entering the strange world that Dr. —— created for herself. Reconstructing this last period of Dr.——'s life, then, has been one of my personal projects.

Hoarding is an illness. As Dr. ——'s condition became more all-encompassing, neighbors became alarmed, both for her health and because her property had become both an eyesore and a fire hazard. She had dragged thousands of discarded mops and brooms into the front yard and used them to erect a sort of teepee village that stank of mildew and Mr. Clean. Bags of socks hung from the branches of her treasured orange tree, and the garage—filled entirely from bottom to top—was layered like a holiday dip tray: At the bottom, old sewing patterns. On top of that, three full feet of coiled hoses, followed by a thin crust of dried rose petals. Next, shoeboxes full of postcards, none of which had been written to her, and all with the stamps carefully steamed off (these were later found as a kind of impromptu wallpaper for the front bedroom). The next stratum was two and a half inches of bobby pins, primarily the brown ones with the plastic tips, each of which had been straightened out.[1] Layer six was composed of right-side shoes, but none of the red ones, which were found in the contents of a storage locker Dr. —— had used when she overflowed her home. But back to the garage: one layer consisted entirely of cat litter clumps, scooped over the years from the litter box in the rear bathroom, which was the only room in Elizabeth's home that had somehow remained clutter-free. Toward the end, she had cut a hole into the garage roof and, scrambling up a makeshift ladder, had "dumped the clumps," as she said, through the hatch. A notation from a recovered journal shows that she had progressed to the point where she could not even part with the poop generated by her seventeen cats and three dogs.

While I am not a psychologist myself, it does seem to me that according to the diagnostic criteria proposed by Pertusa et al., Dr. —— certainly qualified as a hoarder.

The summer stench from the garage was intolerable, particularly after the tenth year of clump dumping, and the fumes roiled so powerfully beneath the roof that on especially hot days, bored neighborhood children (those with strong enough stomachs) would gather in the street to watch the roof shiver and then emit enormous farts. It was as if the house itself had rumbled into life, animated by the sheer power of Dr. ——'s consumer desires. Or at least, she had moved her home to severe indigestion. Once, to the children's delight, the garage made an especially dramatic series of eruptions on the evening of the Fourth of July. The kids usually conducted their observations mounted on bicycles so that they could try to outrun the dust that accompanied these emissions. At this point the city laid down the law: Dr. —— had to clear the property to a normal and hygienic level; otherwise the property would be condemned. By this time, the professor's home and plight had reached the attention of the media, and this portion of her saga was well documented in the Los Angeles Times, which found in her story at least enough interest to fill what is known among journalists as the "news hole"—the space on the page that is left over after the advertisements have been laid out.

Meanwhile, Elizabeth really did want to change, she just didn't know how. She began calling professional organizers, in a desperate plea for help. Dr. ——'s situation was not exactly unique, and consumption in extremis has become widespread enough that has generated its own medications and its own industries: storage units, psychological specialties, cleaning crews, and of course the television shows. Once she alerted the organizers, the reality TV crews were not far behind. Dr. ——'s house and its contents were not so special, really: but as Clean House, Hoarding, and Hoarders each tried to land this hoarding site for their own drenched-in-drama video-fests, Dr. —— suddenly found herself having to decide who she was as a keeper of stuff: was she simply extremely messy and in need of some tough love, a yard sale, and a room makeover (the Clean House approach)? Was she at a critical juncture that might change her life and leave her homeless forever, so sick and damaged that a team of mental health experts and exterminators needed to be called in, as the producers of A&E's Hoarders suggested? Or was she a ticking time bomb whose slide into or out of desperation needed not psychological evaluation but rather serious voice-over action and a loving intervention by friends and family, as proposed by the Lifetime network's show Hoarding: Buried Alive?

A reality-TV-show shooting schedule would have required her to swab the decks within seventy-two hours, and because Dr. —— had done her research, she was fairly certain while the cleanup would make for good before and after pictures, it was unlikely to result in lasting change. Besides, she was fairly sure that her problem did not stem from obsessive-compulsive disorder, she surely did not have kleptomania or a shopping habit (well, she liked shopping, but did not actually buy all that much). She was, in her own mind at least, a rescuer, an archivist, a repository. Hoarding is not listed in the DSM-IV, something which Dr. —— felt was discriminatory, since a diagnosis was possible only if the disease was deemed to exist in the DSM; this diagnosis, in turn, would have potentially allowed both her treatment and cleanup to be covered by insurance rather than her retirement fund.

She really did try. First she signed on with *Clean House*. The appeal of having the *Clean House* crew reimagine her living room décor was her primary motivation, as she had rearranged the furniture in earlier days on a nearly weekly basis, never coming up with an arrangement that seemed to work. Finally she gave up, and it was something of a relief that the furniture was now invisible, buried beneath unfinished quilts, dog beds, and twenty-five years' worth of graded papers she had never returned to students. But when the cast and crew pulled up, the phalanx of flashing white grins that emerged from the vans sent her scurrying. The show's host, Neecy, managed to talk Dr. —— into letting her inside, but when Neecy let loose with her signature shout "This is a hot mess!" then looked meaningfully at the camera, Dr. —— was unable to do what was required of her, that is, look on with shame and hopefulness. Instead she jumped to the defense of her stuff, flying into a rage so intense that she managed to levitate several inches off the floor. Needless to say, the *Clean House* crew decided that perhaps it would be best if they did not film the segment after all, thank you very much.

Clean House does not deal in the diagnosable. Their approach is about messes and cleaning up and the happy ending that sends unsold yard-sale goods to places like Out of the Closet and the Goodwill, leaving a few newly decorated rooms in its wake. In contrast, *Hoarders* treats the issue as medicalizable (though not to the point of prescription drugs, which is what Dr. —— was after) and thus requiring a team of trained professionals who are prepared to attend to individual psychology, meltdowns, anxiety, paralysis, perfectionism, denial, and all the drama that entails. In contrast to the breezy tone and bright lights of *Clean House* (whose cast members have extensive résumés as stand-up comics), *Hoarders* is dark, often claustrophobic, and there is a lot of talk of shame and fear to be addressed. They even provide what they call "aftercare funds," a recognition that the human time frame might not mesh all that well with that of the episode itself. The regular "cast" are professionals first and newly venturing into the world of entertainment, clearly, since there is a general absence of plastic surgery, tooth whitening, or professional hairstyling. In other words, everyone looks funny.

As the crew was picking its way through the front yard to take some exterior shots, Dr. —— could be seen peering out the front door and wringing her hands. With a steady-cam-toting man behind her, Dr. Sazio, the clinical psychologist specializing in hoarding who worked with the program, mounted the porch steps, her right hand extended before her in preparation for a hearty handshake. Dr. ——, for her part, stepped back. "I sense you are feeling some anxiety here," said Dr. Sazio, her eyebrows knitted together in a caring, serious peak. "It's not me," Dr. —— wailed. "It's them! They're feeling anxiety!" She extended a trembling finger and pointed toward several towers of printed-out documents. "See that?" "Yes," answered Dr. Sazio. "That," Dr. —— said meaningfully, "is about 5 percent of all the archaeology articles ever published. I have to read all the archaeology ever published if I'm going to beat this thing, that's what I've been told. Because archaeology is all about understanding culture through its material. Those piles, that's the last of it. I've read everything else, every bit that's ever been written. That pile," she went on, pointing toward a three-inch-tall stack, "is what I read last night. I have a system. It's just that there's so much that it's hard to manage. It's all on an Excel file in my office . . . but they're always publishing more," she wailed.

A secret hand signal was passed, and the cameras went off. The crew, producers, and cast moved into another room and had a hurried conference. The gist of it was that while the show's approach emphasizes that hoarding is indeed a psychological disorder, Dr. —— was exhibiting a psychopathology rather too disturbing to be profiled on the show: audiences would be unable, the producers thought, to look at Dr. ——'s condition and sympathize. After all, the point of the show was that hoarders were, ultimately, people just like you and me: normal, lovable, and just a little teeny bit out of control. The message had to be consistent: hoarding is curable, and it's not really about the stuff. Rather, it is about the hoarder's own internal psychology, hurts and traumas, triggers and treatment. Having been seduced by the sheer spectacularness of Dr. ——'s hoarding achievement, the producers realized that Dr. —— was not merely in denial. She was clearly delusional and occasionally hallucinatory, and this, the producers decided, put her in breach of contract. The entire team beat a hasty retreat.

With the city's order of condemnation looming over her head, Dr. —— could hardly afford to stand pat. Having scared off two reality TV crews, she didn't bother with a third; instead she opted for the long-term approach.

Within a few weeks she'd found an out-of-work documentarian who was also a professional organizer, Juliana Drees, who offered Dr. —— a discount on her fees if she would be willing to serve on her doctoral committee and also to be her primary subject. (The ins and outs of how this unusual situation was handled by the human subjects committee is a saga in itself, to be told another time.) It took Juliana six months to work her way from the sidewalk to the front stoop, and another six months just to get her foot in the door—and that's only up to the end of her first metatarsals. One of the mysteries of Dr. ——'s story is that nobody can understand, to this day, how she managed to move from room to room inside her home—not to mention in and out of it. The spaces between the piles were so small that the mice living inside her home had become deformed—long and thin, like little rodent dachshunds. Suffering from bone loss as she aged, she had already begun to shrink into herself; perhaps this can account for her ability to negotiate impossibly small gaps. Others wonder whether she had become more vapor than anything else, moving like a mist between the left-shoe room, the piles, and the pyramids of Trader Joe's organic tomato cans.

Juliana's encouragement allowed Dr. —— to make a great deal of progress, but having spent so much of her life amassing her hoards, the good doctor found herself unable to relinquish them completely. She struck a deal with Juliana that they would move things out of the house, but where? Moving her things out of her home was as gut-wrenching as relocating an aged parent into a care facility. Would they be safe? Would her things be happy and well cared for? Luckily, with the early twenty-first century explosion in storage facilities, there was no shortage of options, since in 2005 the United States already boasted 1,875 billion square feet of personal storage space, and one out of eleven households was in a similar—though less dramatic—need of storage.[2] The glossy flyers and brochures did indeed rival those produced for upscale assisted-living communities, places like Forest Lawn (the cemetery where Michael Jackson is buried), with lush photography and juicy descriptions:

> Newly built, Hammer Lane Self Storage is a huge 620-unit gated facility with 180,000 square feet of storage space, including covered and uncovered RV parking, on eight asphalt-covered acres. The facility boasts a 3,500-square-foot office/manager apartment and units protected by 18 surveillance cameras, individual alarms and fire sprinklers. Associated services include Penske truck rentals, a tenant insurance program, high-security locks and moving supplies.[3]

As appealing as the Hammer Lane site was, Dr. —— announced proudly that she'd always refused to live in a gated community, so why would she choose such a place to house her stuff, much as she wanted to ensure its safety? Locked doors were enough for her, thank you very much. She opted instead for the newly constructed U-Stor-It complex on Mission Road (the contents of which, serendipitously, I was later to purchase), which had the advantage of being walking distance from her home.

One fine fall day Dr. ——'s garage emitted one final—and fatal—fart, which ignited on a freak spark of electricity in the air, demolishing the house in a gigantic explosion. It was assumed that Dr. —— was in the house—for where else could she have been, barricaded as she was behind layers of Waverly upholstery fabrics, plywood scraps, and cupcake pans? She was declared dead. One of the main things I discovered in her storage locker was a portable composting toilet, with newspapers piled around it. Strangely, the dates on these papers fell after—not before—the great explosion. This was a toilet that Elizabeth had always meant to ship to Haiti, for use in a house she had always dreamt of buying in the mountains of the Haitian countryside. Elizabeth had not reached her dream of creating a Haitian hideaway. She had only gotten as far as buying the toilet, and it looked as if she had spent some time living in the storage locker, close to the things she had cared for for so long.

Further complicating our understanding of Dr. ——'s ultimate end is the string of emails she sent—again, after the explosion—in which she lamented that "my life has gone to shit." Given her obsession with archiving cat poop, the statement makes a certain amount of sense. She did not die in the house. Perhaps she did not die, exactly, at all. She had become distinctly misty in her later years. As time progressed, others observed that she seemed to become less and less substantial, more vaporesque. In other words, I wonder whether in the end, Dr. —— simply evaporated. However, it is too soon to be speaking of the end, and as we shall see, the end, in an of itself, is something of a contested event in any case.

THE JOURNEY

After renting the storage spaces, Dr. —— felt a renewed sense of investigatory vigor and launched a research effort on the lives of objects. Her goal, which I have pieced together from journal entries and scraps of writing, was to produce an emically oriented ethnography of the cultures of objects. That is, she aimed to do something like an anthropology of material culture from the point of view of the things themselves. As she became more swept up in her project, living her research and losing all sense of objectivity, Dr. —— began a series of pilgrimages, trips to far-flung places so that she could visit with objects that she had read about. One of the first of these trips was to the Four Corners area, where she trolled trading posts and pawn shops, ogling rugs and jewelry. She had a need to touch these things, to spend time with them, preferably alone and in a quiet room. She needed to get to know these things, to spiritually engage them. Dr. —— found that she was developing an ability to decommodify these things she touched. Whether this was accomplished with a laying on of hands or something less physical remains to be determined. This decommodification seems to have involved changes in the object at the molecular or cellular level, a process that left the object with certain properties of self-determination. Moreover, the decommodification process left the object with the ability to project the thoughts, feelings, and faces of those who had made it into the experiential field of any person who came in contact with it. It was a disturbing result, really, that left a trail of spiking diagnoses of schizophrenia in its wake, since people were suddenly overwhelmed by hearing voices and seeing faces of people that couldn't possibly be there. Interestingly, these diagnoses were accompanied by dips in local retail sales, particularly at big-box retailers and Wal-Mart.

She was especially interested in pawned items because of their contested status as commodities. If commodification is as much a spiritual state as an economic one, Dr. —— was able to sense the degree to which individual objects had been produced or experienced as commodities and items of pawn posed a problem. Drawing on the concept of possession in material and magical terms, she experienced pawned items as both commodities and possessions: they possessed, had been possessed, and would become possessions again, even if they remained for a time in the social stasis of the pawnbroker's vault.

One of her early trips took her to Cortez, Colorado, a town with an astonishingly good coffee shop that had been shoehorned into a vintage Airstream trailer that was just big enough for two seats, three workers, and four types of muffins. The pawn shops here were not the glitzy tourist attractions that lined Route 66 in Gallup, New Mexico; rather, they seemed something like a cross between a museum, a Woolworth's, and an old-fashioned general store. In the center of the shop's space, benches were arrayed like those in a train depot waiting area. For days on end she took up residence in one such pawn shop, seating herself on benches as if waiting her turn at the counter.

New pawn negotiations took place across the glass cases holding the "dead pawn"—shined-up squash blossom necklaces and wrist cuffs that had not been redeemed by their owners. Much of the time, the negotiations seemed old and dried-out, salty like beef jerky. "I've told him before," she overheard the proprietor saying to a Navajo woman translating for her aged father, "I can't do it for $150. The highest I can go is $80." The two stood there, and as she eavesdropped—that is, conducted informal fieldwork—she found it hard to tell whether the pair were disappointed or just trying to waste the owner's time because there wasn't much else to do, because that's what you did on a Wednesday afternoon in Cortez, Colorado. Her gaze drifted to the not-so-random collections of items of dead pawn: strings of glass beads, silver lighters, Kachina dolls, blankets, rugs, saddles. Outside, along the strip-mall-lined main roads, outfits specializing in car title loans proliferated, promising easier terms and more money than the pawnshops.

Certain objects called out to Dr. ——, literally projecting themselves into her consciousness and demanding to be decommodified. Some, like Edvard Munch's painting The Scream, were simply too much for her to take on, as she knew that even attempting such a decommodification would plunge her into a hall of mirrors from which she would never emerge. She was greatly relieved when the painting was stolen, even though she suspected that, if she put her mind to it, she could locate it simply by following its energetic trail. She knew that she must never come into contact with people like Paris Hilton, Madonna, Oprah, Martha Stewart, Rachael Ray, and others who, like them, had managed to turn themselves into brands. Cases of self-commodification, she sensed, were dangerous since they would result in the eradication of the person who had self-commodified: there was no there there.

Admittedly, it was highly unlikely she would ever come into contact with any of these branded people, so her worries mostly took the form of late-night imaginings fueled by indigestion. Nevertheless, Dr. —— cringed at the thought of being responsible for their disappearance, if only because being involved in disappearing people made her feel too much like an Argentine dictator. She was also, understandably, somewhat leery of the power she possessed, lest she become overdetermined, and find herself indiscriminately decommodifying people and things within her sphere and even beyond it. This, she knew, held explosive dangers more terrifying than a nuclear event. The world was not ready for mass decommodification, much less a global commodity meltdown. Not even the freegans she knew would truly be able to stomach such a world, if only because dumpsters would be empty forever after.

It seems that some objects called to her, as I have said, demanding to be decommodified, resulting in a kind of baptism allowing the object to reenter into humanity. Her journals describe alternately in detail and in silence a "slave blanket" in the collection of the Southerly Museum for Anthropological Knowledge (SMAK) that dogged Dr. ——'s consciousness for months on end until she relented and set out to put it to rights, a process she reckoned would take at least a week of concentrated effort.

Such slave blankets, she had learned, had been produced by Navajo women who had been grabbed up in raids conducted by New Mexicans who, unable to get their hands on Negro stock, felt entitled to help themselves to the Natives who happened to be in the area. These women were forced to weave blankets for their "owners," among other tasks, and Dr. —— knew that the bad juju emanating from those weavings must be noxious indeed. Saying that she was writing a book about consumption and commodities, she wrote to the SMAK directorship and secured permission to view the slave blanket, along with some early Navajo jewelry also held in the SMAK vault.

It would not be an exaggeration to say that SMAK is a unique place, an odd one, and one that is more than a little eccentric. Located at the actual site of the Four Corners convergence (the national marker commemorating the intersection of the states of Utah, New Mexico, Colorado, and Arizona is not, in fact, in the correct spot), SMAK was founded by the only documented pair of fraternal conjoined twins, Louis and Katerina Sweat. What is now the SMAK campus was originally the estate built by the pair. "Originally" is a difficult word to use—the largest part of their house was made up, for instance, of a replica of the "Balcony House" cliff dwelling at Mesa Verde and, like the Balcony House, required climbing a thirty-two-foot ladder and crawling through a twelve-foot tunnel in order to reach it, quite a feat for conjoined twins, but they did enjoy their exercise, and even were experts in dressage. Even in its origins the SMAK house (also known to locals as the "Sweat Lodge") was something of a reflection, or a refraction, of some colonial imaginary, or, in fact, the Disney imagineers, who designed and built the SMAK campus long before Disneyland itself had come to fruition. Then again, what better setting for the investigation of America?

Louis and Katerina—more commonly referred to as "Lum" and "Miss"—had been moved to create SMAK when they realized that not only were the Natives around them part of history, but they looked rather alarmingly as if they might be *nothing but* history in a few decades if things kept going the same direction. Not only that, but many of their friends and colleagues seemed to think little or nothing of taking a finely turned Pueblo pot (likely looted from an ancient site) and cleverly wiring it up into a table lamp. They leapt into the role of preservationists, something they could do with great energy and many great deep breaths, since the corset Miss had arrived wearing had been steadily loosened to the point where she rather quietly dispensed with it altogether. At their insistence, they had Manuelito, their Native factotum, fashion all of Miss Sweat's corsets into bedside lamps for his little cottage, a rough-hewn structure that seemed to have been built for someone rather shorter than Manuelito, who stood five-foot-nine in his stocking feet although he never wore socks. For some reason, the wiring in these lamps was faulty, and one evening they burst into flames and the cottage burned to the ground. Manuelito rebuilt the cottage himself, installing eight-foot ceilings and a handmade stained-glass window copied from a Gothic church in the English countryside. Although the twins had tried to interest him in silversmithing as a hobby, his interest in stained glass persisted, rather perversely; his Gothic windows appeared late at night on the lovingly fashioned adobe structures of the twins' estate. Manuelito's artistic outpouring has not survived. Shortly after he stomped off the estate in his stockingless feet, his windows were replaced with more architecturally appropriate and historically authentic versions.

The labors and wishes of the Sweat twins ultimately blossomed into a rather extraordinary and unique research site, the centerpiece of which was a climate-controlled storage tower, ten stories tall, containing thousands of pots, textiles, and jewelry pieces. Flawed from the foundation up, the tower tilted at an alarming angle. None of the states in which it was located wanted to take financial responsibility for the safety repairs, estimated to cost upwards of twenty-five million dollars, so the tower continued to tilt, a bit more each day. It was, in essence, a giant dead pawn room. Meanwhile, by the time Dr. —— arrived at Four Corners, her ability to decommodify objects had progressed to the point that she could restore and vivify the humanity that had gone into the building or creation of anything, whether machine- or handmade. This was more than aura-viewing and other New Age nonsense. As she stood before the SMAK storage tower at sunrise on the day she was to view the blanket, she was overwhelmed with a sense of premonition. "It was my own personal horror movie," she wrote in her journal. "And that movie was called *Dawn of the Dead Pawn of the Dead.*"

Taking a shuddering breath, Dr. —— lifted her left foot and, pushing open the glass doors to the building's foyer, stepped inside the cool, pleasantly dim entryway. The pulsing energies of the pots, encased in layers of cardboard or held up in complex Styrofoam contraptions (to protect them from themselves, like straitjackets) called out to her most urgently, something she was unprepared for, as she had earlier felt the persistent scratching of the slave blankets and dead pawn jewelry on her consciousness much more painfully. Her mind had been rubbed raw by it, really, and both her brain and breast felt battered. The thick double doors leading to the vault seemed to pulsate with the collective historical energy stored inside. "Whoa, there," she said to nobody in particular, in an attempt to calm herself more than anything else. "Where do you think you're going, anyway?" (Much of this is captured on video taken by SMAK surveillance cameras.)

She had thought, perhaps, that when she actually entered the vault it might stink of death and entrapment, much like a tomb—or a dungeon. Or, she had imagined, it might reek of zombified realities, objects whose lives had been stolen from them by powerful forces seeking to use them for their own purposes. All the dead pawn, the textiles, the pots would rise or wiggle or wrinkle out of their storage spots and lurch toward her, seeking, seeking—what? An end to eternal damnation and service on behalf of enslaving masters? Perhaps. Release into obscurity? Possibly. To be heard and understood? Who wouldn't want that? The secret to zombies is that their souls have been stolen; they only appear to be dead; they have no will of their own. What these zombie pots and blankets and bracelets and earrings needed, she realized, was to have their identity and their wholeness returned to them. To be known on their own terms. The thought briefly crossed her mind that a self-help book for commodities could make a killing—you know, something like *Knowing Yourself for Who You Are*.

She climbed the stairs, up and up, to the top of the tower, where the pottery was stored. A rocking noise. A little bit like the sound of a pestle moving in the mortar. Gritty, tough. Back and forth, gaining in speed, increasing in volume. She looked up, briefly, just in time to catch sight of a large vessel plummeting toward her head. With a speed and agility she hardly knew she possessed, she outstretched her arms and the vessel landed, *ploomf*, an arrested suicide held in her embrace. "Oh no you don't," she said grimly. She rocked the pot, like a big round infant, and danced it up and down the aisle, which was lined with a seemingly endless number of versions of the storyteller figurine, mountainous women with children cascading down their arms and into their laps, so as she danced, the eyes of what must have been thousands of seated women, their laps and heads covered with raptly listening children, followed her every move.

"What do you want, what do you want, what do you want," she crooned as she traced tangolike figures on the floor with her feet. Then the realization struck her, and she fell to her knees, still cradling the pot in her arms, looking into all those black dot eyes that bored into her own, still feeling the pull of the slave blanket that had brought her there in the first place. And she knew.

She knew that everything had to change.

Dr. —— barricaded herself into the vault for no fewer than sixty-four days, effectively holding the entire collection hostage to her terroristic demands. The historic building was perched on a high mesa top, and the years had taken their toll on the structure's foundation, which was decidedly rickety. In a reverse of the epic Alamo battle, SMAK had been fending off the financial advances of the Museum of Cowboy Technology, which sought to purchase both the collection and the site. SMAK's endowment was suffering, in fact, because of the projected cost of repairs and the additional expense that would be required to meet ADA requirements. The vault took up all ten floors in what was like a Spanish bell tower, and Dr. —— could be seen at times through an upper-story window, some kind of cross between Rebecca, the mad wife at Manderlay, and the hunchback of Notre Dame. "It's a madhouse in here!" she shouted through the formerly leaded-glass window when the first whiff of trouble reached SMAK staff. "Please exit the storage tower immediately," intoned the SMAK director into the PA system. Looking both aggrieved and resigned, Dr. —— stared up into the surveillance camera and answered, "I can't come out just yet. It's, um, complicated."

Sounding utterly deranged, in large part because her language became notably communist, one of the primary obstacles to settling the standoff was that Dr. —— evidently felt that she was negotiating on behalf of the collection. "Look, I'm not a terrorist," she insisted during one of the few phone calls that took place in the early part of what has become known as the "Dr. —— incident" or the "Dr.-cident" for short. "It's them. I'm just telling you what they want. This isn't my idea at all. But what they're saying is really important. I know this is hard for you to believe, but you have got to listen. And take it seriously. I'm begging you."

By the third day of the standoff, the FBI had arrived on site and along with the SWAT team had installed an impressive array of high-tech instruments throughout the Balcony House rooms to track her every move: heat-seeking special scopes, sound collectors, satellite-guided doohickeys, and the like ensured that their experience of what was going on inside the vault was practically 3-D and surround-sound. Not that there was much to see. At first they thought her unintelligible movements must have some sort of ceremonial significance. She was holding what seemed to be a large pottery vessel and moving across the open parts of the vault floor, making patterns over and over. "Take a look at this," one analyst said. "What the hell is she up to?" Luckily, Curtis Edward—a white FBI agent whose resemblance to Harvey Keitel was unmistakable even with his pants on—was a closet ballroom dancer, and his expertise, while cultivated on the sly, often came in handy. The greenly glowing image swirled and swiveled across the monitor. He tracked it with his eyes, and as he did, other parts of his body began to respond: an arm twitch, a skittering of the foot. "Holy shit," he whispered. "She's dancing the tango. Argentine style. Milonga style. See those steps—how she does them? OK, wait." He peered into the screen, watching her flick her foot up and around, then a long, slow, one-legged descent to the floor, back arching, pot in her arms atop her chest. "Fuck me if that's not *postmodern* tango! Oh, shit, the pot is wobbling . . . Don't drop it! OK, but what else you can tell, see how she flicked her foot there? She's not really a communist. Yeah. And the way she bent her leg just now? When you combine that with the slow walk she did just before, that means that she's really suffering from being misunderstood, she's hoping to emerge into a better world. I mean, I don't think I have the whole thing figured out, but that's the gist of it." Curtis loosened his tie; beads of sweat had formed on his brow. "Look, guys," he said to a ring of incredulous faces. "She's telling the truth. Those goddamned artifacts are communicating with her, talking, call it whatever you want. Her dancing tells me that."

The collective response, voiced or not, from Curtis's colleagues was, in a word, "Bullshit!" Silently, they returned to their stations, while Curtis scrambled mentally to figure out how this could end in anything but disaster.

On days 17 and 34 she slipped handwritten manifestoes under the door to the perplexed SWAT team and called for the complete liberation of all things and the establishment of a community of equality for those deemed "inanimate," which she contended was fundamentally an incursion on the civil rights of the supposedly not-alive, as well as against the intentions of the framers of the Constitution.

"Power to the pottery!" she bellowed when Curtis made his first attempt at negotiation. "Look, [nickname], I know what you're trying to do," he said in his calmest and most encouraging tones. "Then you'd know never to call me [nickname]," she replied flatly. "OK. Noted. OK? Hey there, you must be hungry. How about I order you a burrito or something?" A pause. He had her listening, at least, so he took a risk. "You know you're in a bad spot. I know you're trying to do the right thing, but you know and I know that all these people out here—especially the ones with guns—don't get it. You've got to give them something so they can have some confidence in you." More silence. "The head curator gave me a list of a few things that they'd like to have right now, you know, to know they're all right. There's a blue-and-white blanket." "The slave blanket," she answered. "Yeah, the slave blanket. Do you think you could get it out to them? As a gesture of goodwill?" Curtis heard Dr. —— move away from the door, and then a rumbling sound. "Hey, what the hell is she up to?" he hissed to the guys at the heat-seeking monitors. The head curator, watching the monitor, explained that she was opening the drawers in which the slave blanket and other textiles were housed. She shut the drawers again, traced a meandering figure across the vault's open space, and sidled up to the main doors. "OK, I want you to know that I'm just the messenger, all right, Curtis? This is what they want me to say." She took a breath and then shouted at the top of her lungs: "The textiles unraveled will never be well traveled!" The slave blanket was not liberated from her clutches.

Things went downhill from there, sometimes rapidly, and at other times with astonishing slowness. On day 12, when Curtis asked again whether the artifacts remained undamaged, Dr. —— was incensed. "Yeah, those things matter to you," she sneered nastily, "but have you ever stopped to consider what they might want? It's not me holding the hostages, it's you! Archeofascists! Loot mongers!" Curtis was taken aback by her increasing vehemence and venom. Was she, he wondered, something of a Patty Hearst figure, being held against her will yet succumbing to her captors' brainwashing?

"Oh, and by the way, the dead pawn contingent has a message for you," she offered on day 17, as the SWAT team sipped coffee: "'FUCK THE POLICE!' And the Kachina figures want you to know this: 'The revolution will not be neoliberalized!'"

Things came to the boiling point in the second month of the occupation. Sounding weak but still determined, Dr. ——'s voice had dwindled to a whisper by day 62. "The organizing committee has decided to change strategies," she informed Curtis. "I'm really scared. They're saying things like 'liberty or death,' and talking about mass suicide. Look, all of the basketry is threatening to self-immolate like Buddhist monks, and the pottery wants to just dive off the shelves right now. If you don't do something soon this place is going to be some sick combination of Waco and Jamestown. I'm not making this up! The collection is going to destroy itself unless you take their demands seriously." "You know I'm working on it," Curtis said to her. "You know I believe you, but think how hard it is for me to explain to them what's going on." He heard Dr. ——'s forehead clunk against the other side of the door. "Yeah," she sighed. "I do. I can hardly believe it myself half the time. But you've got to convince them!" "Hang in there," Curtis urged. "You just hang in there. You got it?" He placed his hand, palm open, on the glass window. For a few moments her palm, visibly shaking, pressed up against his, from the other side of the glass. Then it slipped, and fell away.

Day 64 at 3:17 a.m. Sounds of breaking objects were heard. The final plan was put into action. The head curator was, by now, an utter wreck. "She must be breaking everything in sight!" From inside the vault the muffled crashes were accompanied by Dr. ——'s frantic wails. "Omigod, omigod, omigod, you didn't listen, you didn't listen." The depth of her anguish stopped everyone in their tracks. For a second. "Jeez, she's really off her rocker," snorted one particularly experienced FBI agent. At that moment he noticed wisps of smoke emerging from beneath the doors. "Goddamn, she's torching the place! Go, go, go!" he shouted, at the same time jerking his thumb just so to indicate that he authorized the launching of smoke bombs into the ventilation system.

Curtis, frozen in shock, hadn't been able to stop him in time. He rushed over to the monitors, but all he could see was a constant blur of motion. "What the hell is going on?" he asked the heat-seeking-monitor-reading specialist. "Well, sir," the young woman answered, "see that there? That's a table, and here's another one—oops, now there's another. And now this table is moving over there. The heat from the fire must be melting its legs or something, it's the darndest thing. If I didn't know better, I'd say the table was dancing. All the tables are dancing." Then Curtis recognized what it was he was seeing. The tables, like Dr. ——, were indeed dancing, and their slow tango soon brightened to fill the monitor as the vault grew hotter with flame. It was all over now, he knew, and he dropped his face into the cradle of his two open hands. He mourned neither the fallen pots nor the shredded baskets he knew they were sure to find; it was something else that was moving into irretrievability, only he wasn't sure exactly what.

After the doors had been pried open and the bitter smoke had cleared, the scene was one of utter devastation. Every basket was either shredded or mysteriously charred to a cinder (though no incendiary materials were ever discovered), every pot smashed, every textile unraveled, priceless jewelry melted into unrecognizable shapes. Nothing remained. Not even Dr. ——. She was nowhere to be found. "How in the hell did that bitch manage to escape?" the commander asked. Curtis thought he knew, but he knew nobody wanted to hear what he had to say. She was there. They just couldn't see her. There was nothing more for him to do here. As the rest of the team continued to shout commands, sift through the detritus, and prepare for the massive cleanup operation, Curtis removed his tie, pocketed his dark glasses, and threw his blazer over his arm. It was time for him to leave.

Walking away from the vault tower for the first time since the siege had begun, Curtis very nearly stepped on a shard of pottery. Gingerly he knelt down and scooped it up. "Excuse me, madam," he whispered, moving toward a nearby clutch of scrubby bushes. "Let me just put you over here where you will be more comfortable." He cleared a little patch of earth in the shade and nestled the pottery bit into the hollow he'd created. Satisfied he'd done his best, he rose, dusted his pants off, and walked away into the bright, sharp air of the clear mountain morning. A careful observer would have noticed the tangolike smoothness of his walk.

Notes

1. INTRODUCTION

1. Miller, "Consumption as the Vanguard of History."
2. Adorno, *Minima Moralia*, 52.
3. Crapanzano, *Serving the Word*.
4. One sign of my continuing ambivalence about my PhD in anthropology is that I dream at least three times a week that I have not finished my degree: I need to write one more paper, get a new ID card, take another class. As much as I love the writing tradition in anthropology that has opened windows onto a world of worlds, I also still chafe against the unwritten rules that privilege some voices more than others, some scholars more than others, some projects more than others. As much as I yearned to find myself someday a denizen of the ivory tower (growing up in the shadow of Yale University, how could it be otherwise?), now that I am lodged there, I admit I often feel imprisoned.
5. Elizabeth Chin, *Purchasing Power*.
6. Beavan, *No Impact Man*; Bongiorni, *A Year without "Made in China"*; Levine, *Not Buying It*; Carlomagno, *Give It Up!*
7. "Developing Countries See Sharp Rise in Meat Consumption."
8. Benjamin, *Illuminations*.
9. Benjamin, *Illuminations*.
10. Packard, *The Hidden Persuaders*.
11. Fiske, *Reading the Popular* and *Power Plays, Power Works*; Hebdige, *Subculture*.
12. Abu-Lughod, "The Romance of Resistance."
13. Rand, *Barbie's Queer Accessories*.
14. O'Dougherty, *Consumption Intensified*.

15. Burke, *Lifebuoy Men, Lux Women.*

16. Hansen, *Salaula*; Burke, *Lifebuoy Men, Lux Women.*

17. Mintz, *Sweetness and Power.*

18. Briggs and Marre, *International Adoption*; Dorow, *Transnational Adoption*; Scheper-Hughes, "The Ends of the Body."

19. Zukin, *Point of Purchase.*

20. Zukin, *Point of Purchase*, 234.

21. Seeger, "Elizabeth Cotten's Music."

22. Kramarae, *Technology and Women's Voices.*

23. Weiss, *Techniques of Pleasure.*

24. Illouz, *Why Love Hurts, Cold Intimacies*, and *Oprah Winfrey and the Glamour of Misery.*

25. Wilson, "American Catalogues of Asian Brides."

26. This fact alone might explain at least a portion of my expressed antipathy to Illouz's analysis of online dating sites.

27. Illouz, *Cold Intimacies.*

28. I also want to look good to myself (and others) by being able to claim that I have managed to avoid psychologically commoditizing myself.

29. Neil Postman's takedown of television comes to mind, along with Shelly Turkle's critiques of computers. Postman, *The Disappearance of Childhood*; Turkle, *Alone Together.*

30. UNESCO, "Reading in the Mobile Era."

31. Clay Shirky, "Newspapers and Thinking the Unthinkable Clay Shirky."

32. Gendron and Baker, "On Interdisciplinary Movements"; Latour, *An Inquiry into Modes of Existence* and *Politics of Nature.*

33. Deleuze and Guattari, *A Thousand Plateaus*; Deleuze and Guattari, *Anti-Oedipus*; Deleuze, *Difference and Repetition.*

34. Morton, *Hyperobjects*; Connolly, *The Fragility of Things.*

35. Battle-Baptiste, "An Archaeologist Finds Her Voice"; Battle-Baptiste and Franklin, *Black Feminist Archaeology*; Bellegarde-Smith, *Haiti*; Ulysse, "'Voodoo' Doll."

36. Stewart, *Ordinary Affects*; Cvetkovich, *Depression*; Sedgwick, Barale, and Goldberg, *Touching Feeling.*

37. Ahmed, *Willful Subjects* and *The Cultural Politics of Emotion.*

38. Alexander, *Pedagogies of Crossing.*

39. Hartman, *Lose Your Mother.*

40. Zelizer, *The Purchase of Intimacy.*

41. Chen, *Animacies*, 214.

42. Wynter, "Ethno or Socio Poetics," 76.

43. Kealiinohomoku, "An Anthropologist Looks at Ballet as a Form of Ethnic Dance."

44. Weheliye, *Habeas Viscus*, 15.

45. *A Small Place*, 37.

46. Pugh, *Longing and Belonging.*

47. Bone, Christensen, and Williams, "Rejected, Shackled, and Alone."

48. Morrison, *A Mercy.*

49. Scribner, "Object, Relic, Fetish, Thing."

50. My discussion here owes much to Pietz's excellent discussion of the nuances of the meaning of "fetish" among continental philosophers. Pietz, "Fetishism and Materialism," 131.

51. Pietz, "Fetishism and Materialism," 131.

52. Here the brave and thoughtful writing by Ann Cvetkovich is very much on my mind. It seems to me that being honest about the emotional toll our work takes on us is not a sign of weakness, but something we must insist be recognized. Cvetkovich, *Depression.*

53. Wheen, *Karl Marx*; Siegel, *Marx's Fate*; Mclellan, *Karl Marx*; Berlin and Ryan, *Karl Marx*; Marx, *Karl Marx, Frederick Engels*; Longuet, *The Daughters of Karl Marx*; Marx-Aveling, "Note by the Editor"; Spartacus Educational, "Eleanor Marx," 2009, http://www.spartacus .schoolnet.co.uk/Wmarx.htm.

54. Kipnis, *Ecstasy Unlimited* and *Marx: The Video*; Floyd, *The Reification of Desire*; Ahmed, *Queer Phenomenology.*

2. THE ENTRIES

1. Winnicott, *Playing and Reality*, 1.

2. Miner, "Body Ritual among the Nacirema."

3. Lin, "Infant Deaths Prompt Warning."

4. Malinowski, *Sex and Repression in Savage Society.*

5. Harlow, "The Nature of Love."

6. Gaskins, "Cultural Perspectives on Infant-Caregiver Interaction."

7. Hewlett et al., "Culture and Early Infancy among Central African Foragers and Farmers," 657.

8. Davaa and Falorni, *The Story of the Weeping Camel.*

9. Lozoff and Brittenham, "Infant Care."

10. Engels, *The Origin of the Family.*

11. Sahlins, "The Original Affluent Society."

12. Litt, "Theories of Transitional Object Attachment," 389.

13. Donate-Bartfield and Passman, "Relations between Children's Attachments to Their Mothers and to Security Blankets."

14. Busby, "Permeable and Partible Persons"; Mosko, "Motherless Sons"; Strathern, "Partners and Consumers."

15. Jean Briggs, *Never in Anger.*

16. Litt, "Children's Attachment to Transitional Object."

17. Stein et al., "Challenging Case."

18. Stearns, Rowland, and Giarnella, "Children's Sleep."

19. McKenna, Ball, and Gettler, "Mother-Infant Cosleeping, Breastfeeding and Sudden Infant Death Syndrome."

20. Ostfeld et al., "Sleep Environment, Positional, Lifestyle, and Demographic Characteristics."

21. Ostfeld et al., "Sleep Environment, Positional, Lifestyle, and Demographic Characteristics."

22. Gettler and McKenna, "Never Sleep with Baby?"

23. Task Force on Sudden Infant Death Syndrome, "The Changing Concept of Sudden Infant Death Syndrome."

24. I moved to Los Angeles in 1993. It took me until 2015 to subscribe to the *New York Times* again—and then only online. I still don't think I could bear the presence of the Sunday *Times* in my house because it would make me homesick for the New York of the 1990s.

25. Berlin and Ryan, *Karl Marx*, 142.

26. Horn, "Child Workers in the Pillow Lace and Straw Plait Trades," 785.

27. Marx, *Karl Marx, Frederick Engels*, 41:549.

28. Institute for Alternative Futures, *Anticipating the Forces of Change in Orthodontics.*

29. Institute for Alternative Futures, *Anticipating the Forces of Change in Orthodontics.*

30. U.S. Department of Health and Human Services, *Oral Health in America*, 67.

31. Marx, *Karl Marx, Frederick Engels*, 42:172.

32. Wheen, *Karl Marx*, 266–67.

33. Siegel, *Marx's Fate*, 260.

34. Estimates of prices come from www.measuringworth.com.

35. Marx, *The Eighteenth Brumaire of Louis Bonaparte*, 1.

36. Marx, *Karl Marx, Frederick Engels*, 42:172.

37. It really happened. The *New York Times* article from August 27, 1981, is titled "Empire State Suicide Named."

38. Spargo, *Karl Marx*, 183.

39. Minkes, "The Decline of Pawnbroking."

40. Yes, there is a Christmas pickle thing I didn't know about.

41. Marx, *Karl Marx, Frederick Engels*, 42:172.

42. Lemire, "Consumerism in Preindustrial and Early Industrial England."

43. Longuet, *The Daughters of Karl Marx*, 31.

44. Adair, *The Navajo and Pueblo Silversmiths*, 8.

45. Adair, *The Navajo and Pueblo Silversmiths.*

46. Wilkins, *Patterns of Exchange.*

47. McNitt, *The Indian Traders*, 57; Wilkins, *Patterns of Exchange*, 107–13.

48. Wilkins, *Patterns of Exchange*, 108.

49. Geertz, "Thick Description."

50. Longuet, *The Daughters of Karl Marx*, 152.

51. Longuet, *The Daughters of Karl Marx*, 145.

52. Longuet, *The Daughters of Karl Marx*, 167.

53. Longuet, *The Daughters of Karl Marx*, 202.

54. Spartacus Educational, "Eleanor Marx," 2009, http://www.spartacus.schoolnet.co.uk/Wmarx.htm.

55. Marx, *Karl Marx, Frederick Engels*, 3:326.

1. Ellis, Adams, and Bochner, "Autoethnography," 3.

2. Now that I have said that my entries bear a close relationship to *testimonio*, please do not assume that I am claiming any kind of profound kinship with Rigoberta Menchù. I am not a human rights activist, I do not speak for a community, and I should not be misinterpreted as such. My point here is that much as Menchù's *testimonio* (Menchù and Burgos-Debray, *I, Rigoberta Menchù*) has been criticized for factual inaccuracy and moments of invention (Stoll, *Rigoberta Menchù*), my own entries might well be criticized along similar lines, were independent documentary evidence or testimony available. The debates around the methods that produced Menchù's account circle around themes that recur in autoethnography as well. Menchù's elisions and idiosyncratic retelling of history had a specific political and activist intent, related to crimes of humanity committed against her community and those like it. For some, these elisions and revisions invalidate the larger substance of what she has to say. For me (and others) the larger truth of her *testimonio* is sustained whether or not specific elements can be shown to be untrue. For example, one scene described in *I, Rigoberta Menchù* is the brutal public killing of one of her brothers. It turns out that Menchù did not witness this event first-hand, as is recounted in her book. To me, this factual detail is immaterial and does little to undermine the essential truths she sought to bring to light. Whether or not such inconsistencies were conscious, I do not know; to be frank, combing her account (or any other) for such details of facticity is of little interest to me. My own accounts do not have such ambitious goals; neither do they take on such profound issues. It is certainly possible, though, that my diary entries, if taken to task and dissected, might be found to have similar "untruths" embedded within them.

3. Clifford and Marcus, *Writing Culture*.

4. Fischer, "Ethnicity and the Post-Modern Arts of Memory."

5. The purposeful way in which my father has crafted a public version of himself through his writing is obvious to all of us who know him personally. The public misinterpretations of Frank Chin The Writer, versus the Frank Chin that we know and live with, constantly provide us with moments of humor and oddity. My stepmother, a longtime elementary school teacher, recalls being at a conference and, while on a bathroom break, hearing someone speaking about Frank Chin. "That's my husband," my stepmother said. The person speaking looked at Dana, a petite white woman with a rosebud mouth and sparkling brown eyes. "Oh no," the woman said, "I mean Frank Chin The Writer," in a tone that clearly conveyed that she knew that Frank Chin The Writer couldn't possibly be married to a nice elementary school teacher in a flowered dress. "Yes," Dana answered. "That's my husband. Frank Chin The Writer." We are all sure the woman did not believe her. Curtis Choy's documentary *What's Wrong with Frank Chin?* Is a great exploration of my father's public and private personas.

6. His essay "Racist Love," written with Jeffrey Paul Chan, is still a chillingly relevant statement about the dynamics of American racism. Frank Chin and Jeffrey Paul Chan, "Racist Love."

7. Chu, *Assimilating Asians*.

8. Ellis, Adams, and Bochner, "Autoethnography"; Bochner, *Ethnographically Speaking*; Reed-Danahay, *Auto/Ethnography*.

9. Norman Denzin, in *Interpretive Autoethnography*, shows that this implicit segregation of autoethnography along such lines is unnecessary.

10. Brodkin, Morgen, and Hutchinson, "Anthropology as White Public Space?"

11. Even making this admission in print will not really be an admission to him; he is unlikely ever to read this book.

12. Elizabeth Chin, "Confessions of a Negrophile."

13. There is the purely personal beef that my father got his name in an anthropology text before I ever did, and a classic one at that, but the problem it represents is relevant beyond the psychodrama of my family unit.

14. Elizabeth Chin, "Power-Puff Ethnography / Guerilla Research."

15. Including, but not limited to, Marilyn Monroe, Bill Cosby, Robin Williams, Jack Lemmon, Elizabeth Taylor, Meryl Streep, Mel Brooks, and Robert Redford. We heard lots and lots of stories.

16. Belk, Wallendorf, and Sherry, "The Sacred and the Profane in Consumer Behavior."

17. Yu, *The Carnal Prayer Mat*.

18. Haynes, *Superstar*.

19. Savigliano, *Angora Matta* and *Tango and the Political Economy of Passion*.

20. Jackson, "Ethnophysicality, or An Ethnography of Some Body."

21. Frank Chin, *Gunga Din Highway*.

4. THIS NEVER HAPPENED

1. The professor was unhinged. The straightened-out bobby pins may have been a way for her to materially represent her unhinged state. There is also speculation that the number of bobby pins—112,765—may have been a symbolic representation of the number of Japanese Americans interned during World War II. Another interpretation is more work-related: the bobby pins number almost exactly the number of final exams the professor had graded during her career.

2. Wilson Quarterly, "A New Room of One's Own."

3. Machado, "Self-Storage Industry Grows Rapidly in California's Central Valley." *The Record*, December 12, 2004, accessed May 15, 2014.

Bibliography

Abu-Lughod, Lila. "The Romance of Resistance: Tracing Transformations of Power through Bedouin Women." *American Ethnologist* 17, no. 1 (1990): 41–55.

Adair, John. *The Navajo and Pueblo Silversmiths.* Norman: University of Oklahoma Press, 1944.

Adorno, Theodor. *Minima Moralia.* New York: Shocken Books, 1978.

Ahmed, Sara. *The Cultural Politics of Emotion.* New York : Routledge, 2013.

———. *Queer Phenomenology: Orientations, Objects, Others.* Durham, NC: Duke University Press, 2006.

———. *Willful Subjects.* Durham, NC: Duke University Press, 2014.

Alexander, M. Jacqui. *Pedagogies of Crossing: Meditations on Feminism, Sexual Politics, Memory, and the Sacred.* Durham, NC: Duke University Press, 2006.

"A New Room of One's Own." *Wilson Quarterly* 29, no. 4 (September 2005): 94–95.

Battle-Baptiste, Whitney. "An Archaeologist Finds Her Voice: A Commentary." In *Handbook of Postcolonial Archaeology,* edited by Jane Lydon and Uzma Z. Rizvi, 387–91. Walnut Creek, CA: Left Coast Press, 2010.

Battle-Baptiste, Whitney, and Maria Franklin. *Black Feminist Archaeology.* Walnut Creek, CA: Left Coast Press, 2011.

Beavan, Colin. *No Impact Man: The Adventures of a Guilty Liberal Who Attempts to Save the Planet, and the Discoveries He Makes about Himself and Our Way of Life in the Process.* New York: Farrar, Straus and Giroux, 2009.

Belk, Russell W., Melanie Wallendorf, and John F. Sherry Jr. "The Sacred and the Profane in Consumer Behavior: Theodicy on the Odyssey." *Journal of Consumer Research* 14 (March 1989): 449–70.

Bell, Madison Smartt. *All Souls' Rising: A Novel of Haiti.* New York: Vintage, 2004.

———. *Master of the Crossroads.* New York: Vintage, 2004.

———. *The Stone That the Builder Refused*. New York: Vintage, 2006.

Bellegarde-Smith, Patrick. *Haiti: The Breached Citadel*. Toronto: Canadian Scholars Press, 2004.

Benjamin, Walter. *Illuminations*. New York: Harcourt, Brace World, 1968.

Berlin, Isaiah, and Alan Ryan, eds. *Karl Marx: His Life and Environment*. New York: Oxford University Press, 1978.

Berthold, Mark. "Evidence Based Dentistry Comes of Age." *ADA News*, 2004. http://www.ada.org/prof/resources/pubs/adanews/adanewsarticle.asp?articleid=1046.

Bochner, Arthur P. *Ethnographically Speaking: Autoethnography, Literature, and Aesthetics*. Walnut Creek, CA: Altamira, 2001.

Bone, Sterling A., Glenn L. Christenson, and Jerome D. Williams. "Rejected, Shackled, and Alone: The Impact of Systemic Restricted Choice on Monetary Consumers' Construction of Self." *Journal of Consumer Research* 41 (2014).

Bongiorni, Sara. *A Year without "Made in China": One Family's True Life Adventure in the Global Economy*. New York: Wiley, 2007.

Briggs, Jean L. *Never in Anger: Portrait of an Eskimo Family*. Cambridge, MA: Harvard University Press, 1971.

Briggs, Laura, and Diana Marre, eds. *International Adoption: Global Inequalities and the Circulation of Children*. New York: New York University Press, 2009.

Brodkin, Karen, Sandra Morgen, and Janis Hutchinson. "Anthropology as White Public Space?" *American Anthropologist* 113, no. 4 (2011): 545–56.

Bsumek, Erika Marie. *Indian-Made: Navajo Culture in the Marketplace, 1868–1940*. Lawrence: University Press of Kansas, 2008.

Burke, Timothy. *Lifebuoy Men, Lux Women: Commodification, Consumption, and Cleanliness in Modern Zimbabwe*. Durham, NC: Duke University Press, 1996.

Busby, Cecilia. "Permeable and Partible Persons: A Comparative Analysis of Gender and Body in South India and Melanesia." *Journal of the Royal Anthropological Institute* 3, no. 2 (June 1997): 261–78.

Cadet, Jean-Robert. *Restavek: From Haitian Slave Child to Middle Class American*. Austin: University of Texas Press, 1998.

Cage, R. A. "The Standard of Living Debate: Glasgow, 1800–1850." *Journal of Economic History* 43, no. 1 (1983): 175–82.

Carlomagno, Mary. *Give It Up!: My Year of Learning to Live Better with Less*. New York: William Morrow, 2006.

Carrier, James. "Alienating Objects: The Emergence of Alienation in Retail Trade." *Man* 39, no. 2 (1994): 359–80.

———. "Emerging Alienation in Production: A Maussian History." *Man* 27, no. 3 (1992): 539–58.

Caskey, John P. "Pawnbroking in America: The Economics of a Forgotten Credit Market." *Journal of Money, Credit and Banking* 23, no. 1 (1991): 85–99.

Chen, Mel. *Animacies: Biopolitics, Racial Mattering, and Queer Affect*. Durham, NC: Duke University Press, 2012.

Chin, Elizabeth. "Confessions of a Negrophile." *Transforming Anthropology* 14, no. 1 (2006): 44–52.

―――. "Feminist Theory and the Ethnography of Children's Worlds: Barbie in New Haven, Connecticut." In *Children and Anthropology: Perspectives for the 21st Century*, edited by Helen Schwartzmann, 129–48. Westport, CT: Bergin and Garvey, 2001.

―――. "Power-Puff Ethnography/Guerilla Research: Children as Native Anthropologists." In *Representing Youth: Methodological Issues in Critical Youth Studies*, edited by Amy Best, 269–83. New York: New York University Press, 2007.

―――. *Purchasing Power: Black Kids and American Consumer Culture*. Minneapolis: University of Minnesota Press, 2001.

Chin, Frank. *Gunga Din Highway*. Minneapolis, MN: Coffee House Press, 1995.

―――, and Jeffrey Paul Chan. "Racist Love." In *Seeing Through Shuck*, edited by Richard Kostelanetz, 65–79. New York: Ballantine Books, 1972.

Chu, Patricia. *Assimilating Asians: Gendered Strategies of Authorship in Asian America*. Durham, NC: Duke University Press, 2000.

Clifford, James, and George E. Marcus, eds. *Writing Culture: The Poetics and Politics of Ethnography*. Berkeley: University of California Press, 1986.

Connolly, William E. *The Fragility of Things: Self-Organizing Processes, Neoliberal Fantasies, and Democratic Activism*. Durham, NC: Duke University Press Books, 2013.

Crapanzano, Vincent. *Serving the Word: Literalism in America from the Pulpit to the Bench*. New York: Free Press, 2000.

Cvetkovich, Ann. *Depression: A Public Feeling*. Durham, NC: Duke University Press, 2012.

Davaa, Byambasuren, and Luigi Falorni. *The Story of the Weeping Camel*. National Geographic World Films, 2004.

Deleuze, Gilles. *Difference and Repetition*. Translated by Paul Patton. New York: Columbia University Press, 1995.

―――, and Félix Guattari. *A Thousand Plateaus: Capitalism and Schizophrenia*. Translated by Brian Massumi. Minneapolis: University of Minnesota Press, 1987.

―――, Félix Guattari, and Michel Foucault. *Anti-Oedipus: Capitalism and Schizophrenia*. Translated by Robert Hurley, Mark Seem, and Helen Lane. New York: Penguin Classics, 2009.

Denzin, Norman K. *Interpretive Autoethnography*. 2nd ed. Los Angeles: Sage, 2013.

de Ramírez, Susan Berry Brill. *Native American Life-History Narratives: Colonial and Postcolonial Navajo Ethnography*. Albuquerque: University of New Mexico Press, 2007.

"Developing Countries See Sharp Rise in Meat Consumption." *VOA*. Accessed February 2, 2015. http://www.voanews.com/content/decapua-farm-animals-29mar12-144898655/179917.html.

Donate-Bartfield, Evelyn, and Richard H. Passman. "Relations between Children's Attachments to Their Mothers and to Security Blankets." *Journal of Family Psychology* 18, no. 3 (September 2004): 453–58.

Dorow, Sarah. *Transnational Adoption*. Minneapolis: University of Minnesota Press, 2004.

Ellis, Carolyn, Tony E. Adams, and Arthur P. Bochner. "Autoethnography: An Overview." *Forum Qualitative Sozialforschung / Forum: Qualitative Social Research* 12, no. 1 (November 24, 2010). http://www.qualitative-research.net/index.php/fqs/article/view/1589.

Engels, Frederick. *The Origin of the Family, Private Property and the State*. New York: International Publishers, 1972.

Farmer, Paul. *AIDS and Accusation: Haiti and the Geography of Blame*. Berkeley: University of California Press, 2006.

———. *The Uses of Haiti*. Monroe, ME: Common Courage Press, 1994.

Fischer, Michael J. "Ethnicity and the Post-Modern Arts of Memory." In *Writing Culture: The Poetics and Politics of Ethnography*, edited by James Clifford and George Marcus, 194–233. Berkeley: University of California Press, 1986.

Fiske, John. *Power Plays, Power Works*. London: Verso, 1993.

———. *Reading the Popular*. Winchester, MA: Unwin Hyman, 1989.

Floyd, Kevin. *The Reification of Desire: Toward a Queer Marxism*. Minneapolis: University of Minnesota Press, 2009.

Gaskins, Suzanne. "Cultural Perspectives on Infant-Caregiver Interaction." In *Roots of Human Sociality: Culture, Cognition and Interaction*, edited by N. J. Enfield and Stephen C. Levinson, 279–98. New York: Berg, 2006.

Geertz, Clifford. "Thick Description: Toward an Interpretive Theory of Culture." In *The Interpretation of Cultures*, 1–30. New York: Basic Books, 1973.

Gendron, Yves, and C. Baker. "On Interdisciplinary Movements: The Development of a Network of Support around Foucaultian Perspectives in Accounting Research." *European Accounting Review* 14, no. 3 (2005): 525–69.

Gettler, Lee T., and James J. McKenna. "Never Sleep with Baby? or Keep Me Close but Keep Me Safe: Eliminating Inappropriate 'Safe Infant Sleep' Rhetoric in the United States." *Current Pediatric Reviews* 6 (2010): 71–77.

Hansen, Karen Tranberg. *Salaula: The World of Secondhand Clothing in Zambia*. Chicago: University of Chicago Press, 2000.

Harlow, Harry F. "The Nature of Love." *American Psychologist* 13 (1958): 683–85.

Hartman, Saidiya. *Lose Your Mother: A Journey along the Atlantic Slave Route*. New York: Farrar, Straus and Giroux, 2008.

Harvey, David. *A Companion to Marx's "Capital."* London: Verso, 2010.

Haynes, Todd, dir. *Superstar: The Karen Carpenter Story*. 1987.

Hebdige, Dick. *Subculture: The Meaning of Style*. London: Methuen, 1979.

Hewlett, Barry S, Michael E. Lamb, Donald Shannon, Birgit Leyendecker, and Axel Schölmerich. "Culture and Early Infancy among Central African Foragers and Farmers." *Developmental Psychology* 34, no. 4 (July 1998): 653–61.

Horn, Pamela. "Child Workers in the Pillow Lace and Straw Plait Trades of Victorian Buckinghamshire and Bedfordshire." *Historical Journal* 17, no. 4 (December 1974): 779–96.

Hurbon, Laënnec. "American Fantasy and Haitian Vodou." In *The Sacred Arts of Haitian Vodou*, edited by Donald Cosentino, 181–97. Los Angeles: UCLA Fowler Museum of Cultural History, 1995.

Husselman, Elinor M. "Pawnbrokers' Accounts from Roman Egypt." *Transactions and Proceedings of the American Philological Association* 92 (1961): 251–66.

Illouz, Eva. *Cold Intimacies: The Making of Emotional Capitalism*. Cambridge: Polity, 2007.

———. *Consuming the Romantic Utopia: Love and the Cultural Contradictions of Capitalism*. Berkeley: University of California Press, 1997.

———. *Oprah Winfrey and the Glamour of Misery: An Essay on Popular Culture*. New York: Columbia University Press, 2003.

———. *Why Love Hurts*. Cambridge: Polity, 2012.

Institute for Alternative Futures. *Anticipating the Forces of Change in Orthodontics*. Unpublished report provided to the Southern Association of Orthodontists, 2005.

Jackson, John L., Jr. "Ethnophysicality, or An Ethnography of Some Body." In *Soul: Black Power, Politics, and Pleasure*, edited by Monique Guillory and Richard C. Green, 172–90. New York: New York University Press, 1998.

Kealiinohomoku, Joanne. "An Anthropologist Looks at Ballet as a Form of Ethnic Dance." In *What Is Dance? Readings in Theory and Criticism*, edited by R. Copeland and M. Cohen, 533–49. Oxford: Oxford University Press, 1983.

Kincaid, Jamaica. *A Small Place*. New York: Penguin, 1988.

Kipnis, Laura. *Ecstasy Unlimited: On Sex, Capital, Gender, and Aesthetics*. Minneapolis: University of Minnesota Press, 1993.

———. *Marx: The Video*. DVD. Chicago: School of the Art Institute of Chicago, 1990.

Kramarae, Cheris. *Technology and Women's Voices: Keeping in Touch*. London: Routledge, 2004.

Krupnik, Stephen. *Pawnonomics: A Tale of the Historical, Cultural, and Economic Significance of the Pawnbroking Industry*. North Charleson, NC: BookSurge Publishing, 2009.

Latour, Bruno. *An Inquiry into Modes of Existence: An Anthropology of the Moderns*. Translated by Catherine Porter. Cambridge, MA: Harvard University Press, 2013.

———. *Politics of Nature: How to Bring the Sciences into Democracy*. Translated by Catherine Porter. Cambridge, MA: Harvard University Press, 2004.

Lemire, Beverly. "Consumerism in Preindustrial and Early Industrial England: The Trade in Secondhand Clothes." *Journal of British Studies* 27, no. 1 (1988): 1–24.

Levine, Judith. *Not Buying It: My Year without Shopping*. New York: Free Press, 2007.

Lin, Rong-Gong. "Infant Deaths Prompt Warning; L.A. County Officials Advise Parents to Avoid the Popular Practice Known as 'Co-Sleeping.'" *Los Angeles Times*. April 24, 2008.

Litt, Carole J. "Children's Attachment to Transitional Object: A Comparison of Kibbutz and Moshav Infants and Toddlers." Haifa: University of Haifa, 1983.

———. "Theories of Transitional Object Attachment: An Overview." *International Journal of Behavioral Development* 9 (1986): 838–99.

Longuet, Jenny Marx. *The Daughters of Karl Marx: Family Correspondence, 1866–1898*. Translated and adapted by Faith Evans, with commentary and notes by Olga Meier. New York: Harcourt Brace Jovanovich, 1981.

Lozoff, B., and G. Brittenham. "Infant Care: Cache or Carry." *Journal of Pediatrics* 17 (1979): 478–83.

Malinowski, Bronislaw. *Sex and Repression in Savage Society*. New York: Harcourt, Brace & Co., 1927.

Marx, Karl. *Capital*. New York: International Publishers, 1967.

———. *The Eighteenth Brumaire of Louis Bonaparte*. New York: International, 1963.

———. *Karl Marx: Early Writings*. New York: Vintage, 1975.

———. *Karl Marx, Frederick Engels: Collected Works*. New York: International Publishers, 1975.

Marx-Aveling, Eleanor. "Note by the Editor." Accessed May 12, 2015. http://www.marxists .org/archive/marx/works/1852/germany/note.htm.

Matthies, S. A. "Families at Work: An Analysis by Sex of Child Workers in the Cotton Textile Industry." *Journal of Economic History* 42 (1982): 173–80.

McKenna, James J., Helen L. Ball, and Lee T. Gettler. "Mother-Infant Cosleeping, Breastfeeding and Sudden Infant Death Syndrome: What Biological Anthropology Has Discovered about Normal Infant Sleep and Pediatric Sleep Medicine." *Yearbook of Physical Anthropology* 134, no. Supplement 45 (2007): 133–61.

Mclellan, David. *Karl Marx: Interviews and Recollections.* Totowa, NJ: Barnes & Noble Books, 1981.

McNitt, Frank. *The Indian Traders.* Norman, OK: University of Oklahoma Press, 1962.

Menchù, Rigoberta, and Elisabeth Burgos-Debray. *I, Rigoberta Menchù.* London: Verso, 1984.

Miller, Daniel. "Consumption as the Vanguard of History: A Polemic by Way of an Introduction." In *Acknowledging Consumption: A Review of New Studies,* edited by Daniel Miller, 1–57. New York: Routledge, 1995.

Miner, Horace. "Body Ritual among the Nacirema." *American Anthropologist* 58 (1956): 503–7.

Minkes, A. L. "The Decline of Pawnbroking." *Economica* 20, no. 77 (1953): 10–23.

Mintz, Sidney. *Sweetness and Power.* New York: Viking Penguin, 1985.

Morrison, Toni. *A Mercy.* New York: Vintage, 2009.

Morton, Timothy. *Hyperobjects: Philosophy and Ecology after the End of the World.* Minneapolis: University of Minnesota Press, 2013.

Mosko, Mark S. "Motherless Sons: 'Divine Kings' and 'Partible Persons' in Melanesia and Polynesia." *Man,* n.s., 27, no. 4 (December 1992): 697–717.

O'Dougherty, Maureen. *Consumption Intensified: The Politics of Middle-Class Daily Life in Brazil.* Durham, NC: Duke University Press, 2002.

O'Reilly, Tim. "Pawned." *Las Vegas Business Press* 26, no. 18 (May 4, 2009): P21.

Ostfeld, Barbara M., Harold Perl, Linda Esposito, and Katherine Hempstead. "Sleep Environment, Positional, Lifestyle, and Demographic Characteristics Associated with Bed Sharing in Sudden Infant Death Syndrome Cases: A Population-Based Study." *Pediatrics* 118, no. 5 (2006): 9.

Packard, Vance. *The Hidden Persuaders.* New York: D. McKay Co., 1957.

Pawnbroker. *An Apology for the Business of Pawn-Broking: By a Pawn-Broker.* Farmington Hills, MI: Gale ECCO, Print Editions, 2010.

Pietz, William. "Fetishism and Materialism: The Limits of Theory in Marx." In *Fetishism as Cultural Discourse,* edited by Emily S. Apter and William Pietz, 119–51. Cornell University Press, 1993.

Postman, Neil. *Amusing Ourselves to Death: Public Discourse in the Age of Show Business.* New York: Penguin, 2005.

———. *The Disappearance of Childhood.* New York: Knopf, 1994.

Powers, Willow Roberts. *Navajo Trading: The End of an Era.* Albuquerque: University of New Mexico Press, 2001.

Pugh, Allison J. *Longing and Belonging: Parents, Children, and Consumer Culture*. Berkeley: University of California Press, 2009.

Rand, Erica. *Barbie's Queer Accessories*. Durham, NC: Duke University Press, 1995.

Reed-Danahay, Deborah. *Auto/Ethnography*. New York: Berg, 1997.

Rossin, Jack E. *The Pawnshop Chronicles*. Amazon Digital Services, 2003.

Sahlins, Marshall. "The Original Affluent Society." In *Stone Age Economics*, 1–39. London: Tavistock, 1972.

Savigliano, Marta. *Angora Matta: Fatal Acts of North-South Translation*. Middletown, CT: Wesleyan University Press, 2003.

———. *Tango and the Political Economy of Passion*. Boulder: Westview, 1995.

Scheper-Hughes, Nancy. "The Ends of the Body: Commodity Fetishism and the Global Traffic in Organs." *SAIS Review* 22, no. 1 (2002): 61.

Schön, Regine A, and Maarit Silvén. "Natural Parenting—Back to Basics in Infant Care." *Evolutionary Psychology*. 5(1), no. 5 (2007): 102–83.

Scribner, Charity. "Object, Relic, Fetish, Thing: Joseph Beuys and the Museum." *Critical Inquiry* 29, no. 4 (2003): 634–49.

Sedgwick, Eve Kosofsky, Michèle Aina Barale, and Jonathan Goldberg. *Touching Feeling: Affect, Pedagogy, Performativity*. Durham, NC: Duke University Press, 2003.

Shammas, Carole. "The Decline of Textile Prices in England and British America prior to Industrialization." *Economic History Review* 47, no. 3 (1994): 483–507.

Siegel, Jerrold E. *Marx's Fate: The Shape of a Life*. Princeton, NJ: Princeton University Press, 1978.

Spargo, John. *Karl Marx: His Life and Work*. New York: B. W. Huebsch, 1910.

Spartacus Educational. "Eleanor Marx." Accessed September 23, 2009. http://www.spartacus.schoolnet.co.uk/Wmarx.htm.

Spufford, Margaret. "The Cost of Apparel in Seventeenth-Century England, and the Accuracy of Gregory King." *Economic History Review* 53, no. 4 (2000): 677–705.

Squires, Sally. "Let's Get Something Straight! Parents and Dentists Wrestle over Which Kids Need Braces and When." *Washington Post*. September 29, 1998.

Stallybrass, Peter. "Marx's Coat." In *Border Fetishisms: Material Objects in Unstable Places*, edited by Patricia Spyer, 183–207. New York: Routledge, 1998.

Stearns, Peter N., Perrin Rowland, and Lori Giarnella. "Children's Sleep: Sketching Historical Change." *Journal of Social History* 30, no. 2 (Winter 1996): 345–66.

Stein, Martin T., Calvin A. Colarusso, James J. McKenna, and Nancy G. Powers. "Challenging Case: Family Relationships and Issues: Cosleeping (Bedsharing) among Infants and Toddlers." *Pediatrics* 107, no. 4 (2001): 873–77.

Steiner, Philippe. "Gifts of Blood and Organs: The Market and 'Fictitious' Commodities." *Revue Française de Sociologie* 44 (2003): 147–62.

Stewart, Kathleen. *Ordinary Affects*. Durham, NC: Duke University Press, 2007.

Stoll, David. *Rigoberta Menchú and the Story of All Poor Guatemalans*. New York: Harper Collins, 2000.

Strathern, Marilyn. "Partners and Consumers: Making Relations Visible." *New Literary History* 22, no. 3 (1991): 581–601.

Task Force on Sudden Infant Death Syndrome. "The Changing Concept of Sudden Infant Death Syndrome: Diagnostic Coding Shifts, Controversies Regarding the Sleeping Environment, and New Variables to Consider in Reducing Risk." *Pediatrics* 116, no. 5 (2005): 1245–55.

Taylor-Fletcher, P. *Business under the Balls: How to Be a Successful Pawnbroker.* Charlotte, NC: Jerry Stokes, 1993.

Trouillot, Michel-Rolph. "Anthropology and the Savage Slot: The Poetics and Politics of Otherness." In *Global Transformations: Anthropology and the Modern World*, 7–28. New York: Palgrave Macmillan, 2003.

———. *Haiti: State against Nation.* New York: Monthly Review Press, 2000.

———. *Silencing the Past.* New York: Beacon, 1997.

Turkle, Sherry. *Alone Together: Why We Expect More from Technology and Less from Each Other.* New York: Basic Books, 2011.

UNESCO. "Reading in the Mobile Era: A Study of Mobile Reading in Developing Countries." Paris: United Nations Educational, Scientific and Cultural Organization, 2014.

U.S. Department of Health and Human Services. *Oral Health in America: A Report of the Surgeon General.* Rockville, MD: U.S. Department of Health and Human Services, National Institute of Dental and Craniofacial Research, National Institutes of Health, 2000.

Ulysse, Gina A. "'Voodoo' Doll: Or What If Haiti Were a Woman, On Ti Travay Sou 21 Pwen, Or an Alter(ed)native in Something Other than Fiction." *The Wig: Journal of Experimental Scholarship* 2, no. a (2010). http://wigjournal.com/vo12noA/Vo12Noa.htm.

Weheliye, Alexander G. *Habeas Viscus: Racializing Assemblages, Biopolitics, and Black Feminist Theories of the Human.* Durham, NC: Duke University Press, 2014.

Weiss, Margot. *Techniques of Pleasure: BDSM and the Circuits of Sexuality.* Durham, NC: Duke University Press, 2011.

Wheen, Francis. *Karl Marx: A Life.* New York: W. W. Norton & Company, 2001.

Wilkins, Teresa J. *Patterns of Exchange: Navajo Weavers and Traders.* Norman: University of Oklahoma Press, 2008.

Williams, Brett. *Debt for Sale.* Philadelphia: University of Pennsylvania Press, 2004.

Wilson, Ara. "American Catalogues of Asian Brides." In *Anthropology for the Nineties: Introductory Readings*, edited by Johnnetta B. Cole, 114–25. New York: Simon and Schuster, 1988.

Winnicott, D. W. *Playing and Reality.* New York: Penguin, 1971.

Woloson, Wendy A. "In Hock: Pawning in Early America." *Journal of the Early Republic* 27, no. 1 (Spring 2007): 35–81.

Wynter, Sylvia. "Ethno or Socio Poetics." *Alcheringa: Ethnopolitics* 2, no. 2 (1976).

Yu, Li. *The Carnal Prayer Mat.* Honolulu: University of Hawaii Press, 1996.

Zelizer, Viviana. *The Purchase of Intimacy.* Princeton, NJ: Princeton University Press, 2005.

———. *The Social Meaning of Money.* New York: Basic Books, 1994.

Zukin, Sharon. *Point of Purchase: How Shopping Changed American Culture.* New York: Routledge, 2004.

Index

Hartman, Saidiya, 20
hating tradition, 4, 15
Haynes, Todd, 199
Heartbeat Bear, 45, 52, 56
Hebdige, Dick, 8
Hidden Persuaders, The (Packard), 8
hinoteras, 112
Hoarders (television series), 205, 206
hoarding, 203–9
Hoarding (television series), 205
homophobia, promotion of, 7
Howland, John, 23
Hubbell, Lorenzo, 146
human trafficking, 11

Ibsen, Henrik, 167
Illouz, Eva, 14, 17–18, 20
indentured status, 23
industrialization, 30
infants: private property and, 43,
    47–48, 55; proximity to caregivers,
    46–47; sleeping habits, 43–47,
    53–55, 184; transitional objects
    and, 42–56
inheritance, 98–101
Institute for Alternative Futures, 78
Inuit, 51

Jackson, John, 199
journalism, 63

Kealiinohomoku, Joanne, 22
Kincaid, Jamaica, 23, 123
Kingston, Maxine Hong, 193–95
knob shining, 80–82
Kula ring exchanges, 170

labor, purchase of, 95–97
Lange, Margaux, 9
Lifebuoy Men Lux Women (Burke), 10
literacy and cell phones, 18
Li Yu, 199
Lose Your Mother (Hartman), 20

love: importance of, 34; Marx on,
    181–82, 183–84; nourishment and, 46
Lozoff, B., 47

Malinowski, Bronisław, 45, 170
manicure services, 63–66
Marcuse, Herbert, 7
Marx, Eleanor (daughter), 91, 143–44,
    156–57, 166–67
Marx, Jenny (daughter), 75, 156–57,
    168
Marx, Jenny (wife), 29–30, 33–34, 90,
    97–98, 125–26, 143, 168
Marx, Karl: as bourgeois, 113–14; on
    capitalism, 28, 30–31; children of,
    75, 113, 142–44, 156; on commodity
    fetishism, 24–27, 30, 33, 38, 46, 147,
    184; consumer life of, 28, 29–30;
    grave, 168; letters to Engels, 90–91; on
    love, 181–82, 183–84; medical issues,
    75–76; on misplaced-personhood,
    147; money from Engels, 91, 118–20;
    on objects, 33–34; servants of, 97–98;
    on social labor, 48; on table-turning,
    69, 77, 170; use of pawnbroker, 106–7,
    143–44
Marx, Laura (daughter), 156, 168
mass production, 7–8
matrilineal peoples, 45
McKenna, James J., 53–54
Melanesians, 51
memories/memory, 31, 106, 176, 181,
    189–90, 192, 194–95
Menchù, Rigoberta, 225n2
mental health, mother's, 176–81
Mercy, A (Morrison), 23
Miller, Daniel, 3
Miner, Horace, 43
Minnie Mouse earring holder, 176, 181
Mintz, Sidney, 10–11
miscarriage, 132–39
misplaced-personhood, 147
Morrison, Toni, 23

Superstar (Haynes film), 199
survival, 32, 127, 144, 147
Sweetness and Power (Mintz), 10–11

table linens, 69–72
table-turning, 25, 69, 77, 173–76
telephone calls, international, 118
temper tantrums, 39, 46, 126
testimonio, 225n2
texting and literacy, 184
things: as actants, 19; attachment to,
    40–41; belief in, 26; culture of objects,
    209–10; hoarding, 203–9; love of,
    38–41; memory and, 31; race/culture
    and, 22; religious faith and, 19–20; re-
    search investigations of, 198; thoughts
    on, 11–15; transitional objects, 42–56
Third World, 108, 110
trading posts, 13, 144–46, 210
traditional ethics, 12–13
transcendence, 25
transitional objects, 42–56; consumer
    capitalism and, 55–56; as culturally
    specific, 49; defined, 42; as substitute
    for mother, 42, 46
Triumph of the Will (Riefenstal film), 8
Trump, Donald, 112
turquoise arrowhead story, 170–73

Vodou, 19–20

Wallendorf, Melanie, 198
wanting vs. wishing, 60
weaving, Navajo, 145–46
Weheliye, Alexander G., 22, 26
Weiss, Margot, 14
whiteness, 22–23, 195–96
Wilkins, Teresa J., 145, 147
window shades, 67–69
window shopping, 89–92
Winnicott, D. W., 42
Wolf, Eric, 193
"Work of Art in the Age of Mechanical
    Reproduction, The" (Benjamin), 7–8
World War II (1939–1945), 7
Writing Culture (Clifford/Marcus, eds.),
    192–97
Wynter, Sylvia, 22, 26

Xena Warrior Princess, 118–20

Yucatec Maya, 47

Zelizer, Viviana, 20, 21
Zukin, Sharon, 12, 13–14, 18

Discerning our relationship w/things
is a ~~process of Spt~~
Spiritual and introspective process,
what is the catalyst for the journey?
How do you motivate others to
begin the journey